Learning Resource Centre

Park Road, Uxbridge, Middlesex UB8 1NQ
Renewals: 01895 853344

JOHN WAGNER ★ ALAN GRANT
Writers

BRIAN BOLLAND ★ BRETT EWINS
CLIFF ROBINSON ★ ROBIN SMITH
Artists

BRIAN BOLLAND
Cover Artist

Creative Director and CEO: Jason Kingsley
Chief Technical Officer: Chris Kingsley
Publishing Manager: Ben Smith
2000 AD Editor in Chief: Matt Smith
Graphic Novels Editor: Keith Richardson
Graphic Design: Simon Parr
PR: Michael Molcher
Reprographics: Kathryn Symes
Original Commissioning Editor:
Steve MacManus

Originally serialised in *2000 AD* Progs 149-151, 224-228, 416-427. Copyright
© 1980, 1981, 1985, 2012 Rebellion A/S. All Rights Reserved. *Judge Dredd,
Judge Death & the Dark Judges* and all related characters, their distinctive
likenesses and related elements featured in this publication are trademarks of
Rebellion A/S. No portion of this book may be reproduced without the express
permission of the publisher. Names, character, places and incidents featured
in the publication are either the product of the author's imagination or used
fictitiously. Any resemblance to actual persons, living or dead (except for satirical
purposes) is entirely coincidental.

Published by Rebellion, Riverside House, Osney Mead, Oxford, OX2 0ES, UK.
www.rebellion.co.uk

ISBN: 978-1-78108-045-0
Printed by CPI Bookmarque
First published: September 2012
10 9 8 7 6 5 4 3 2 1

Printed on FSC Accredited Paper

A CIP catalogue record for this book is available from the British Library.

For information on other 2000 AD graphic novels, or if you have any comments
on this book, please email books@2000ADonline.com

To find out more about 2000 AD, visit www.2000ADonline.com

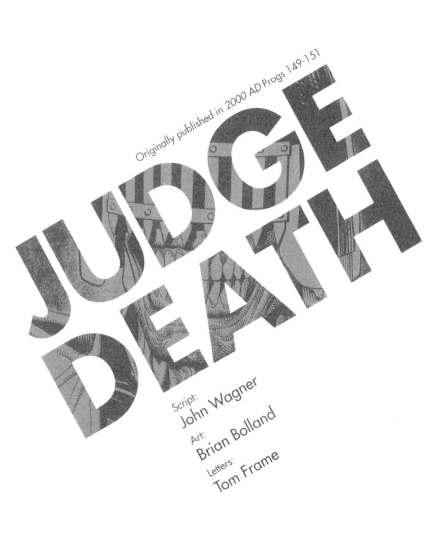

Originally published in 2000 AD Progs 149-151

JUDGE DEATH

Script:
John Wagner

Art:
Brian Bolland

Letters:
Tom Frame

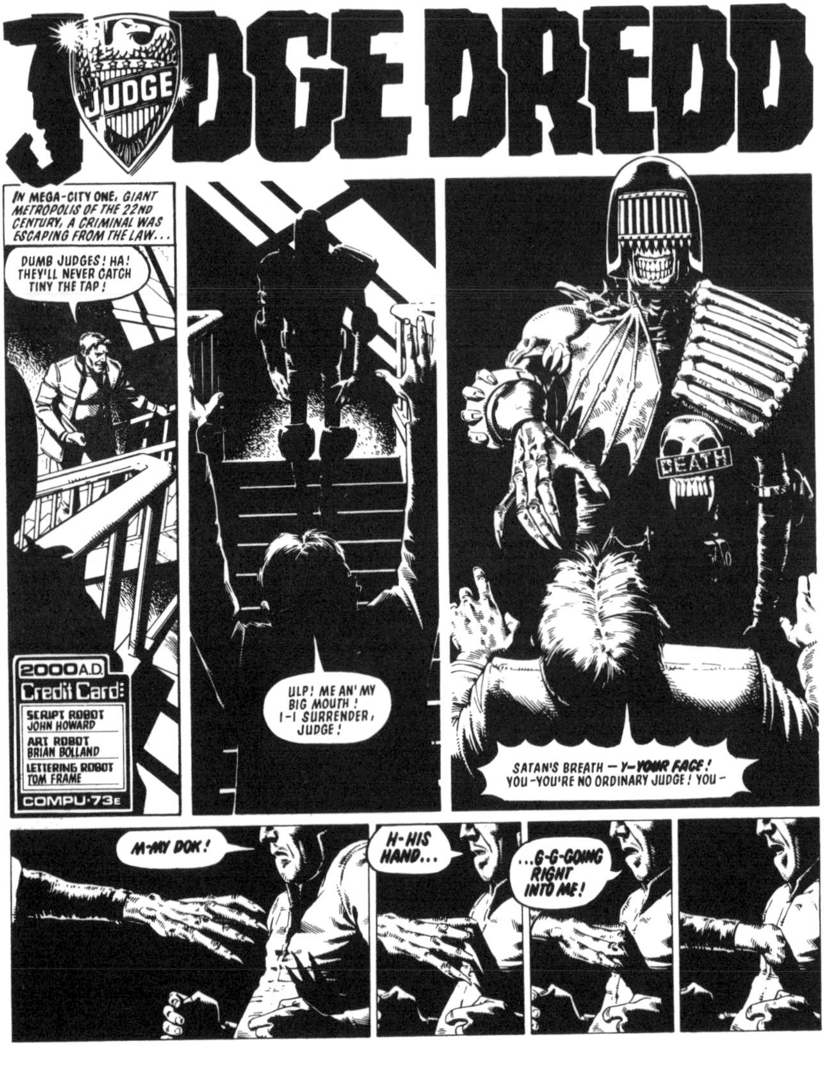
JUDGE DREDD
JUDGE
IN MEGA-CITY ONE, GIANT METROPOLIS OF THE 22ND CENTURY, A CRIMINAL WAS ESCAPING FROM THE LAW...
DUMB JUDGES! HA! THEY'LL NEVER CATCH TINY THE TAP!
2000 A.D. Credit Card:
SCRIPT ROBOT JOHN HOWARD
ART ROBOT BRIAN BOLLAND
LETTERING ROBOT TOM FRAME
COMPU-73E
ULP! ME AN' MY BIG MOUTH! I-I SURRENDER, JUDGE!
DEATH
SATAN'S BREATH — Y-YOUR FACE! YOU-YOU'RE NO ORDINARY JUDGE! YOU-
M-MY DOK!
H-HIS HAND...
...G-G-GOING RIGHT INTO ME!

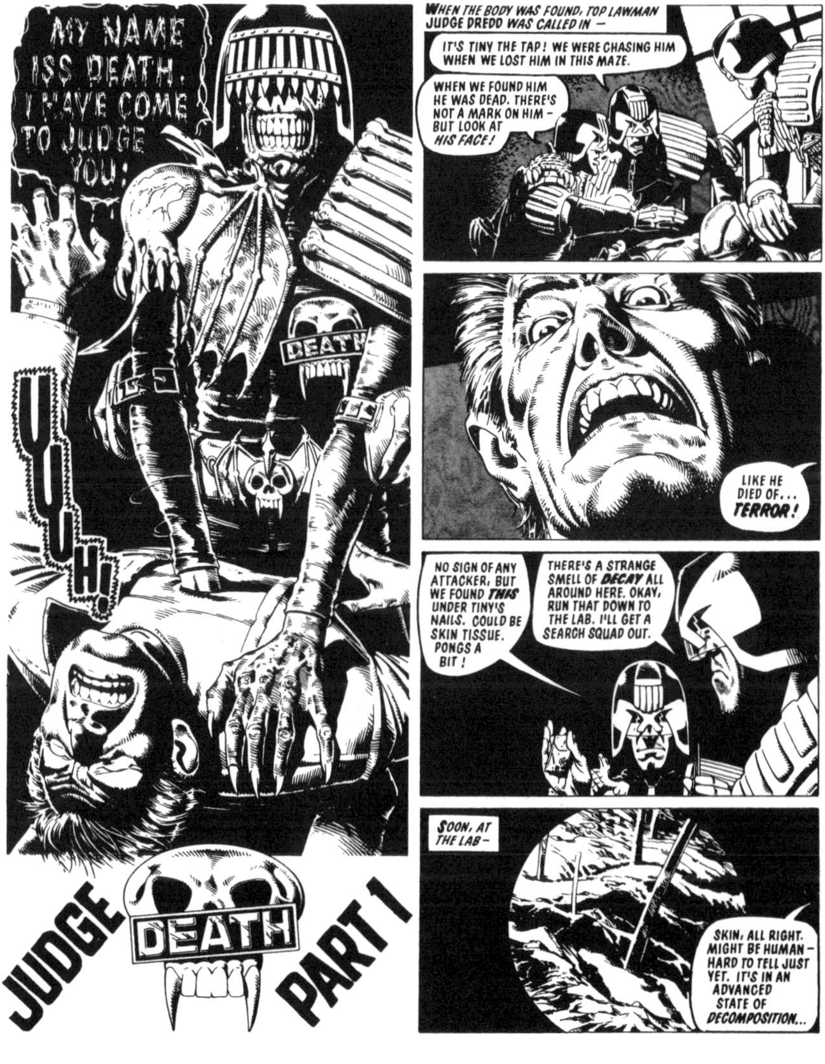
MY NAME ISS DEATH. I HAVE COME TO JUDGE YOU!
UUUH!
JUDGE DEATH PART 1
WHEN THE BODY WAS FOUND, TOP LAWMAN JUDGE DREDD WAS CALLED IN –
IT'S TINY THE TAP! WE WERE CHASING HIM WHEN WE LOST HIM IN THIS MAZE.
WHEN WE FOUND HIM HE WAS DEAD. THERE'S NOT A MARK ON HIM – BUT LOOK AT HIS FACE!
LIKE HE DIED OF... TERROR!
NO SIGN OF ANY ATTACKER, BUT WE FOUND THIS UNDER TINY'S NAILS. COULD BE SKIN TISSUE. PONGS A BIT!
THERE'S A STRANGE SMELL OF DECAY ALL AROUND HERE. OKAY, RUN THAT DOWN TO THE LAB. I'LL GET A SEARCH SQUAD OUT.
SOON, AT THE LAB–
SKIN, ALL RIGHT. MIGHT BE HUMAN – HARD TO TELL JUST YET. IT'S IN AN ADVANCED STATE OF DECOMPOSITION...

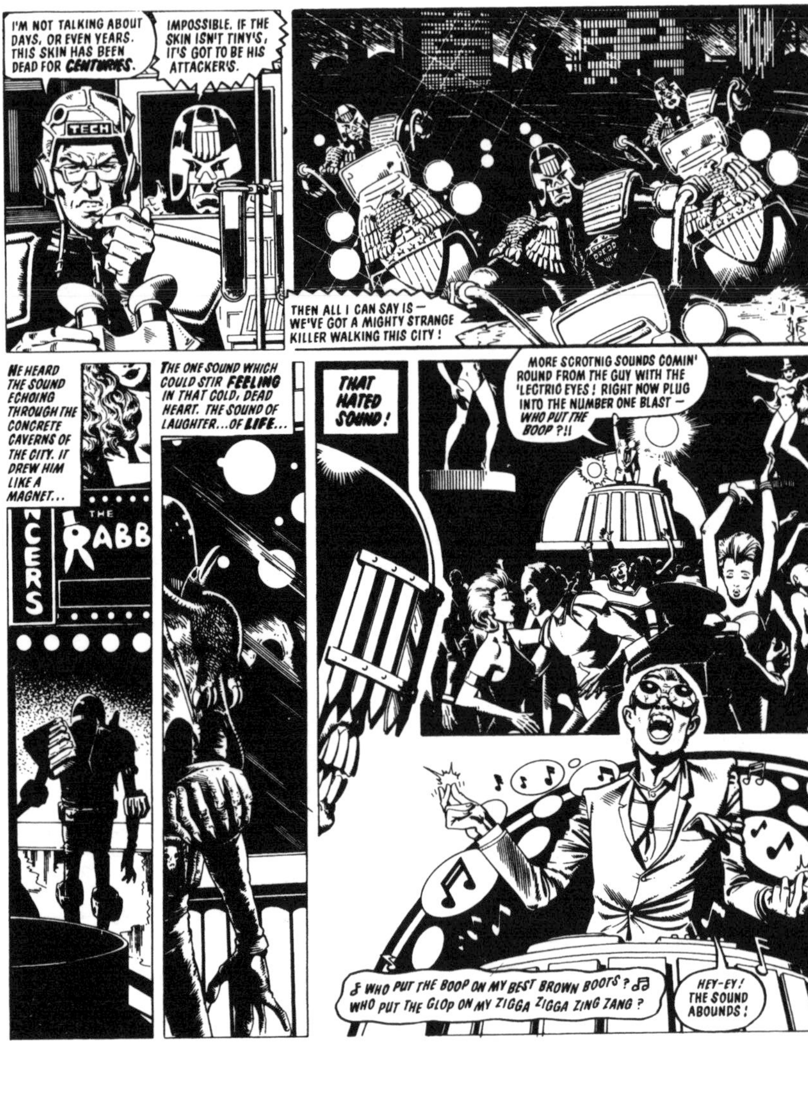
I'M NOT TALKING ABOUT DAYS, OR EVEN YEARS. THIS SKIN HAS BEEN DEAD FOR CENTURIES.
IMPOSSIBLE. IF THE SKIN ISN'T TINY'S, IT'S GOT TO BE HIS ATTACKER'S.
TECH
THEN ALL I CAN SAY IS — WE'VE GOT A MIGHTY STRANGE KILLER WALKING THIS CITY!
HE HEARD THE SOUND ECHOING THROUGH THE CONCRETE CAVERNS OF THE CITY. IT DREW HIM LIKE A MAGNET...
THE RABB
NCERS
THE ONE SOUND WHICH COULD STIR FEELING IN THAT COLD, DEAD HEART. THE SOUND OF LAUGHTER...OF LIFE...
THAT HATED SOUND!
MORE SCROTNIG SOUNDS COMIN' ROUND FROM THE GUY WITH THE 'LECTRIC EYES! RIGHT NOW PLUG INTO THE NUMBER ONE BLAST — WHO PUT THE BOOP?!!
WHO PUT THE BOOP ON MY BEST BROWN BOOTS? WHO PUT THE GLOP ON MY ZIGGA ZIGGA ZING ZANG?
HEY-EY! THE SOUND ABOUNDS!

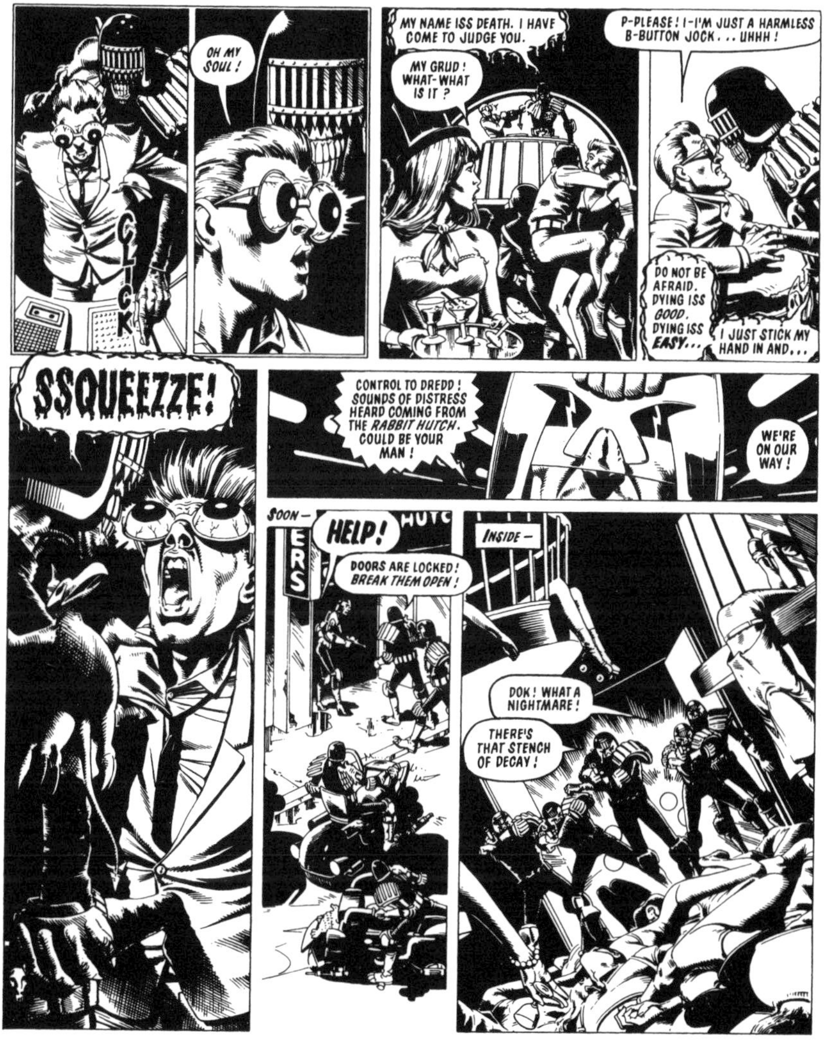
CLICK
OH MY SOUL!
MY NAME ISS DEATH. I HAVE COME TO JUDGE YOU.
MY GRUD! WHAT-WHAT IS IT?
P-PLEASE! I-I'M JUST A HARMLESS B-BUTTON JOCK... UHHH!
DO NOT BE AFRAID. DYING ISS GOOD. DYING ISS EASY...
I JUST STICK MY HAND IN AND...
SSQUEEZZE!
CONTROL TO DREDD! SOUNDS OF DISTRESS HEARD COMING FROM THE RABBIT HUTCH. COULD BE YOUR MAN!
WE'RE ON OUR WAY!
SOON—
HELP!
DOORS ARE LOCKED! BREAK THEM OPEN!
INSIDE—
DOK! WHAT A NIGHTMARE!
THERE'S THAT STENCH OF DECAY!

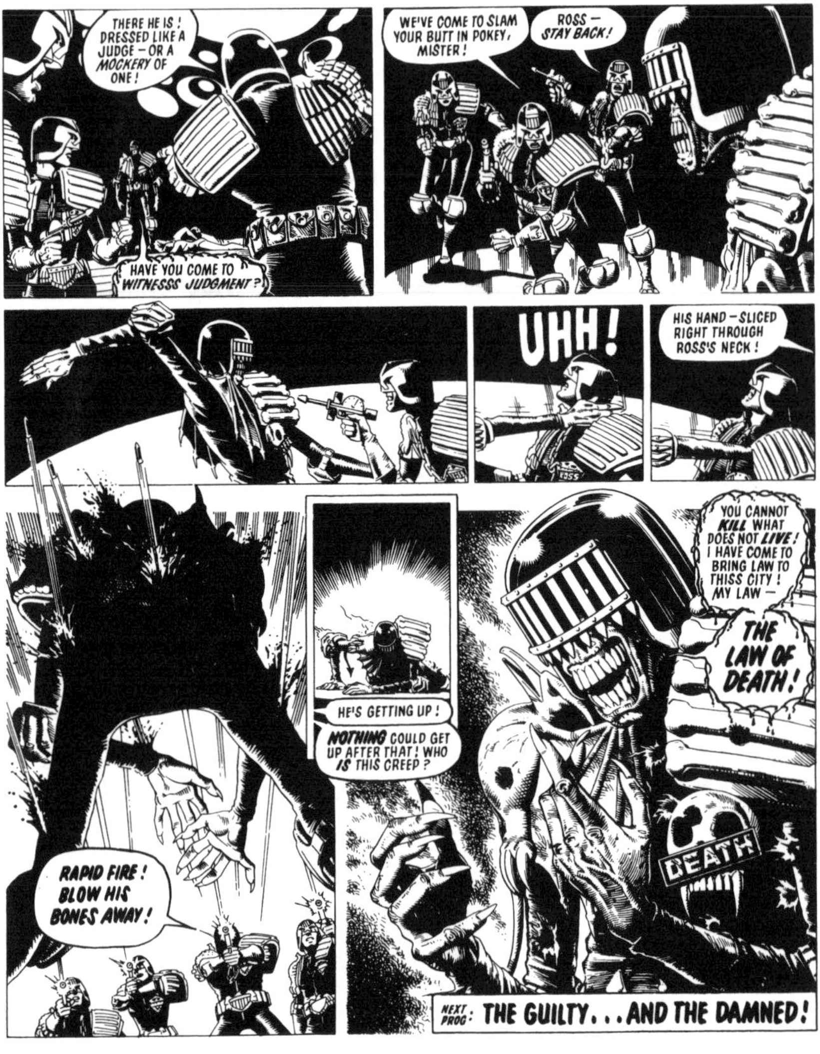
THERE HE IS! DRESSED LIKE A JUDGE — OR A MOCKERY OF ONE!
HAVE YOU COME TO WITNESSS JUDGMENT?
WE'VE COME TO SLAM YOUR BUTT IN POKEY, MISTER!
ROSS — STAY BACK!
UHH!
HIS HAND — SLICED RIGHT THROUGH ROSS'S NECK!
RAPID FIRE! BLOW HIS BONES AWAY!
HE'S GETTING UP!
NOTHING COULD GET UP AFTER THAT! WHO IS THIS CREEP?
YOU CANNOT KILL WHAT DOES NOT LIVE! I HAVE COME TO BRING LAW TO THISS CITY! MY LAW —
THE LAW OF DEATH!
DEATH
NEXT PROG: THE GUILTY... AND THE DAMNED!

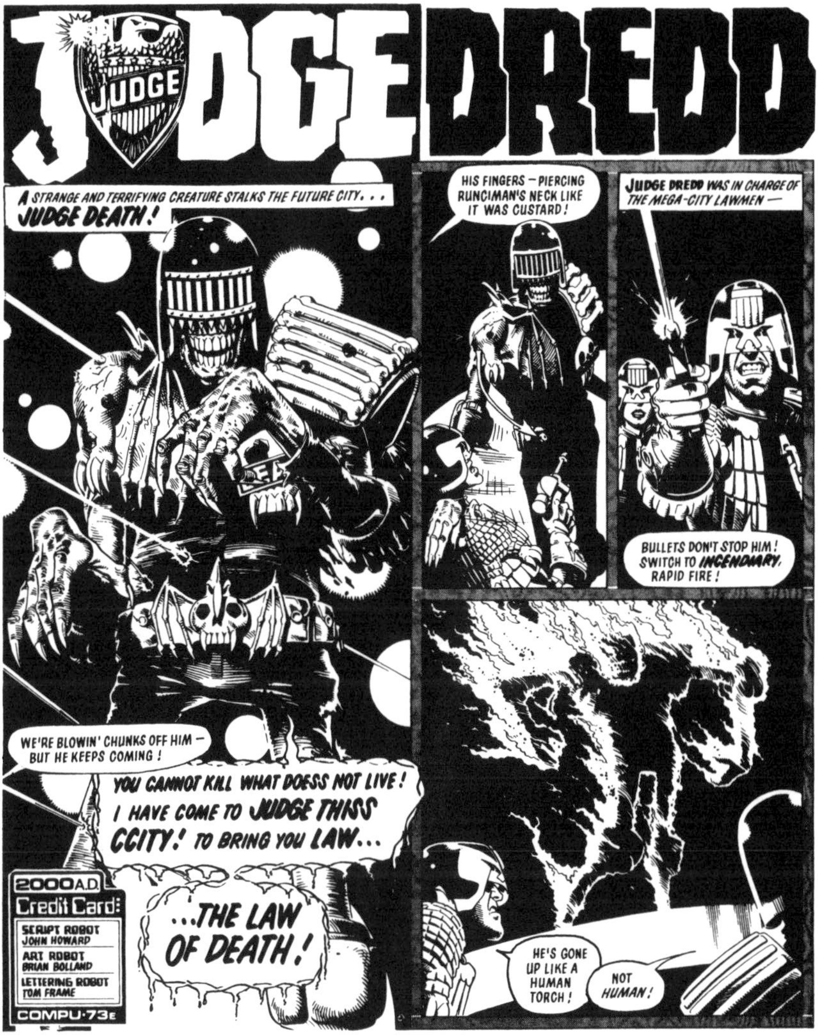
JUDGE DREDD
JUDGE
A STRANGE AND TERRIFYING CREATURE STALKS THE FUTURE CITY. . . JUDGE DEATH!
WE'RE BLOWIN' CHUNKS OFF HIM — BUT HE KEEPS COMING!
YOU CANNOT KILL WHAT DOESS NOT LIVE! I HAVE COME TO JUDGE THISS CCITY! TO BRING YOU LAW...
...THE LAW OF DEATH!
2000 A.D. Credit Card:
SCRIPT ROBOT JOHN HOWARD
ART ROBOT BRIAN BOLLAND
LETTERING ROBOT TOM FRAME
COMPU-73E
HIS FINGERS — PIERCING RUNCIMAN'S NECK LIKE IT WAS CUSTARD!
JUDGE DREDD WAS IN CHARGE OF THE MEGA-CITY LAWMEN —
BULLETS DON'T STOP HIM! SWITCH TO INCENDIARY, RAPID FIRE!
HE'S GONE UP LIKE A HUMAN TORCH!
NOT HUMAN!

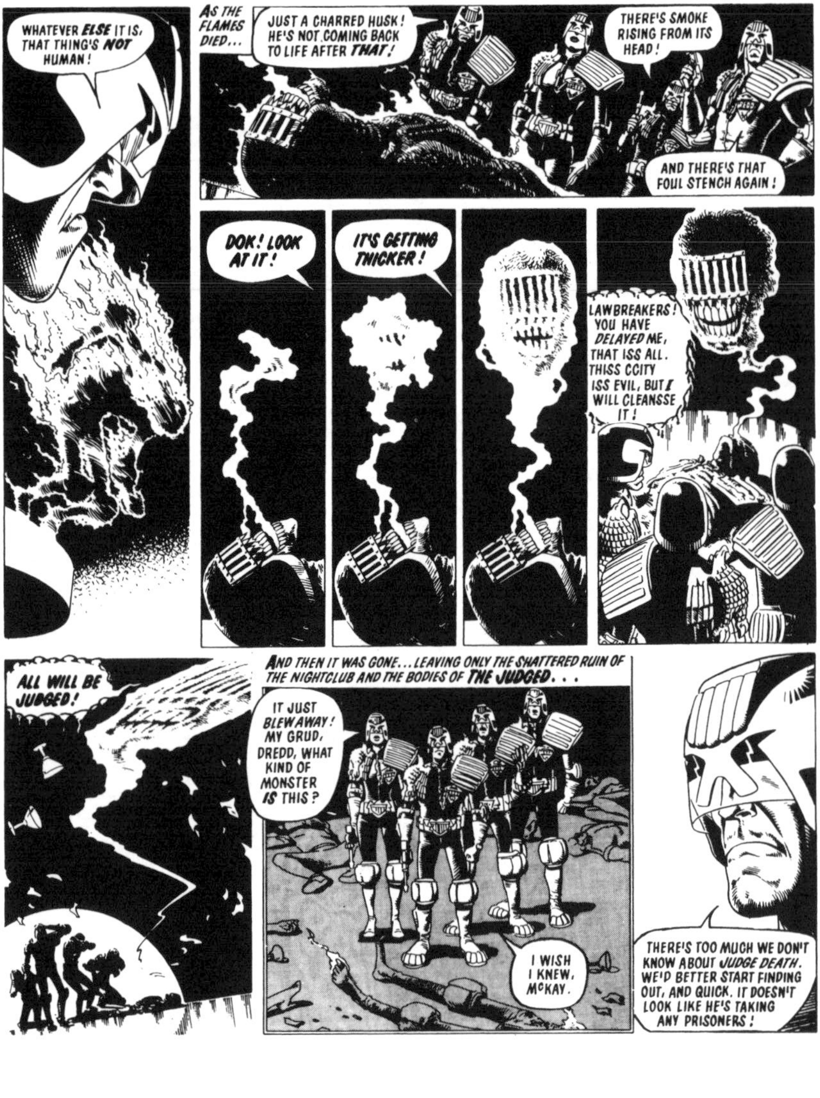
WHATEVER ELSE IT IS, THAT THING'S NOT HUMAN!
AS THE FLAMES DIED...
JUST A CHARRED HUSK! HE'S NOT COMING BACK TO LIFE AFTER THAT!
THERE'S SMOKE RISING FROM ITS HEAD!
AND THERE'S THAT FOUL STENCH AGAIN!
DOK! LOOK AT IT!
IT'S GETTING THICKER!
LAWBREAKERS! YOU HAVE DELAYED ME, THAT ISS ALL. THISS CCITY ISS EVIL, BUT I WILL CLEANSSE IT!
ALL WILL BE JUDGED!
AND THEN IT WAS GONE... LEAVING ONLY THE SHATTERED RUIN OF THE NIGHTCLUB AND THE BODIES OF THE JUDGED...
IT JUST BLEW AWAY! MY GRUD, DREDD, WHAT KIND OF MONSTER IS THIS?
I WISH I KNEW, McKAY.
THERE'S TOO MUCH WE DON'T KNOW ABOUT JUDGE DEATH. WE'D BETTER START FINDING OUT, AND QUICK. IT DOESN'T LOOK LIKE HE'S TAKING ANY PRISONERS!

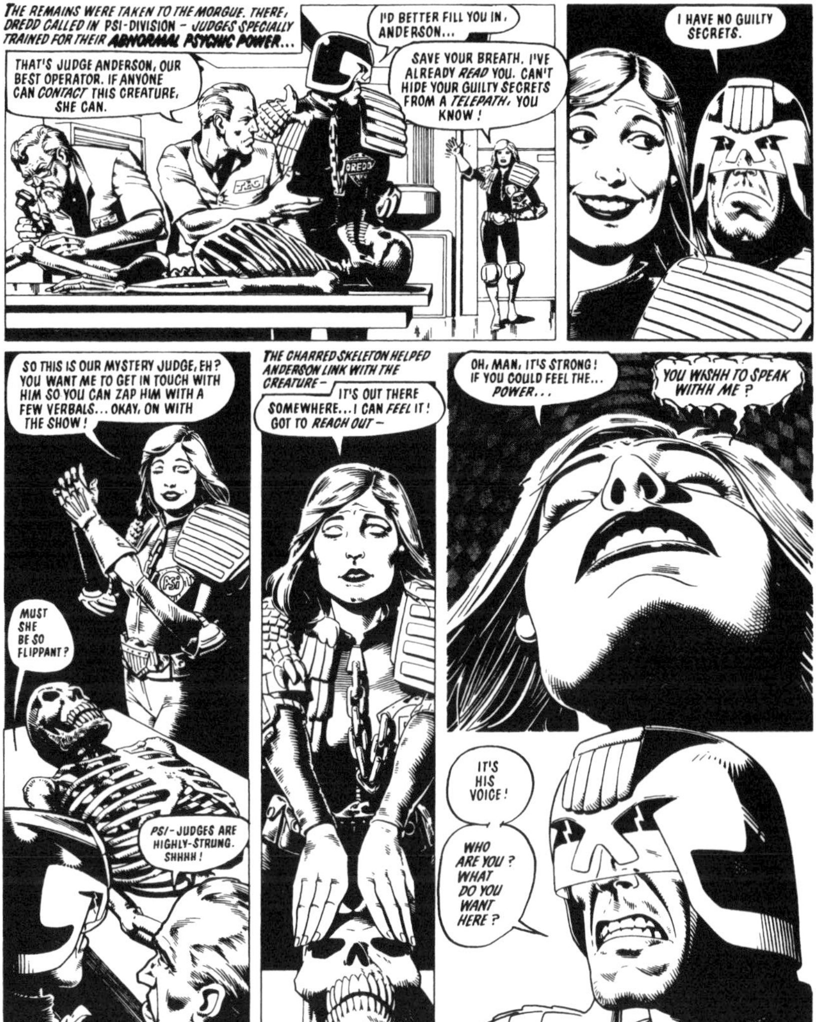
THE REMAINS WERE TAKEN TO THE MORGUE. THERE, DREDD CALLED IN PSI-DIVISION - JUDGES SPECIALLY TRAINED FOR THEIR ABNORMAL PSYCHIC POWER...
THAT'S JUDGE ANDERSON, OUR BEST OPERATOR. IF ANYONE CAN CONTACT THIS CREATURE, SHE CAN.
I'D BETTER FILL YOU IN, ANDERSON...
SAVE YOUR BREATH. I'VE ALREADY READ YOU. CAN'T HIDE YOUR GUILTY SECRETS FROM A TELEPATH, YOU KNOW!
I HAVE NO GUILTY SECRETS.
SO THIS IS OUR MYSTERY JUDGE, EH? YOU WANT ME TO GET IN TOUCH WITH HIM SO YOU CAN ZAP HIM WITH A FEW VERBALS... OKAY, ON WITH THE SHOW!
MUST SHE BE SO FLIPPANT?
PSI-JUDGES ARE HIGHLY-STRUNG. SHHHH!
THE CHARRED SKELETON HELPED ANDERSON LINK WITH THE CREATURE-
IT'S OUT THERE SOMEWHERE... I CAN FEEL IT! GOT TO REACH OUT-
OH, MAN, IT'S STRONG! IF YOU COULD FEEL THE... POWER...
YOU WISHH TO SPEAK WITHH ME?
IT'S HIS VOICE!
WHO ARE YOU? WHAT DO YOU WANT HERE?

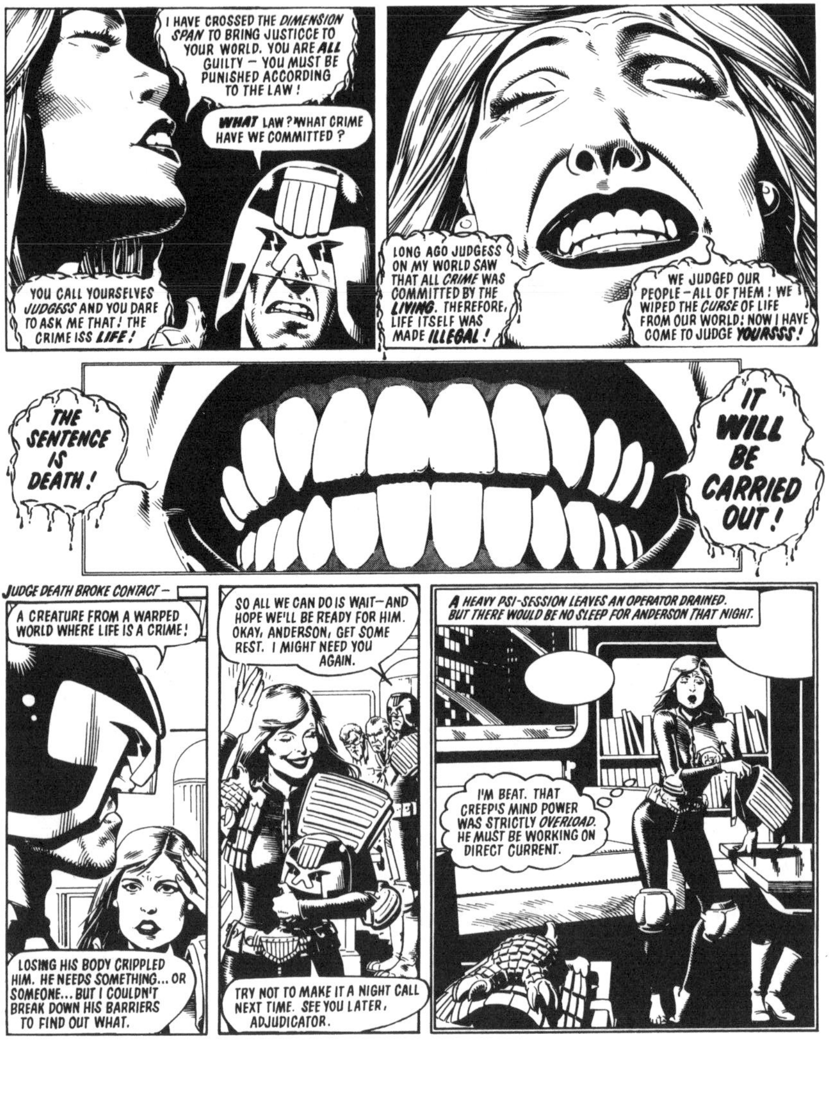
I HAVE CROSSED THE DIMENSION SPAN TO BRING JUSTICCE TO YOUR WORLD. YOU ARE ALL GUILTY — YOU MUST BE PUNISHED ACCORDING TO THE LAW!
WHAT LAW? WHAT CRIME HAVE WE COMMITTED?
YOU CALL YOURSELVES JUDGESS AND YOU DARE TO ASK ME THAT! THE CRIME ISS LIFE!
LONG AGO JUDGESS ON MY WORLD SAW THAT ALL CRIME WAS COMMITTED BY THE LIVING. THEREFORE, LIFE ITSELF WAS MADE ILLEGAL!
WE JUDGED OUR PEOPLE — ALL OF THEM! WE WIPED THE CURSE OF LIFE FROM OUR WORLD! NOW I HAVE COME TO JUDGE YOURSSS!
THE SENTENCE IS DEATH!
IT WILL BE CARRIED OUT!
JUDGE DEATH BROKE CONTACT —
A CREATURE FROM A WARPED WORLD WHERE LIFE IS A CRIME!
LOSING HIS BODY CRIPPLED HIM. HE NEEDS SOMETHING... OR SOMEONE... BUT I COULDN'T BREAK DOWN HIS BARRIERS TO FIND OUT WHAT.
SO ALL WE CAN DO IS WAIT—AND HOPE WE'LL BE READY FOR HIM. OKAY, ANDERSON, GET SOME REST. I MIGHT NEED YOU AGAIN.
TRY NOT TO MAKE IT A NIGHT CALL NEXT TIME. SEE YOU LATER, ADJUDICATOR.
A HEAVY PSI-SESSION LEAVES AN OPERATOR DRAINED. BUT THERE WOULD BE NO SLEEP FOR ANDERSON THAT NIGHT.
I'M BEAT. THAT CREEP'S MIND POWER WAS STRICTLY OVERLOAD. HE MUST BE WORKING ON DIRECT CURRENT.

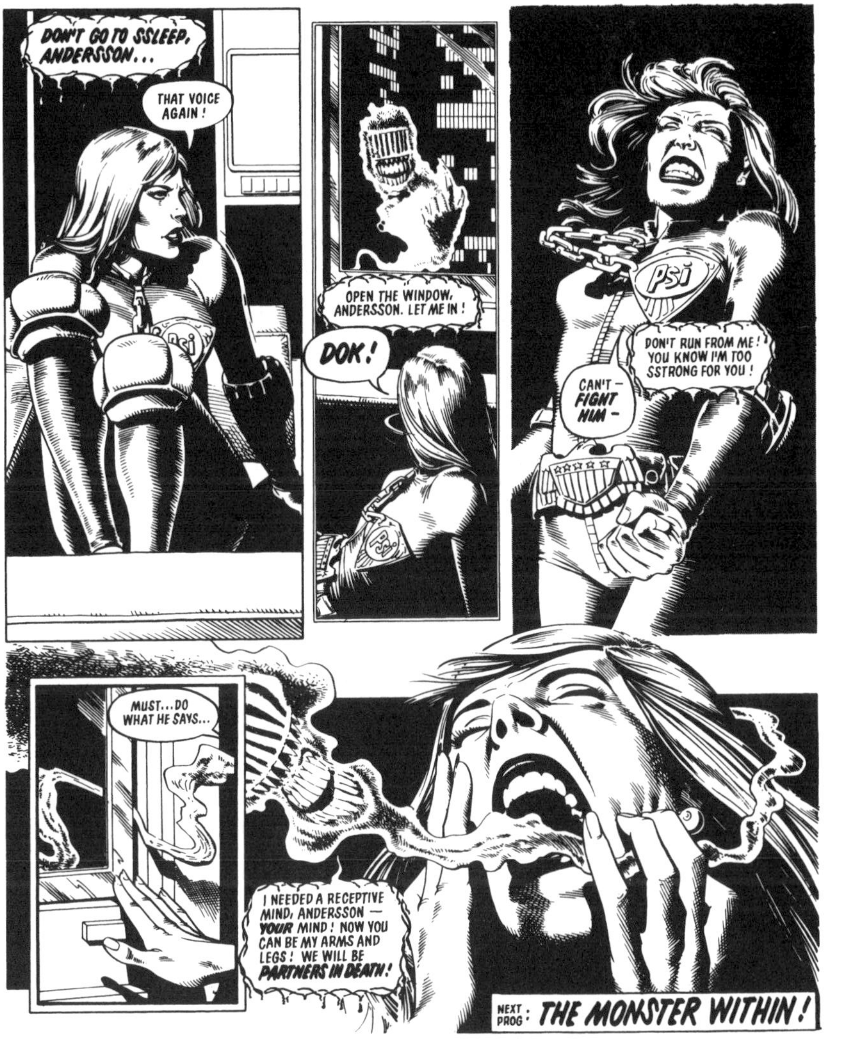
DON'T GO TO SSLEEP, ANDERSSON...
THAT VOICE AGAIN!
OPEN THE WINDOW, ANDERSSON. LET ME IN!
DOK!
DON'T RUN FROM ME! YOU KNOW I'M TOO SSTRONG FOR YOU!
CAN'T — FIGHT HIM —
MUST...DO WHAT HE SAYS...
I NEEDED A RECEPTIVE MIND, ANDERSSON — YOUR MIND! NOW YOU CAN BE MY ARMS AND LEGS! WE WILL BE PARTNERS IN DEATH!
NEXT PROG: THE MONSTER WITHIN!

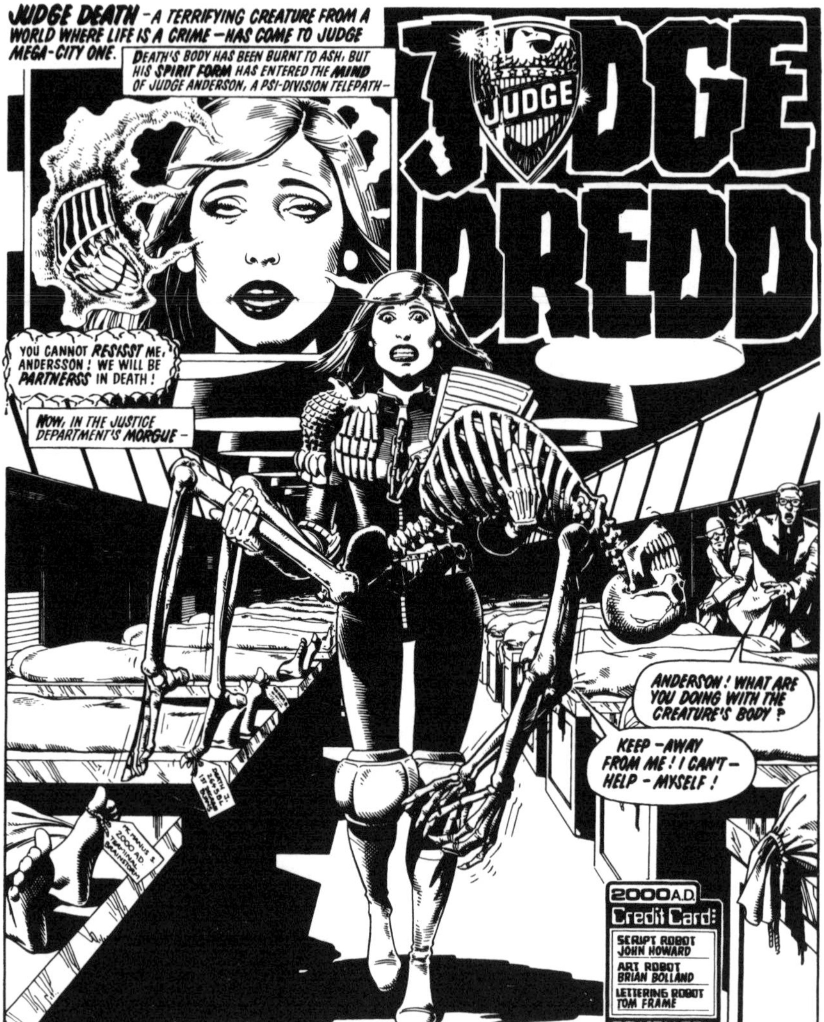
JUDGE DEATH - A TERRIFYING CREATURE FROM A WORLD WHERE LIFE IS A CRIME - HAS COME TO JUDGE MEGA-CITY ONE.
DEATH'S BODY HAS BEEN BURNT TO ASH, BUT HIS SPIRIT FORM HAS ENTERED THE MIND OF JUDGE ANDERSON, A PSI-DIVISION TELEPATH-
JUDGE DREDD
JUDGE
YOU CANNOT RESISST ME, ANDERSSON! WE WILL BE PARTNERSS IN DEATH!
NOW, IN THE JUSTICE DEPARTMENT'S MORGUE -
ANDERSON! WHAT ARE YOU DOING WITH THE CREATURE'S BODY?
KEEP -AWAY FROM ME! I CAN'T- HELP - MYSELF!
2000 A.D.
Credit Card:
SCRIPT ROBOT JOHN HOWARD
ART ROBOT BRIAN BOLLAND
LETTERING ROBOT TOM FRAME
COMPU·73E

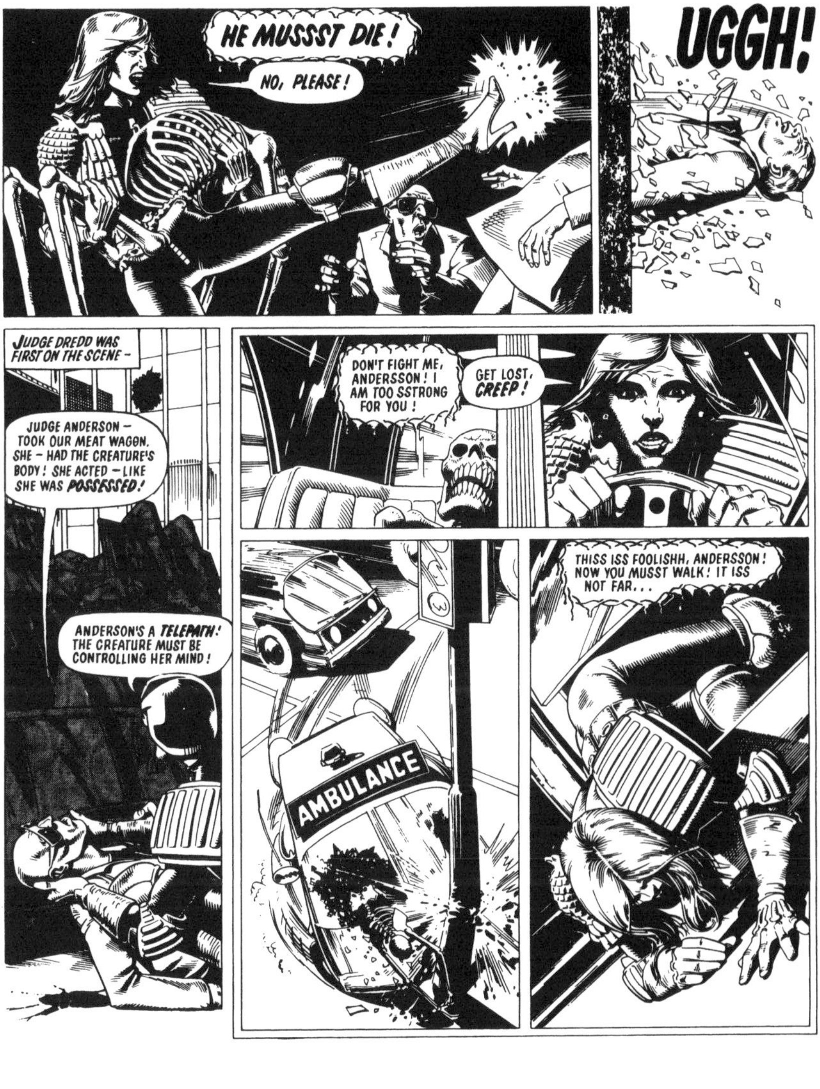
HE MUSSST DIE!
NO, PLEASE!
UGGH!
JUDGE DREDD WAS FIRST ON THE SCENE –
JUDGE ANDERSON – TOOK OUR MEAT WAGON. SHE – HAD THE CREATURE'S BODY! SHE ACTED – LIKE SHE WAS POSSESSED!
ANDERSON'S A TELEPATH! THE CREATURE MUST BE CONTROLLING HER MIND!
DON'T FIGHT ME, ANDERSSON! I AM TOO SSTRONG FOR YOU!
GET LOST, CREEP!
AMBULANCE
THISS ISS FOOLISHH, ANDERSSON! NOW YOU MUSST WALK! IT ISS NOT FAR...

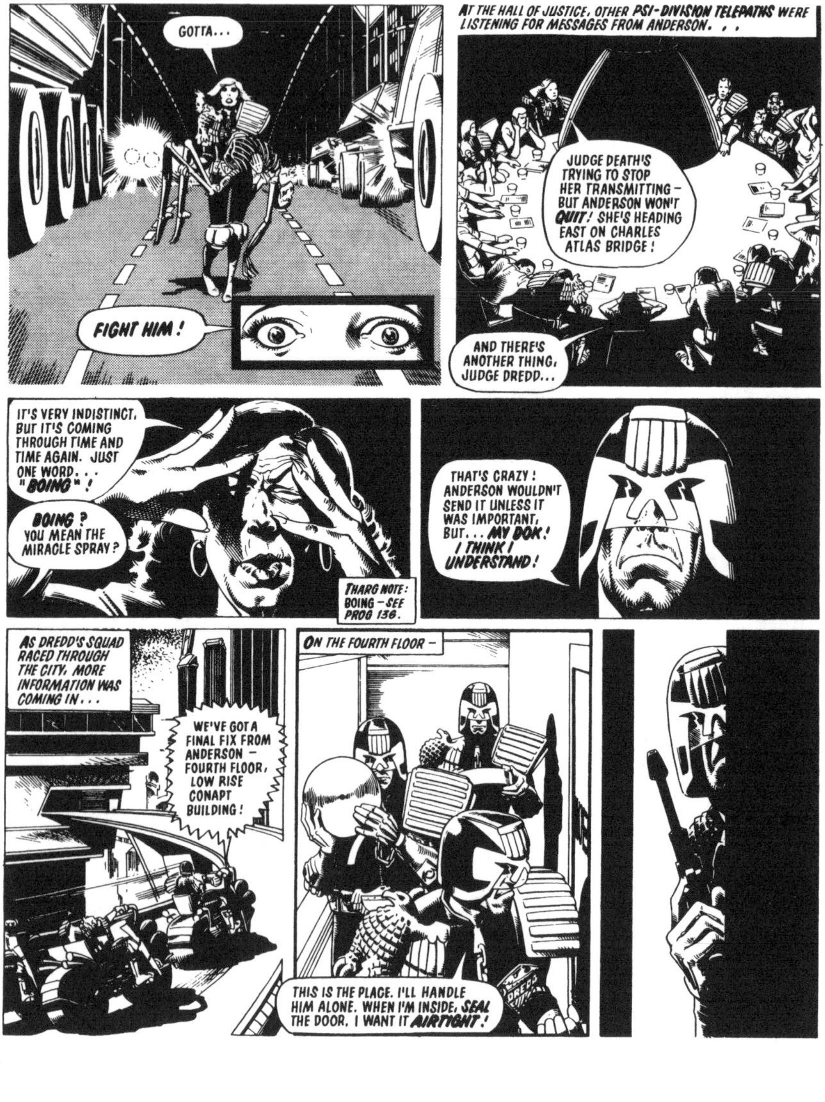
GOTTA...
FIGHT HIM!
AT THE HALL OF JUSTICE, OTHER PSI-DIVISION TELEPATHS WERE LISTENING FOR MESSAGES FROM ANDERSON. . .
JUDGE DEATH'S TRYING TO STOP HER TRANSMITTING – BUT ANDERSON WON'T QUIT! SHE'S HEADING EAST ON CHARLES ATLAS BRIDGE!
AND THERE'S ANOTHER THING, JUDGE DREDD...
IT'S VERY INDISTINCT, BUT IT'S COMING THROUGH TIME AND TIME AGAIN. JUST ONE WORD. . . "BOING"!
BOING? YOU MEAN THE MIRACLE SPRAY?
THARG NOTE: BOING – SEE PROG 136.
THAT'S CRAZY! ANDERSON WOULDN'T SEND IT UNLESS IT WAS IMPORTANT, BUT. . . MY DOK! I THINK I UNDERSTAND!
AS DREDD'S SQUAD RACED THROUGH THE CITY, MORE INFORMATION WAS COMING IN...
WE'VE GOT A FINAL FIX FROM ANDERSON – FOURTH FLOOR, LOW RISE CONAPT BUILDING!
ON THE FOURTH FLOOR –
THIS IS THE PLACE. I'LL HANDLE HIM ALONE. WHEN I'M INSIDE, SEAL THE DOOR. I WANT IT AIRTIGHT!

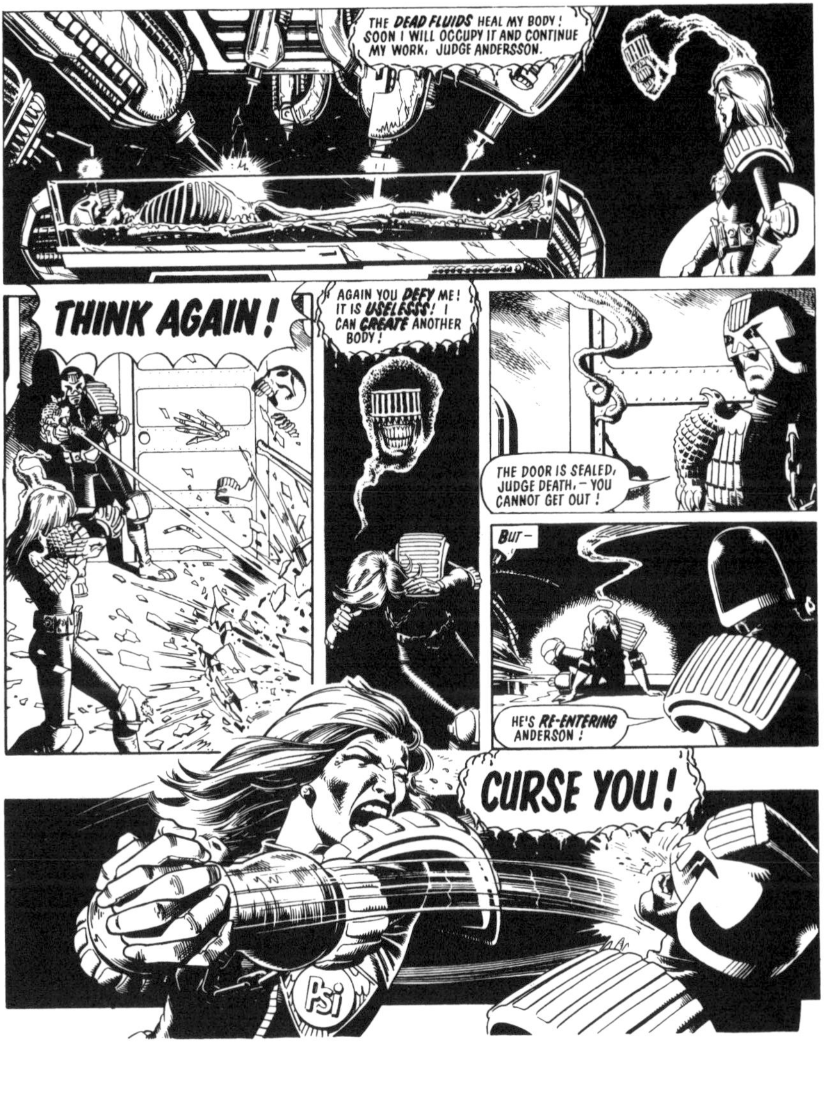
THE DEAD FLUIDS HEAL MY BODY! SOON I WILL OCCUPY IT AND CONTINUE MY WORK, JUDGE ANDERSSON.
THINK AGAIN!
AGAIN YOU DEFY ME! IT IS USELESSS! I CAN CREATE ANOTHER BODY!
THE DOOR IS SEALED, JUDGE DEATH, – YOU CANNOT GET OUT!
BUT –
HE'S RE-ENTERING ANDERSON!
CURSE YOU!
PSI

NOW, DREDD! DO IT — THE BOING TIN!

THE MIRACLE PLASTIC SWELLED AROUND ANDERSON —

GRUD! **WHAT ON EARTH** —?

YOU CAN'T KILL **DEATH**. WE HAD TO **TRAP** HIM. THERE WAS ONLY ONE WAY, AND ANDERSON REALISED IT...

HE'S TRAPPED IN ANDERSON'S HEAD — ENCASED IN... **BOING!**

WE CAN'T EVER RISK JUDGE DEATH BREAKING FREE. ANDERSON CAN NEVER COME OUT OF THERE... AND SHE KNEW IT. HER BRAVERY WILL BE REMEMBERED!

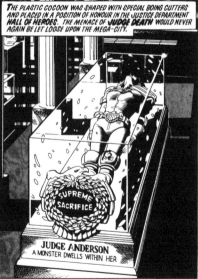

THE PLASTIC COCOON WAS SHAPED WITH SPECIAL BOING CUTTERS AND PLACED IN A POSITION OF HONOUR IN THE JUSTICE DEPARTMENT **HALL OF HEROES**. THE MENACE OF **JUDGE DEATH** WOULD NEVER AGAIN BE LET LOOSE UPON THE MEGA-CITY.

SUPREME SACRIFICE

JUDGE ANDERSON
A MONSTER DWELLS WITHIN HER

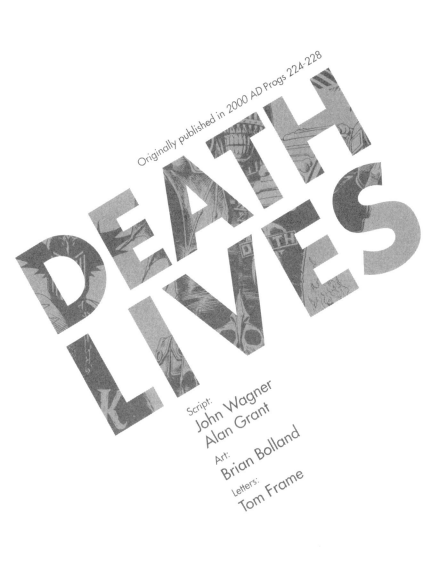

Originally published in 2000 AD Progs 224-228

DEATH LIVES

Script:
John Wagner
Alan Grant

Art:
Brian Bolland

Letters:
Tom Frame

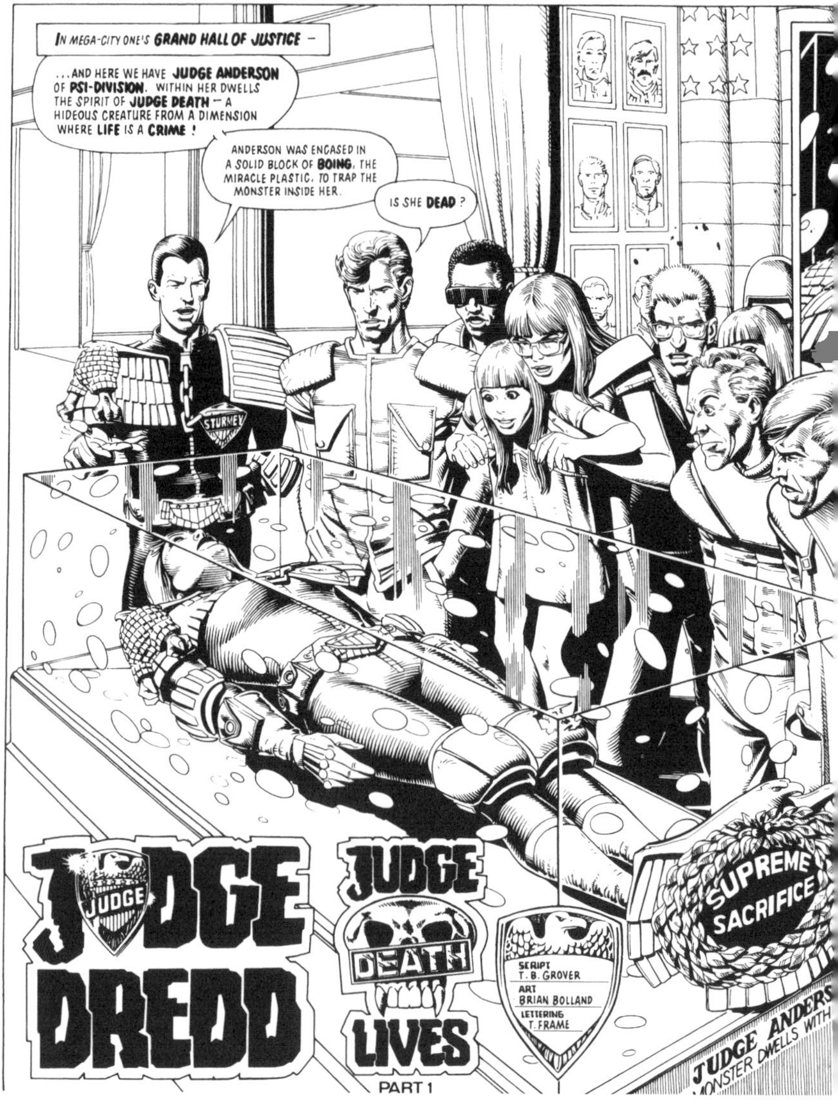
IN MEGA-CITY ONE'S GRAND HALL OF JUSTICE –
...AND HERE WE HAVE JUDGE ANDERSON OF PSI-DIVISION. WITHIN HER DWELLS THE SPIRIT OF JUDGE DEATH – A HIDEOUS CREATURE FROM A DIMENSION WHERE LIFE IS A CRIME!
ANDERSON WAS ENCASED IN A SOLID BLOCK OF BOING, THE MIRACLE PLASTIC, TO TRAP THE MONSTER INSIDE HER.
IS SHE DEAD?
STURMEY
JUDGE
JUDGE DREDD
JUDGE DEATH LIVES
PART 1
SCRIPT T. B. GROVER
ART BRIAN BOLLAND
LETTERING T. FRAME
SUPREME SACRIFICE

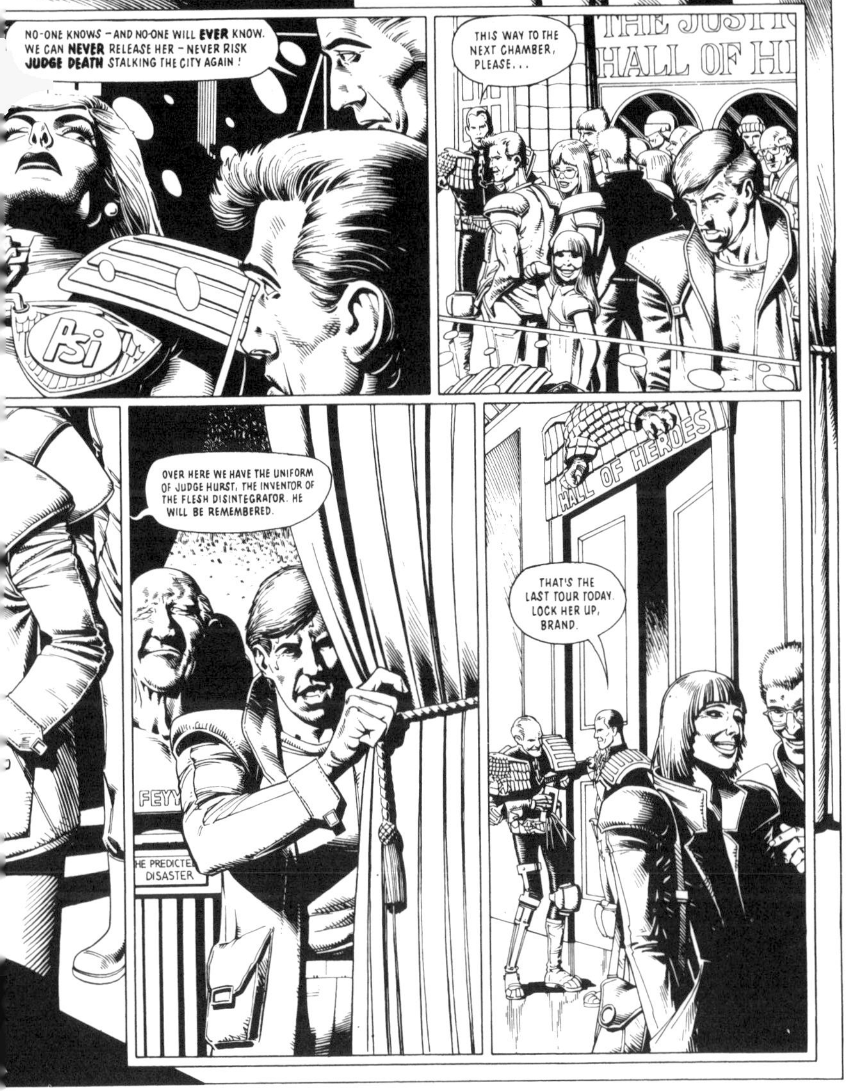
NO-ONE KNOWS – AND NO-ONE WILL **EVER** KNOW. WE CAN **NEVER** RELEASE HER – NEVER RISK **JUDGE DEATH** STALKING THE CITY AGAIN!
THIS WAY TO THE NEXT CHAMBER, PLEASE...
THE JUSTI
HALL OF HI
OVER HERE WE HAVE THE UNIFORM OF JUDGE HURST, THE INVENTOR OF THE FLESH DISINTEGRATOR. HE WILL BE REMEMBERED.
FEYY
HE PREDICTE
DISASTER
HALL OF HEROES
THAT'S THE LAST TOUR TODAY. LOCK HER UP, BRAND.

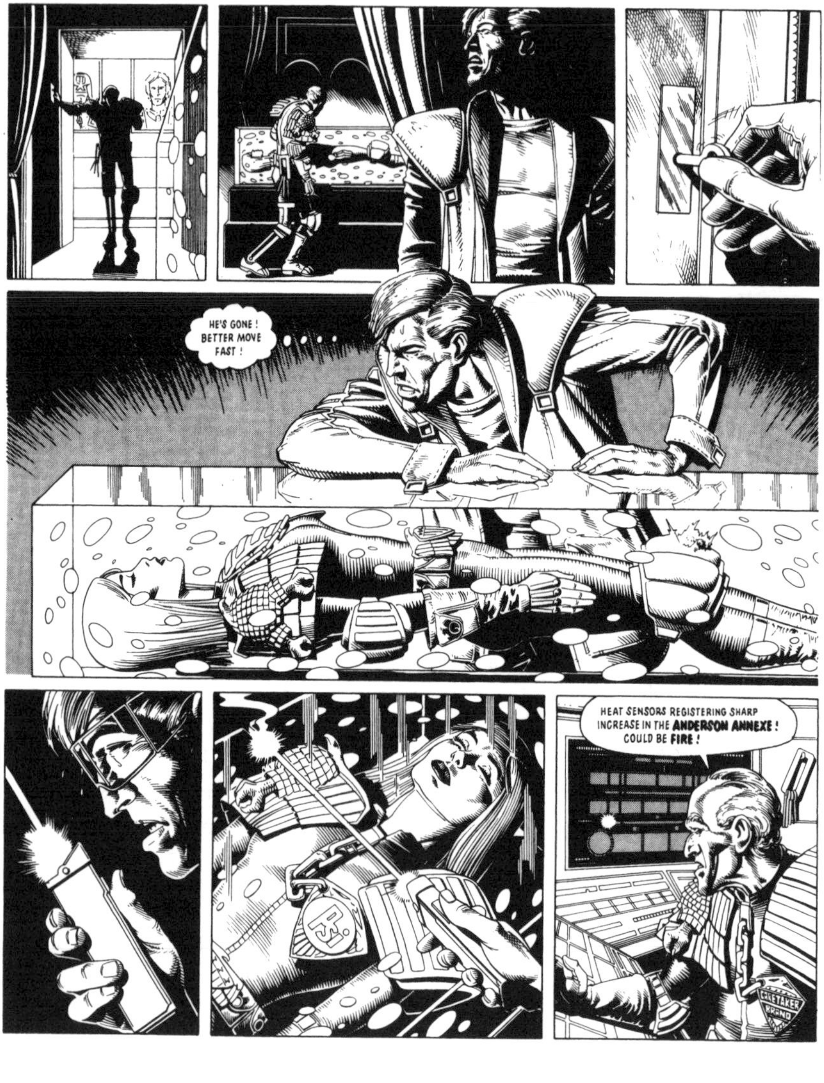
HE'S GONE ! BETTER MOVE FAST !
HEAT SENSORS REGISTERING SHARP INCREASE IN THE ANDERSON ANNEXE ! COULD BE FIRE !
CARETAKER
BRAND

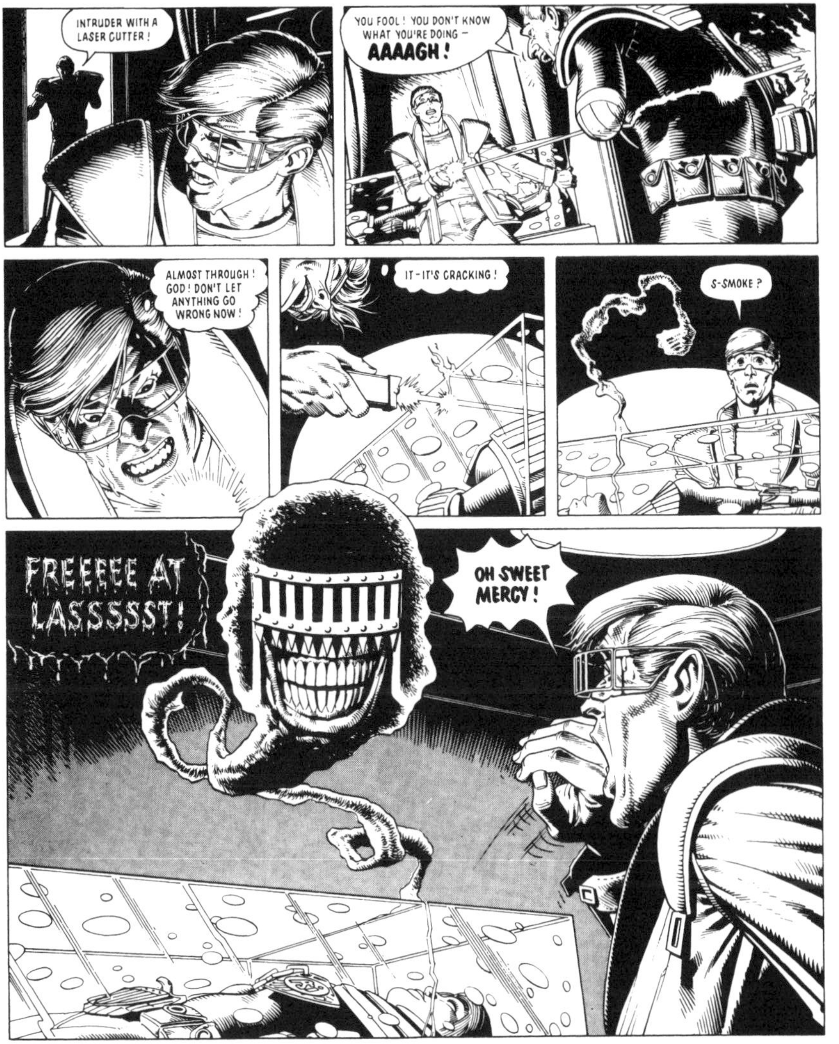
INTRUDER WITH A LASER CUTTER!
YOU FOOL! YOU DON'T KNOW WHAT YOU'RE DOING — AAAAGH!
ALMOST THROUGH! GOD! DON'T LET ANYTHING GO WRONG NOW!
IT-IT'S CRACKING!
S-SMOKE?
FREEEEE AT LASSSSST!
OH SWEET MERCY!

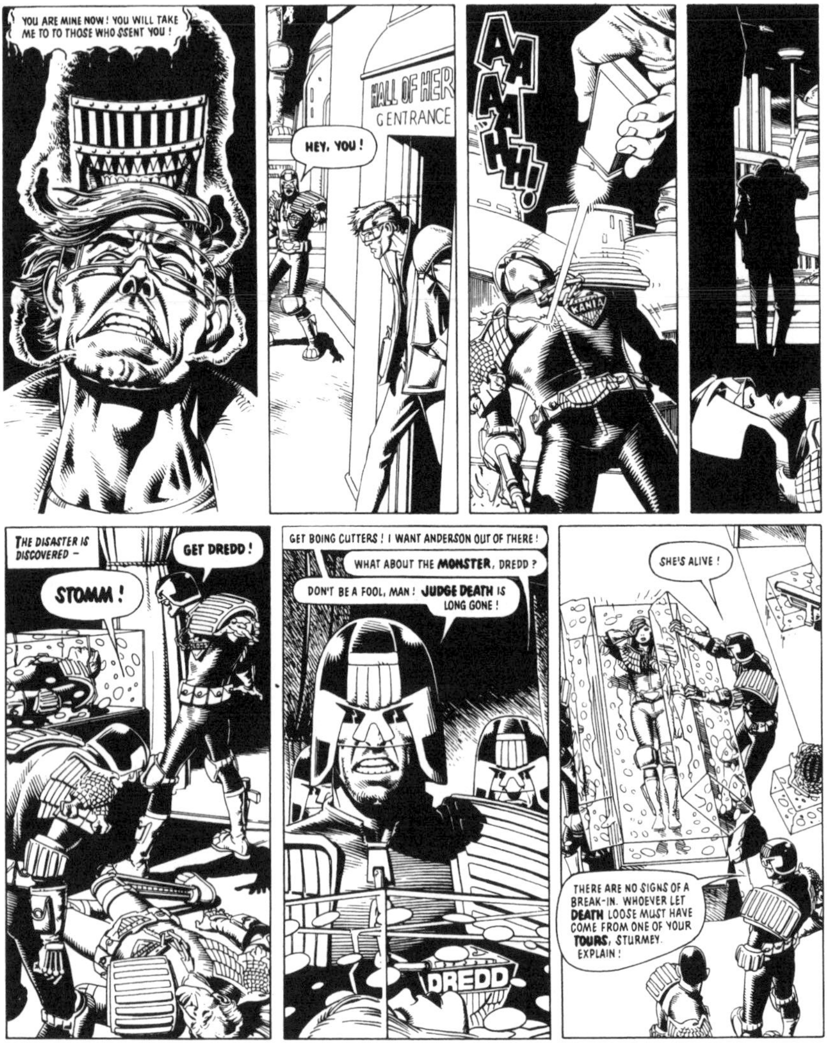
YOU ARE MINE NOW! YOU WILL TAKE ME TO TO THOSE WHO SSENT YOU!
HALL OF HER
GENTRANCE
HEY, YOU!
AAAAHH!
KANIA
THE DISASTER IS DISCOVERED –
GET DREDD!
STOMM!
GET BOING CUTTERS! I WANT ANDERSON OUT OF THERE!
WHAT ABOUT THE MONSTER, DREDD?
DON'T BE A FOOL, MAN! JUDGE DEATH IS LONG GONE!
DREDD
SHE'S ALIVE!
THERE ARE NO SIGNS OF A BREAK-IN. WHOEVER LET DEATH LOOSE MUST HAVE COME FROM ONE OF YOUR TOURS, STURMEY. EXPLAIN!

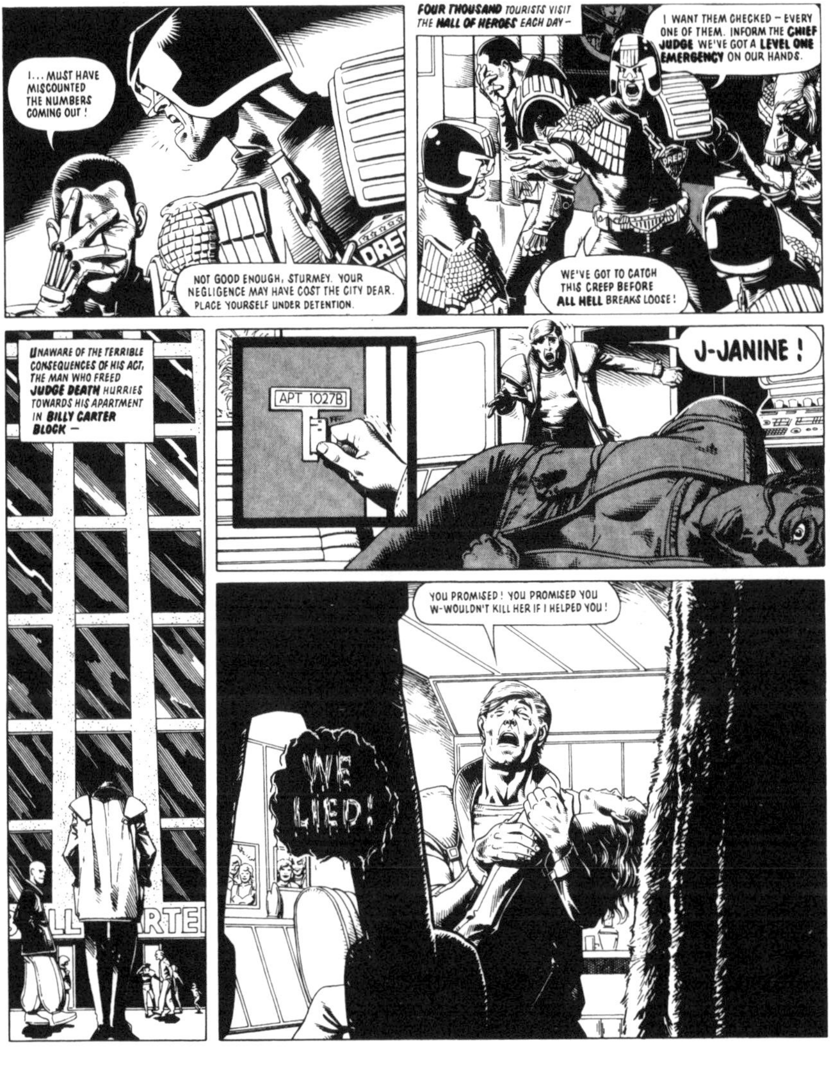
I... MUST HAVE MISCOUNTED THE NUMBERS COMING OUT!
NOT GOOD ENOUGH, STURMEY. YOUR NEGLIGENCE MAY HAVE COST THE CITY DEAR. PLACE YOURSELF UNDER DETENTION.
FOUR THOUSAND TOURISTS VISIT THE HALL OF HEROES EACH DAY –
I WANT THEM CHECKED – EVERY ONE OF THEM. INFORM THE CHIEF JUDGE WE'VE GOT A LEVEL ONE EMERGENCY ON OUR HANDS.
WE'VE GOT TO CATCH THIS CREEP BEFORE ALL HELL BREAKS LOOSE!
UNAWARE OF THE TERRIBLE CONSEQUENCES OF HIS ACT, THE MAN WHO FREED JUDGE DEATH HURRIES TOWARDS HIS APARTMENT IN BILLY CARTER BLOCK –
APT 1027B
J-JANINE!
YOU PROMISED! YOU PROMISED YOU W-WOULDN'T KILL HER IF I HELPED YOU!
WE LIED!

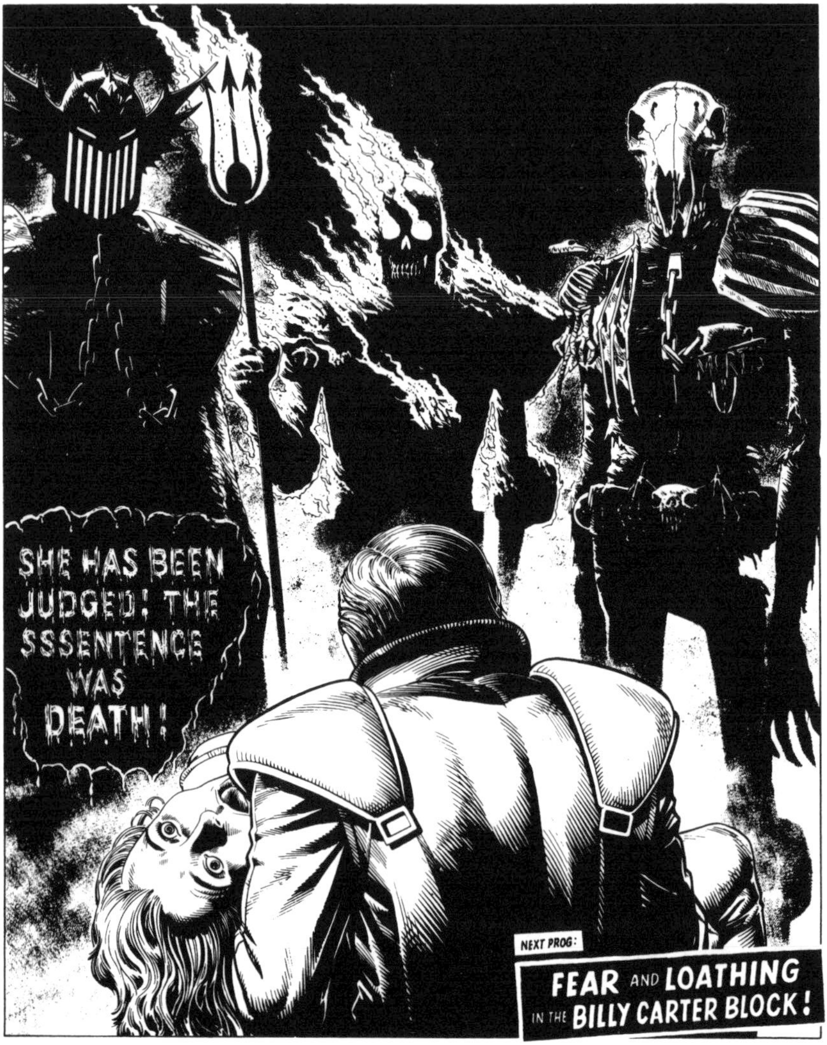
SHE HAS BEEN JUDGED! THE SSSENTENCE WAS DEATH!
NEXT PROG:
FEAR AND LOATHING IN THE BILLY CARTER BLOCK!

THE DARK JUDGES

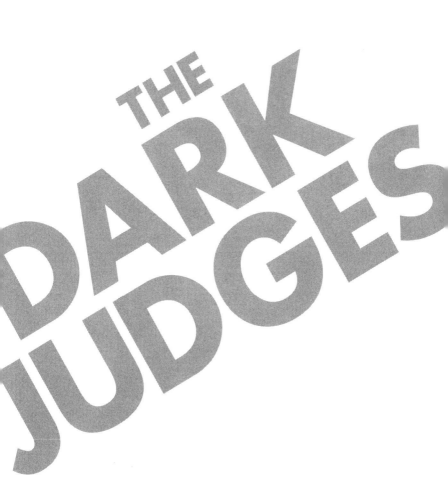

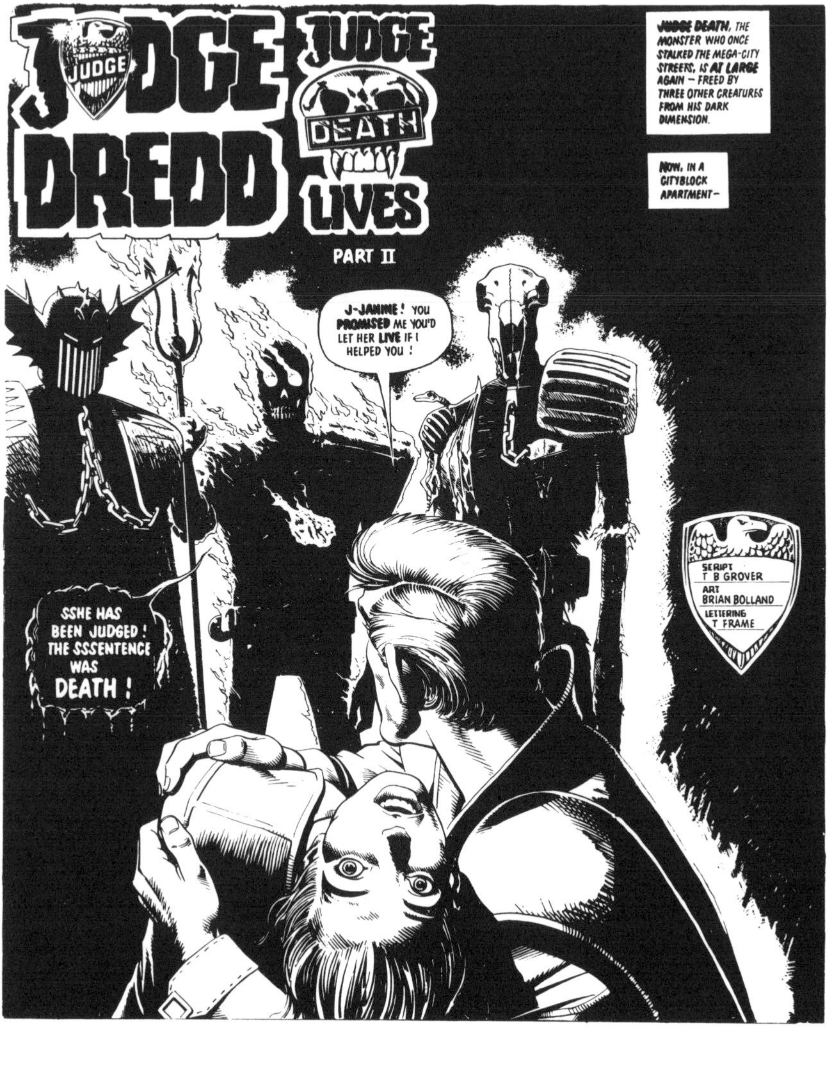
JUDGE DREDD
JUDGE
JUDGE DEATH LIVES
PART II
JUDGE DEATH, THE MONSTER WHO ONCE STALKED THE MEGA-CITY STREETS, IS AT LARGE AGAIN — FREED BY THREE OTHER CREATURES FROM HIS DARK DIMENSION.
NOW, IN A CITYBLOCK APARTMENT—
J-JANNIE! YOU PROMISED ME YOU'D LET HER LIVE IF I HELPED YOU!
SSHE HAS BEEN JUDGED! THE SSSENTENCE WAS DEATH!
SCRIPT T B GROVER
ART BRIAN BOLLAND
LETTERING T FRAME

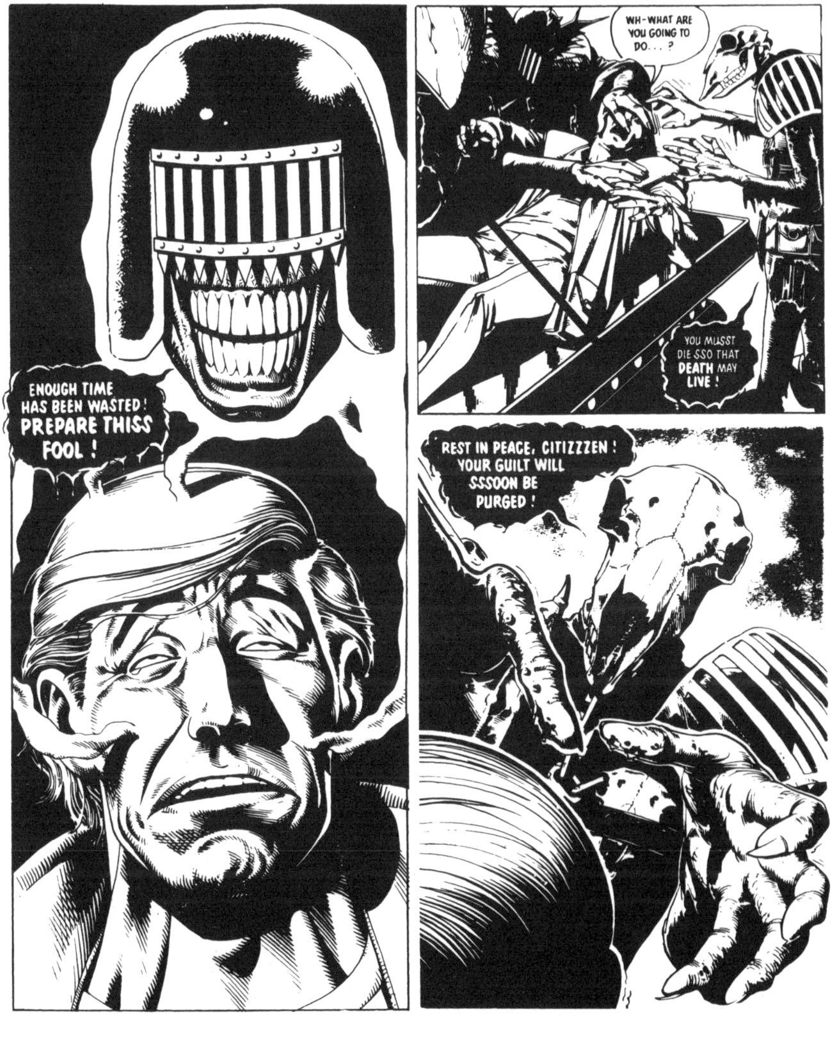
ENOUGH TIME HAS BEEN WASTED! PREPARE THISS FOOL!
WH-WHAT ARE YOU GOING TO DO...?
YOU MUSST DIE SSO THAT DEATH MAY LIVE!
REST IN PEACE, CITIZZZEN! YOUR GUILT WILL SSSOON BE PURGED!

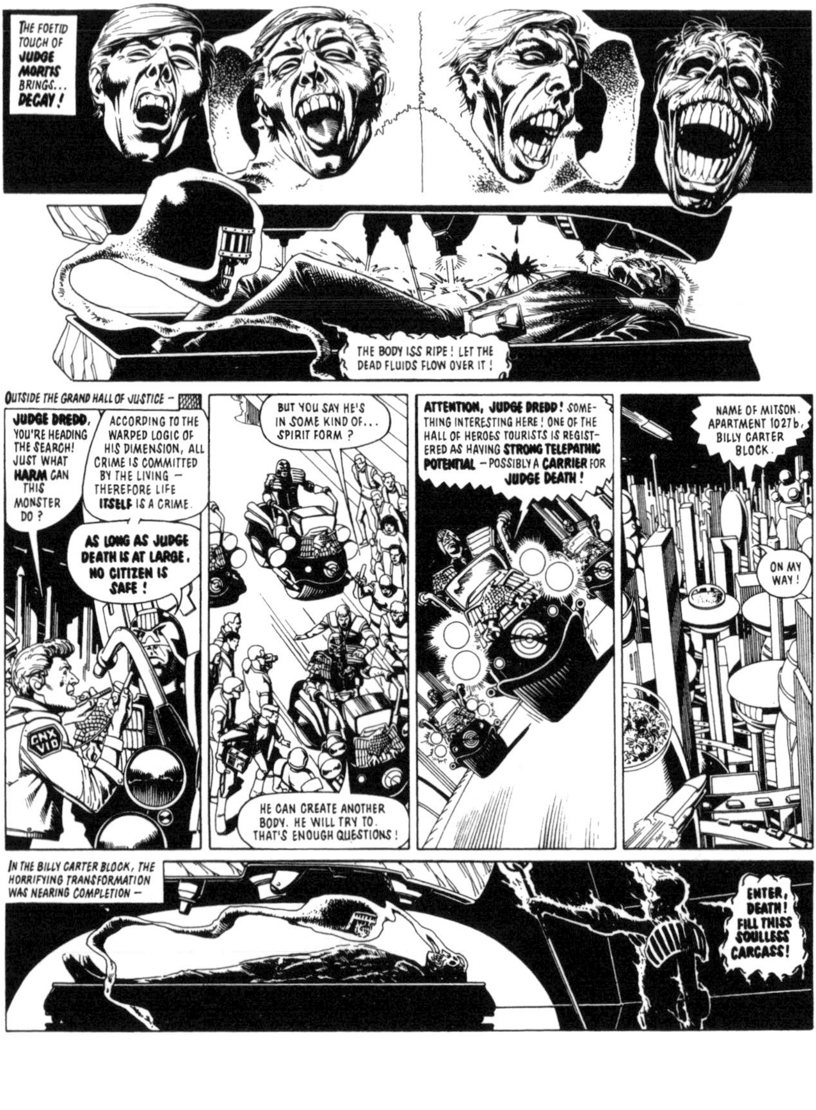
THE FOETID TOUCH OF JUDGE MORTIS BRINGS... DECAY!
THE BODY ISS RIPE! LET THE DEAD FLUIDS FLOW OVER IT!
OUTSIDE THE GRAND HALL OF JUSTICE —
JUDGE DREDD, YOU'RE HEADING THE SEARCH! JUST WHAT HARM CAN THIS MONSTER DO?
ACCORDING TO THE WARPED LOGIC OF HIS DIMENSION, ALL CRIME IS COMMITTED BY THE LIVING — THEREFORE LIFE ITSELF IS A CRIME.
AS LONG AS JUDGE DEATH IS AT LARGE, NO CITIZEN IS SAFE!
CNX VID
BUT YOU SAY HE'S IN SOME KIND OF... SPIRIT FORM?
HE CAN CREATE ANOTHER BODY. HE WILL TRY TO. THAT'S ENOUGH QUESTIONS!
ATTENTION, JUDGE DREDD! SOMETHING INTERESTING HERE! ONE OF THE HALL OF HEROES TOURISTS IS REGISTERED AS HAVING STRONG TELEPATHIC POTENTIAL — POSSIBLY A CARRIER FOR JUDGE DEATH!
NAME OF MITSON. APARTMENT 1027b, BILLY CARTER BLOCK.
ON MY WAY!
IN THE BILLY CARTER BLOCK, THE HORRIFYING TRANSFORMATION WAS NEARING COMPLETION —
ENTER, DEATH! FILL THISS SOULLESS CARCASS!

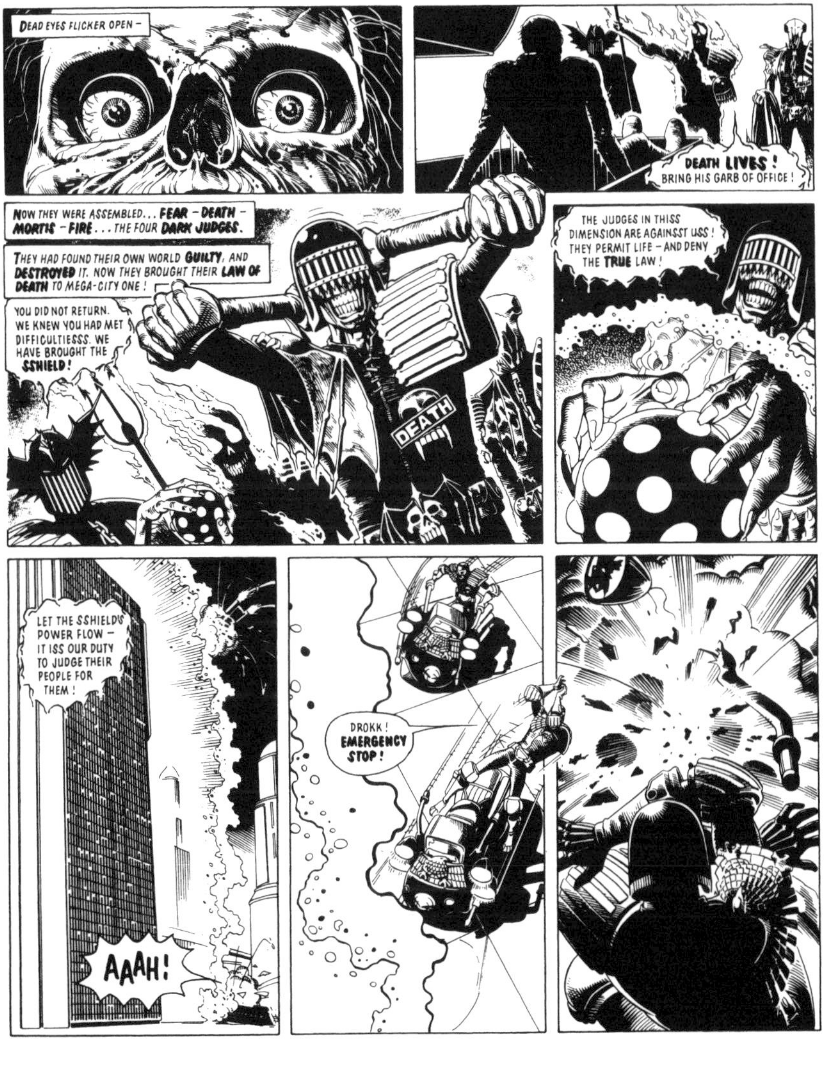
DEAD EYES FLICKER OPEN –
DEATH LIVES! BRING HIS GARB OF OFFICE!
NOW THEY WERE ASSEMBLED... FEAR – DEATH – MORTIS – FIRE... THE FOUR DARK JUDGES.
THEY HAD FOUND THEIR OWN WORLD GUILTY, AND DESTROYED IT. NOW THEY BROUGHT THEIR LAW OF DEATH TO MEGA-CITY ONE!
YOU DID NOT RETURN. WE KNEW YOU HAD MET DIFFICULTIESSS. WE HAVE BROUGHT THE SSHIELD!
DEATH
THE JUDGES IN THISS DIMENSION ARE AGAINSST USS! THEY PERMIT LIFE – AND DENY THE TRUE LAW!
LET THE SSHIELD'S POWER FLOW – IT ISS OUR DUTY TO JUDGE THEIR PEOPLE FOR THEM!
AAAH!
DROKK! EMERGENCY STOP!

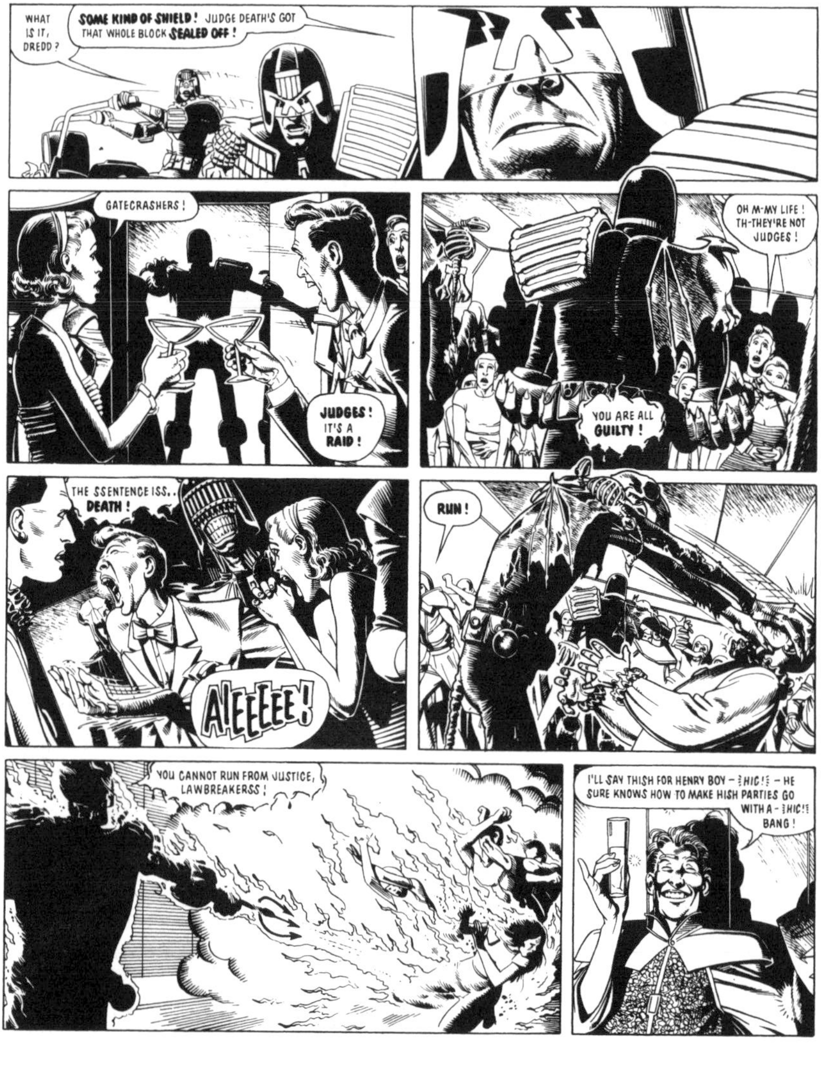
WHAT IS IT, DREDD?
SOME KIND OF SHIELD! JUDGE DEATH'S GOT THAT WHOLE BLOCK SEALED OFF!
GATECRASHERS!
JUDGES! IT'S A RAID!
OH M-MY LIFE! TH-THEY'RE NOT JUDGES!
YOU ARE ALL GUILTY!
THE SSENTENCE ISS.. DEATH!
AIEEEEE!
RUN!
YOU CANNOT RUN FROM JUSTICE, LAWBREAKERSS!
I'LL SAY THISH FOR HENRY BOY - HIC! - HE SURE KNOWS HOW TO MAKE HISH PARTIES GO WITH A - HIC! BANG!

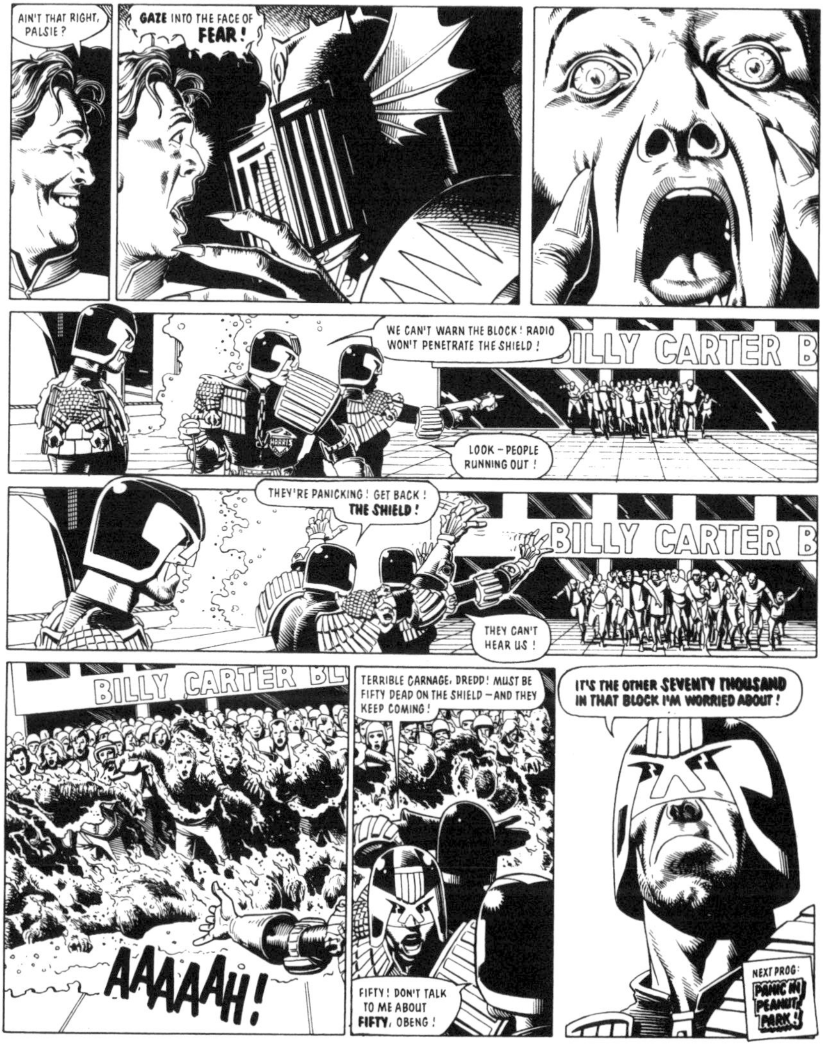
AIN'T THAT RIGHT, PALSIE?
GAZE INTO THE FACE OF FEAR!
WE CAN'T WARN THE BLOCK! RADIO WON'T PENETRATE THE SHIELD!
BILLY CARTER B
LOOK – PEOPLE RUNNING OUT!
THEY'RE PANICKING! GET BACK! THE SHIELD!
BILLY CARTER B
THEY CAN'T HEAR US!
BILLY CARTER BL
AAAAAH!
TERRIBLE CARNAGE, DREDD! MUST BE FIFTY DEAD ON THE SHIELD – AND THEY KEEP COMING!
FIFTY! DON'T TALK TO ME ABOUT FIFTY, OBENG!
IT'S THE OTHER SEVENTY THOUSAND IN THAT BLOCK I'M WORRIED ABOUT!
NEXT PROG: PANIC IN PEANUT PARK!

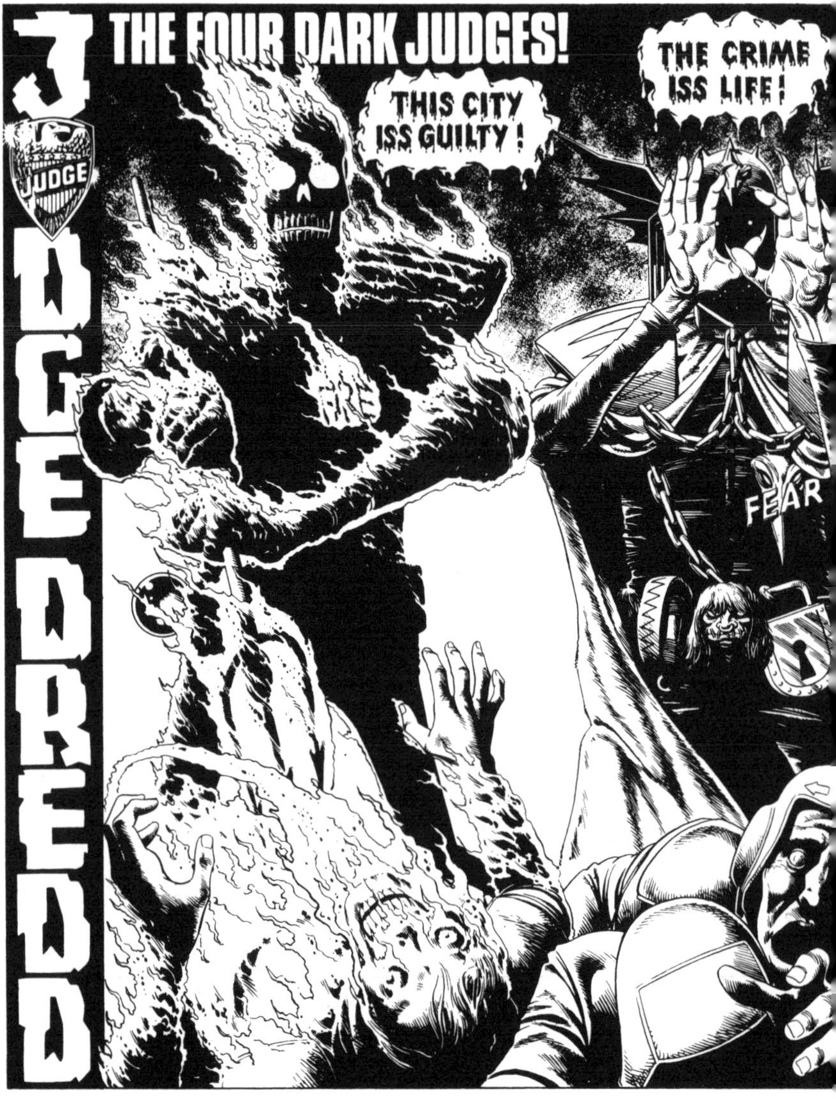
JUDGE DREDD
3
JUDGE
THE FOUR DARK JUDGES!
THIS CITY ISS GUILTY!
THE CRIME ISS LIFE!
FEAR

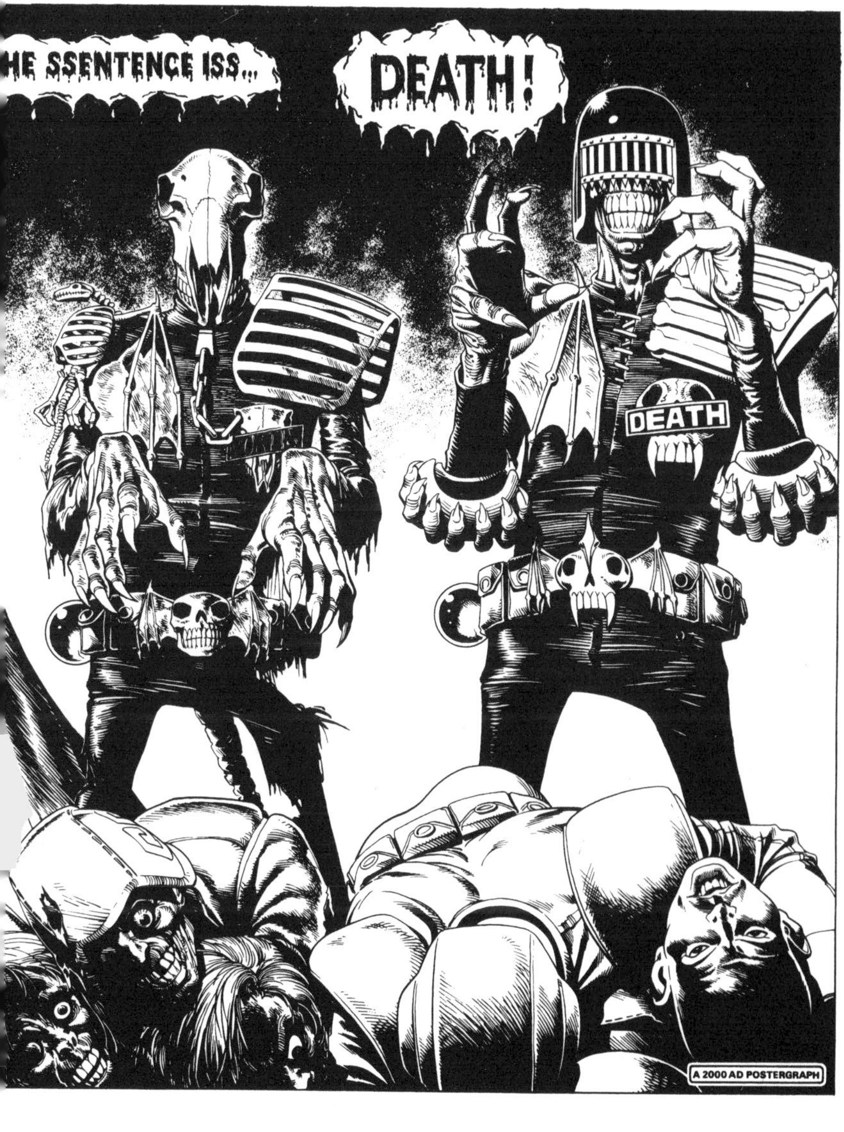
HE SSENTENCE ISS...
DEATH!
DEATH
A 2000 AD POSTERGRAPH

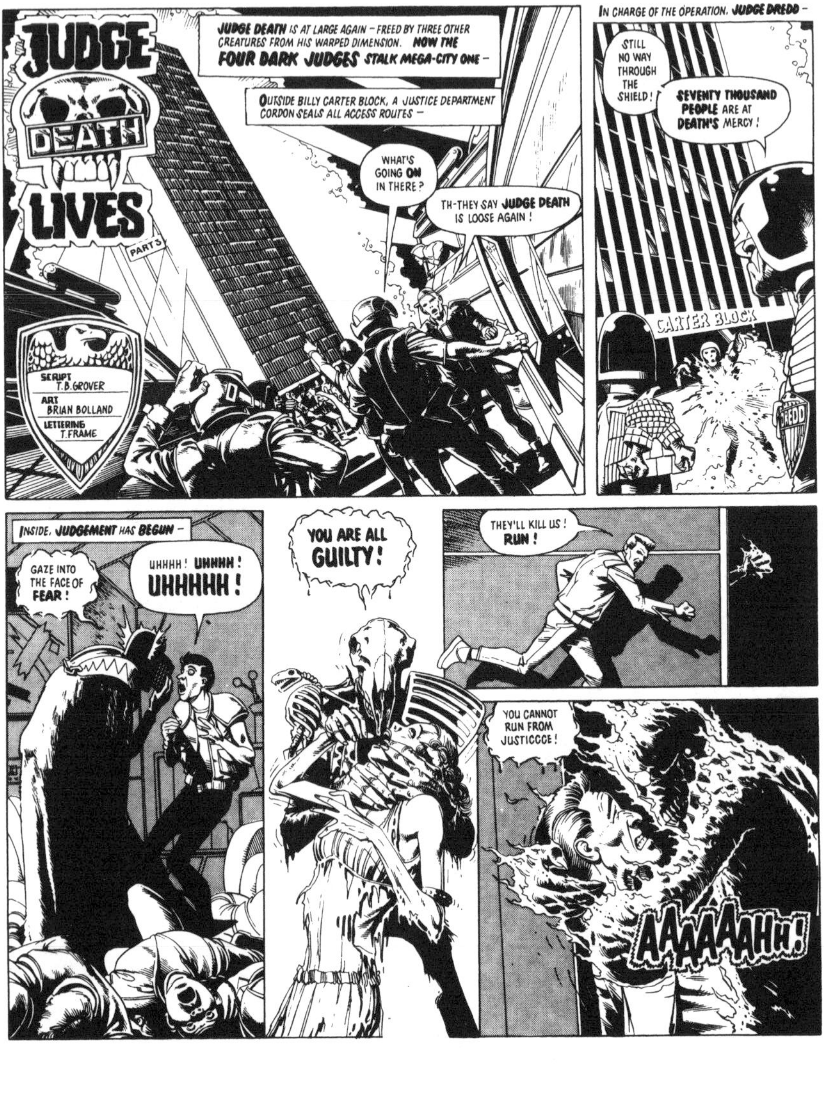
JUDGE DEATH LIVES
PART 3
SCRIPT T.B.GROVER
ART BRIAN BOLLAND
LETTERING T.FRAME
JUDGE DEATH IS AT LARGE AGAIN – FREED BY THREE OTHER CREATURES FROM HIS WARPED DIMENSION. NOW THE FOUR DARK JUDGES STALK MEGA-CITY ONE –
OUTSIDE BILLY CARTER BLOCK, A JUSTICE DEPARTMENT CORDON SEALS ALL ACCESS ROUTES –
WHAT'S GOING ON IN THERE?
TH-THEY SAY JUDGE DEATH IS LOOSE AGAIN!
IN CHARGE OF THE OPERATION, JUDGE DREDD –
STILL NO WAY THROUGH THE SHIELD!
SEVENTY THOUSAND PEOPLE ARE AT DEATH'S MERCY!
CARTER BLOCK
DREDD
INSIDE, JUDGEMENT HAS BEGUN –
GAZE INTO THE FACE OF FEAR!
UHHHH! UHHHH! UHHHHH!
YOU ARE ALL GUILTY!
THEY'LL KILL US! RUN!
YOU CANNOT RUN FROM JUSTICCCE!
AAAAAAHH!

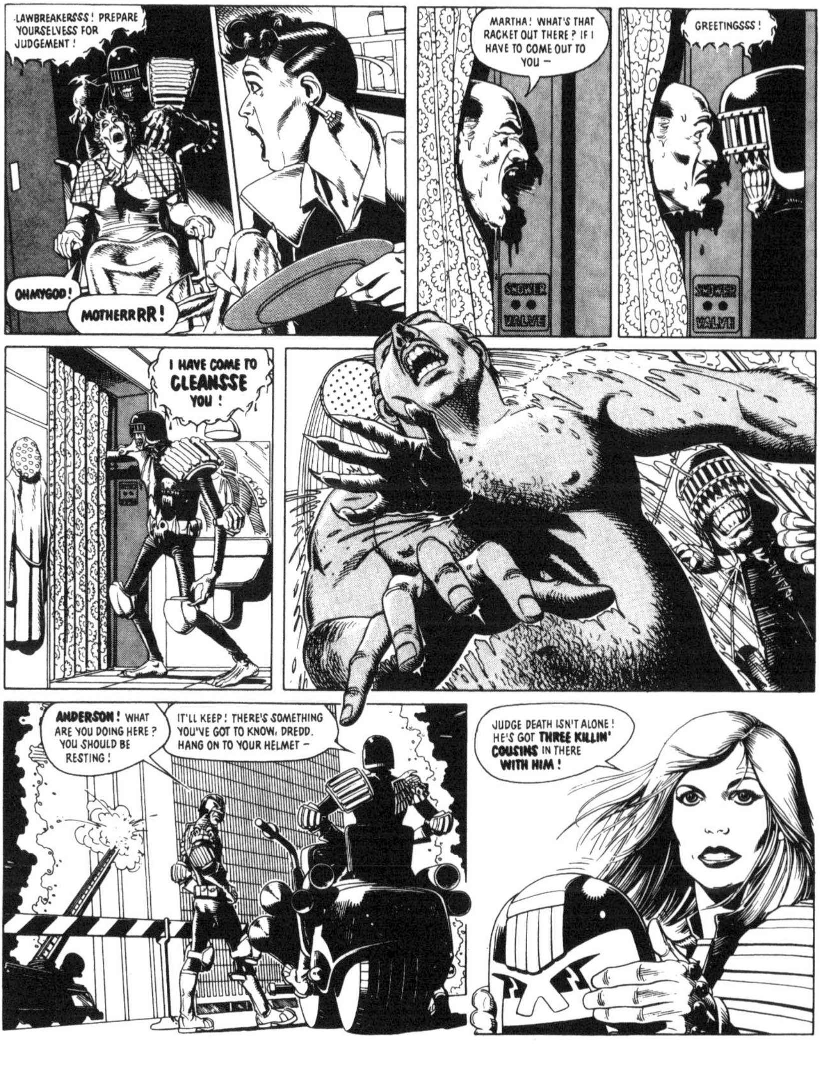
LAWBREAKERSSS! PREPARE YOURSELVESS FOR JUDGEMENT!
OHMYGOD!
MOTHERRRRR!
MARTHA! WHAT'S THAT RACKET OUT THERE? IF I HAVE TO COME OUT TO YOU –
SHOWER
VALVE
GREETINGSSS!
I HAVE COME TO CLEANSSE YOU!
ANDERSON! WHAT ARE YOU DOING HERE? YOU SHOULD BE RESTING!
IT'LL KEEP! THERE'S SOMETHING YOU'VE GOT TO KNOW, DREDD. HANG ON TO YOUR HELMET –
JUDGE DEATH ISN'T ALONE! HE'S GOT THREE KILLIN' COUSINS IN THERE WITH HIM!

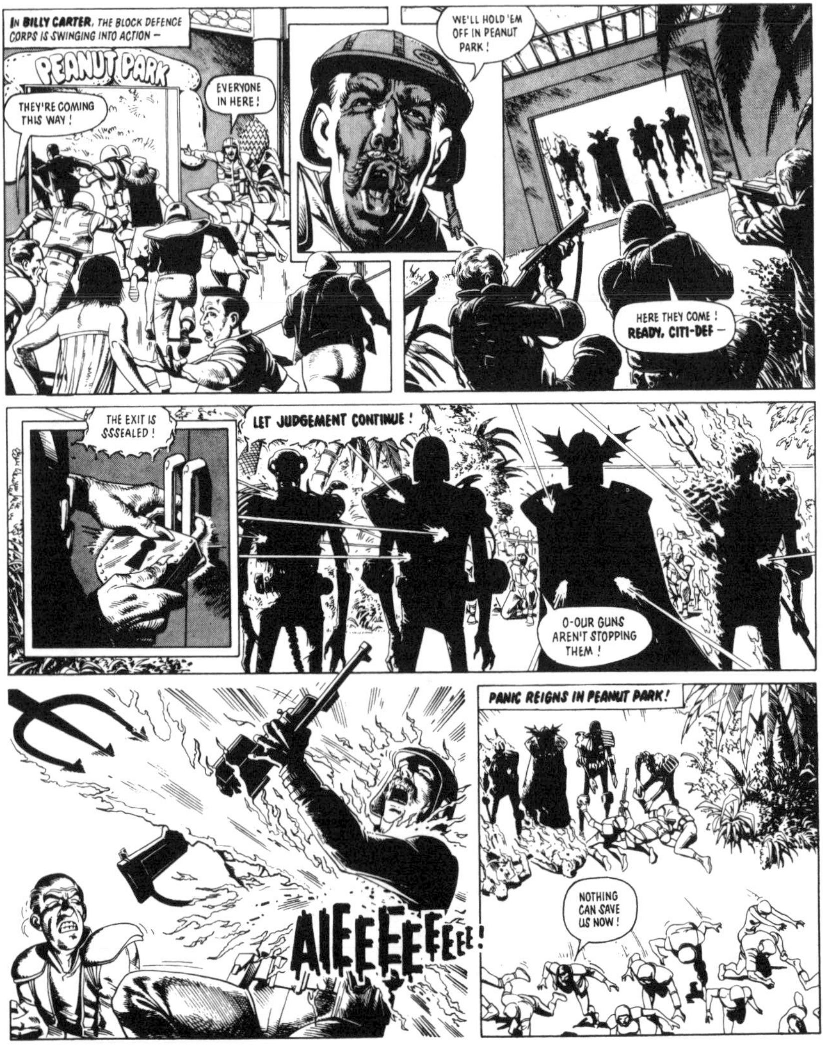
IN BILLY CARTER, THE BLOCK DEFENCE CORPS IS SWINGING INTO ACTION —
PEANUT PARK
THEY'RE COMING THIS WAY!
EVERYONE IN HERE!
WE'LL HOLD 'EM OFF IN PEANUT PARK!
HERE THEY COME! READY, CITI-DEF —
THE EXIT IS SSSEALED!
LET JUDGEMENT CONTINUE!
O-OUR GUNS AREN'T STOPPING THEM!
AIEEEEEEEE!
PANIC REIGNS IN PEANUT PARK!
NOTHING CAN SAVE US NOW!

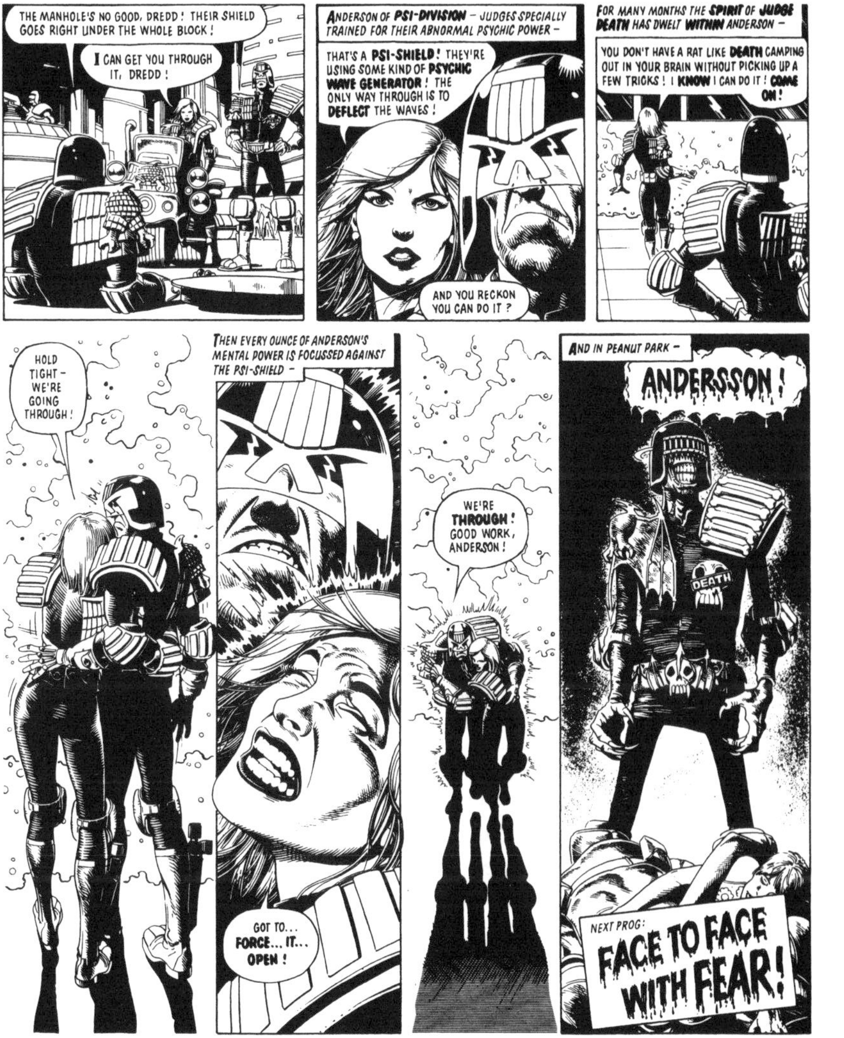
THE MANHOLE'S NO GOOD, DREDD! THEIR SHIELD GOES RIGHT UNDER THE WHOLE BLOCK!
I CAN GET YOU THROUGH IT, DREDD!
ANDERSON OF PSI-DIVISION – JUDGES SPECIALLY TRAINED FOR THEIR ABNORMAL PSYCHIC POWER –
THAT'S A PSI-SHIELD! THEY'RE USING SOME KIND OF PSYCHIC WAVE GENERATOR! THE ONLY WAY THROUGH IS TO DEFLECT THE WAVES!
AND YOU RECKON YOU CAN DO IT?
FOR MANY MONTHS THE SPIRIT OF JUDGE DEATH HAS DWELT WITHIN ANDERSON –
YOU DON'T HAVE A RAT LIKE DEATH CAMPING OUT IN YOUR BRAIN WITHOUT PICKING UP A FEW TRICKS! I KNOW I CAN DO IT! COME ON!
HOLD TIGHT – WE'RE GOING THROUGH!
THEN EVERY OUNCE OF ANDERSON'S MENTAL POWER IS FOCUSSED AGAINST THE PSI-SHIELD –
GOT TO... FORCE... IT... OPEN!
WE'RE THROUGH! GOOD WORK, ANDERSON!
AND IN PEANUT PARK –
ANDERSSON!
DEATH
NEXT PROG:
FACE TO FACE WITH FEAR!

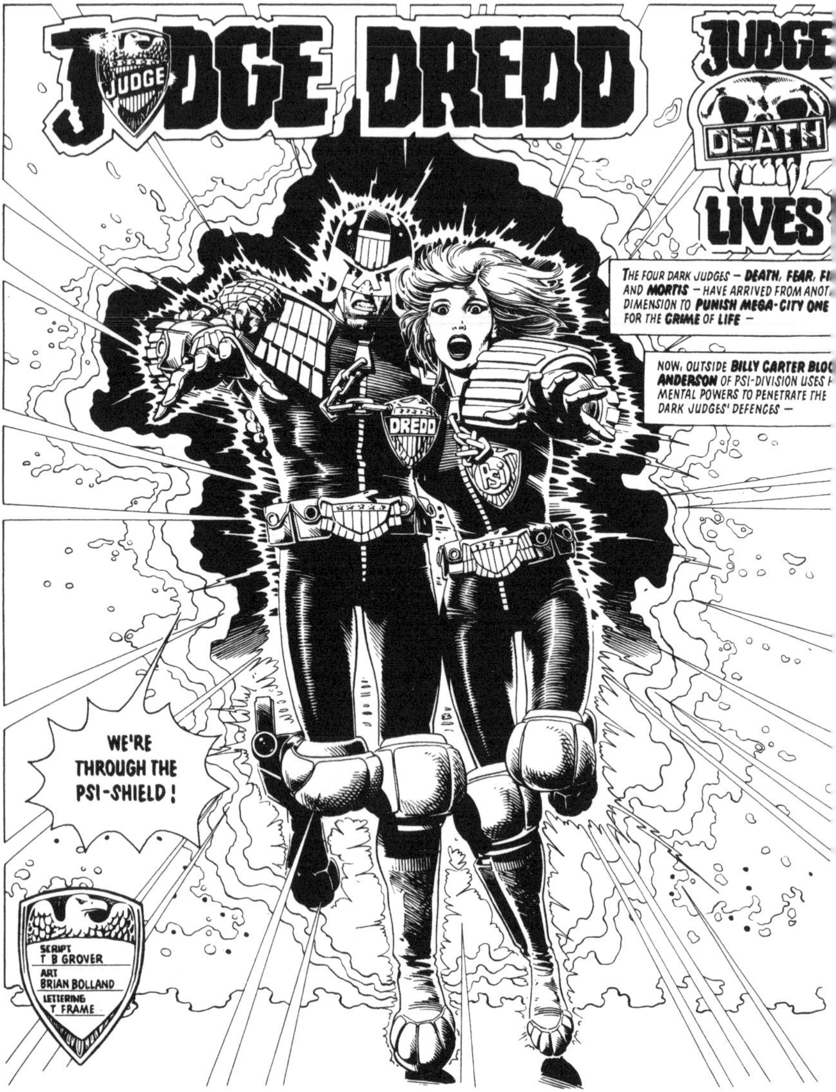
JUDGE DREDD
JUDGE DEATH LIVES
THE FOUR DARK JUDGES – DEATH, FEAR, AND MORTIS – HAVE ARRIVED FROM DIMENSION TO PUNISH MEGA-CITY ONE FOR THE CRIME OF LIFE –
NOW, OUTSIDE BILLY CARTER ANDERSON OF PSI-DIVISION USES MENTAL POWERS TO PENETRATE THE DARK JUDGES' DEFENCES –
WE'RE THROUGH THE PSI-SHIELD!
SCRIPT T B GROVER
ART BRIAN BOLLAND
LETTERING T FRAME

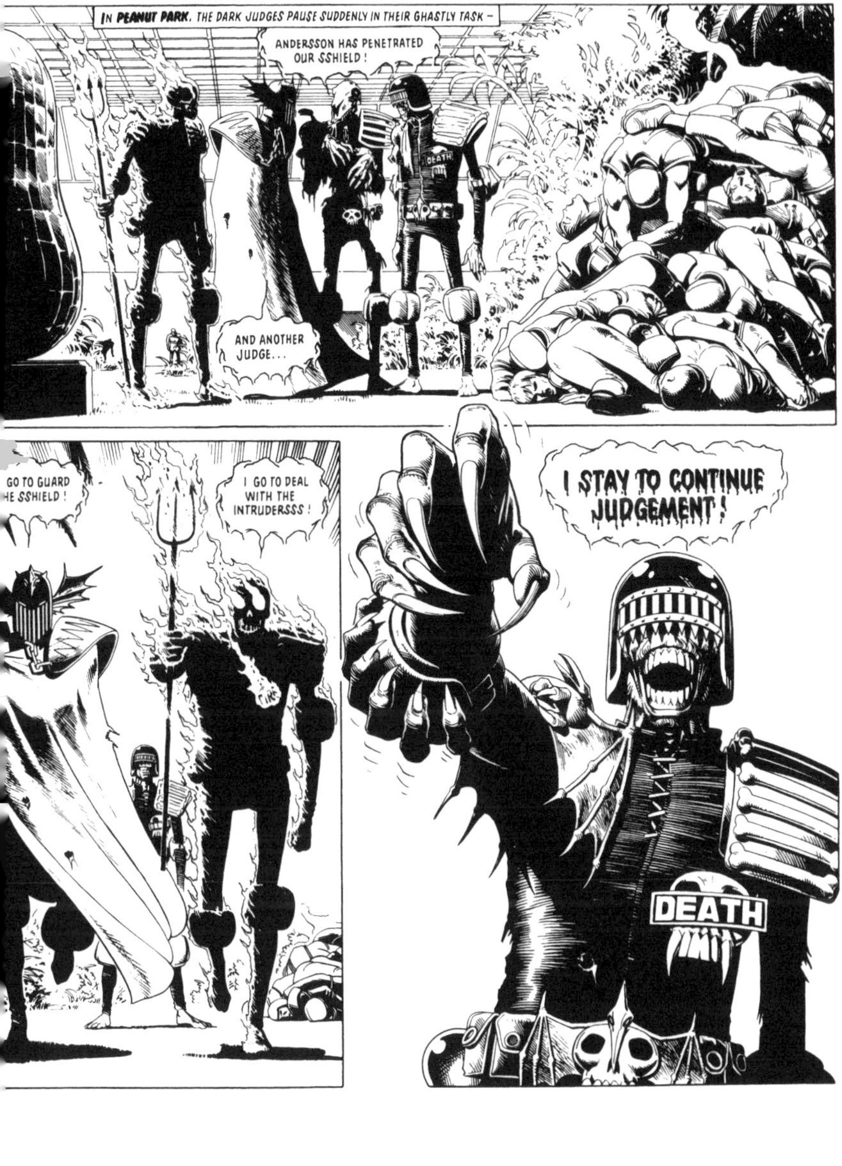
IN PEANUT PARK, THE DARK JUDGES PAUSE SUDDENLY IN THEIR GHASTLY TASK –
ANDERSSON HAS PENETRATED OUR SSHIELD!
AND ANOTHER JUDGE...
DEATH
JUDGE
GO TO GUARD HE SSHIELD!
I GO TO DEAL WITH THE INTRUDERSSS!
I STAY TO CONTINUE JUDGEMENT!
DEATH

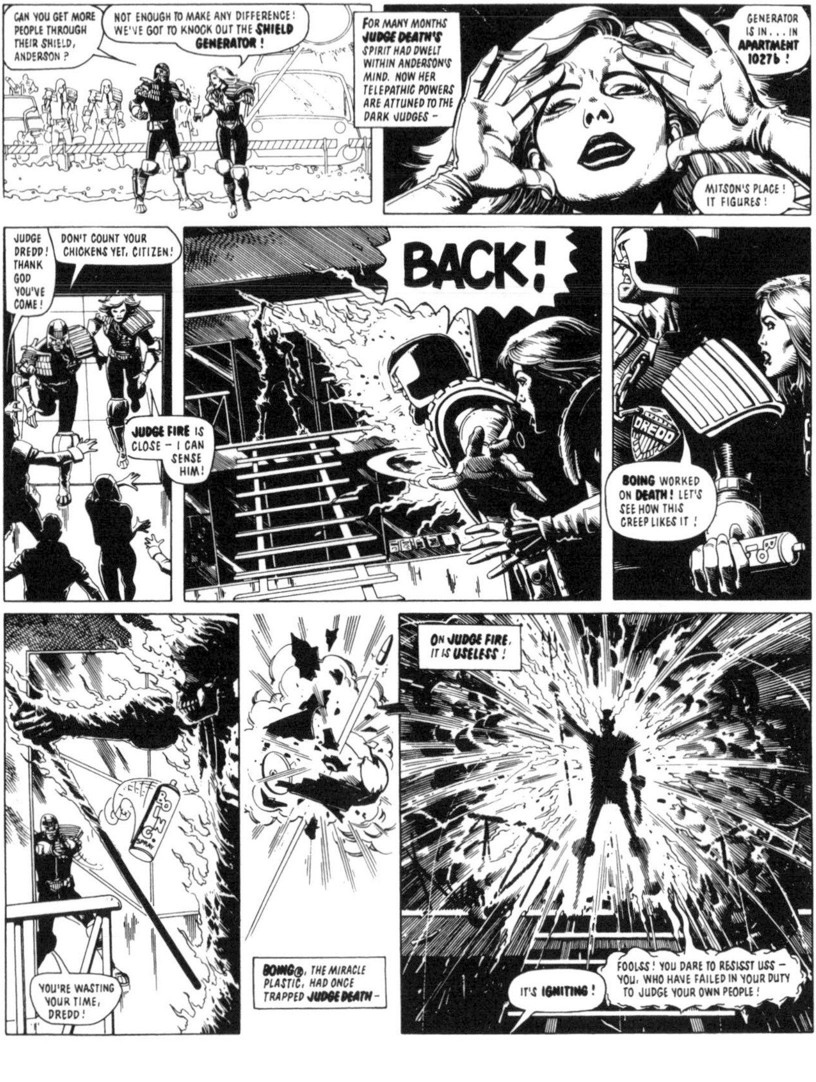
CAN YOU GET MORE PEOPLE THROUGH THEIR SHIELD, ANDERSON ?
NOT ENOUGH TO MAKE ANY DIFFERENCE! WE'VE GOT TO KNOCK OUT THE SHIELD GENERATOR !
FOR MANY MONTHS JUDGE DEATH'S SPIRIT HAD DWELT WITHIN ANDERSON'S MIND. NOW HER TELEPATHIC POWERS ARE ATTUNED TO THE DARK JUDGES –
GENERATOR IS IN . . . IN APARTMENT 1027b !
MITSON'S PLACE ! IT FIGURES !
JUDGE DREDD ! THANK GOD YOU'VE COME !
DON'T COUNT YOUR CHICKENS YET, CITIZEN!
JUDGE FIRE IS CLOSE – I CAN SENSE HIM!
BACK!
BOING WORKED ON DEATH ! LET'S SEE HOW THIS CREEP LIKES IT !
YOU'RE WASTING YOUR TIME, DREDD !
BOING®, THE MIRACLE PLASTIC, HAD ONCE TRAPPED JUDGE DEATH –
ON JUDGE FIRE, IT IS USELESS !
IT'S IGNITING !
FOOLSS ! YOU DARE TO RESISST USS – YOU, WHO HAVE FAILED IN YOUR DUTY TO JUDGE YOUR OWN PEOPLE !

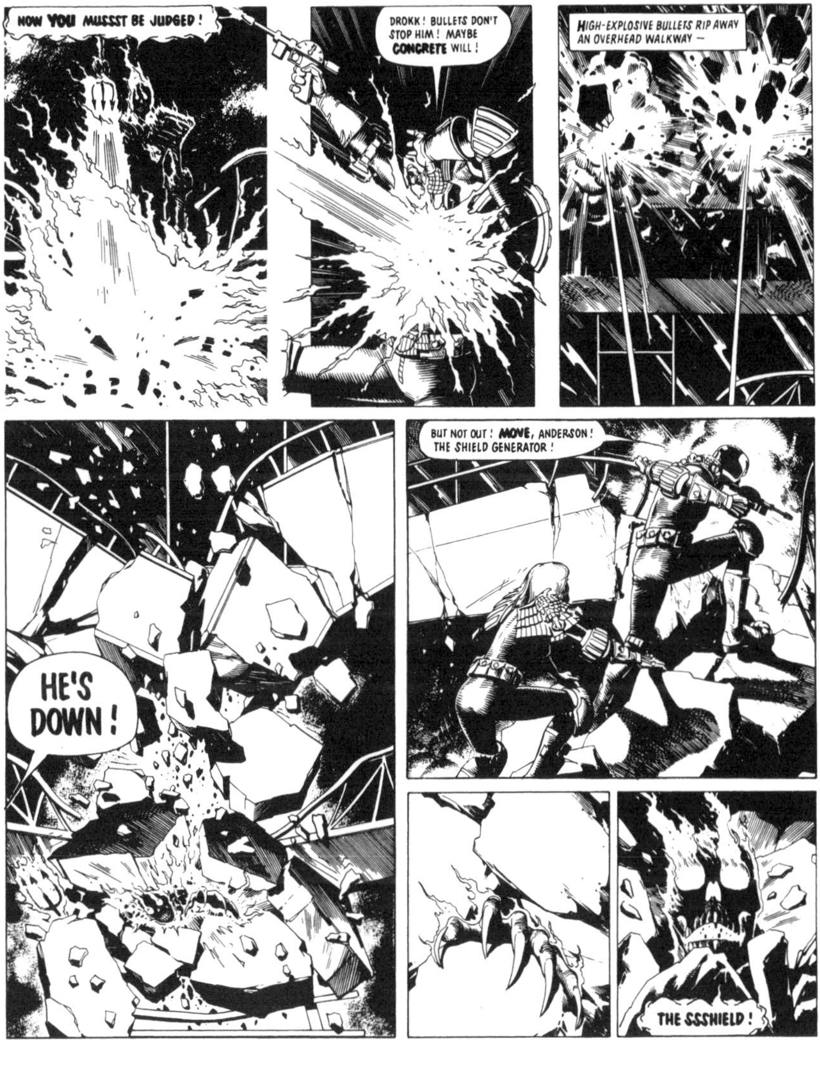
NOW YOU MUSSST BE JUDGED!
DROKK! BULLETS DON'T STOP HIM! MAYBE CONCRETE WILL!
HIGH-EXPLOSIVE BULLETS RIP AWAY AN OVERHEAD WALKWAY —
HE'S DOWN!
BUT NOT OUT! MOVE, ANDERSON! THE SHIELD GENERATOR!
THE SSSHIELD!

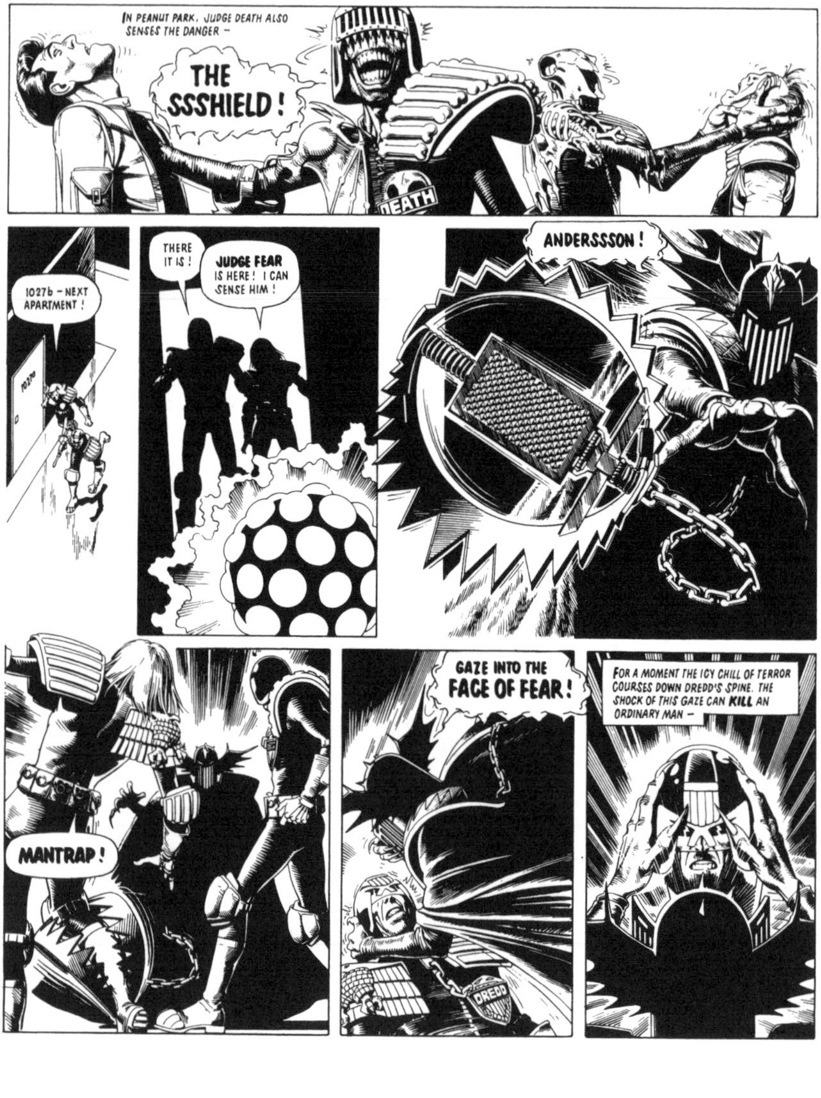
IN PEANUT PARK, JUDGE DEATH ALSO SENSES THE DANGER –
THE SSSHIELD!
DEATH
1027b – NEXT APARTMENT!
THERE IT IS!
JUDGE FEAR IS HERE! I CAN SENSE HIM!
ANDERSSSON!
MANTRAP!
GAZE INTO THE FACE OF FEAR!
DREDD
FOR A MOMENT THE ICY CHILL OF TERROR COURSES DOWN DREDD'S SPINE. THE SHOCK OF THIS GAZE CAN KILL AN ORDINARY MAN –

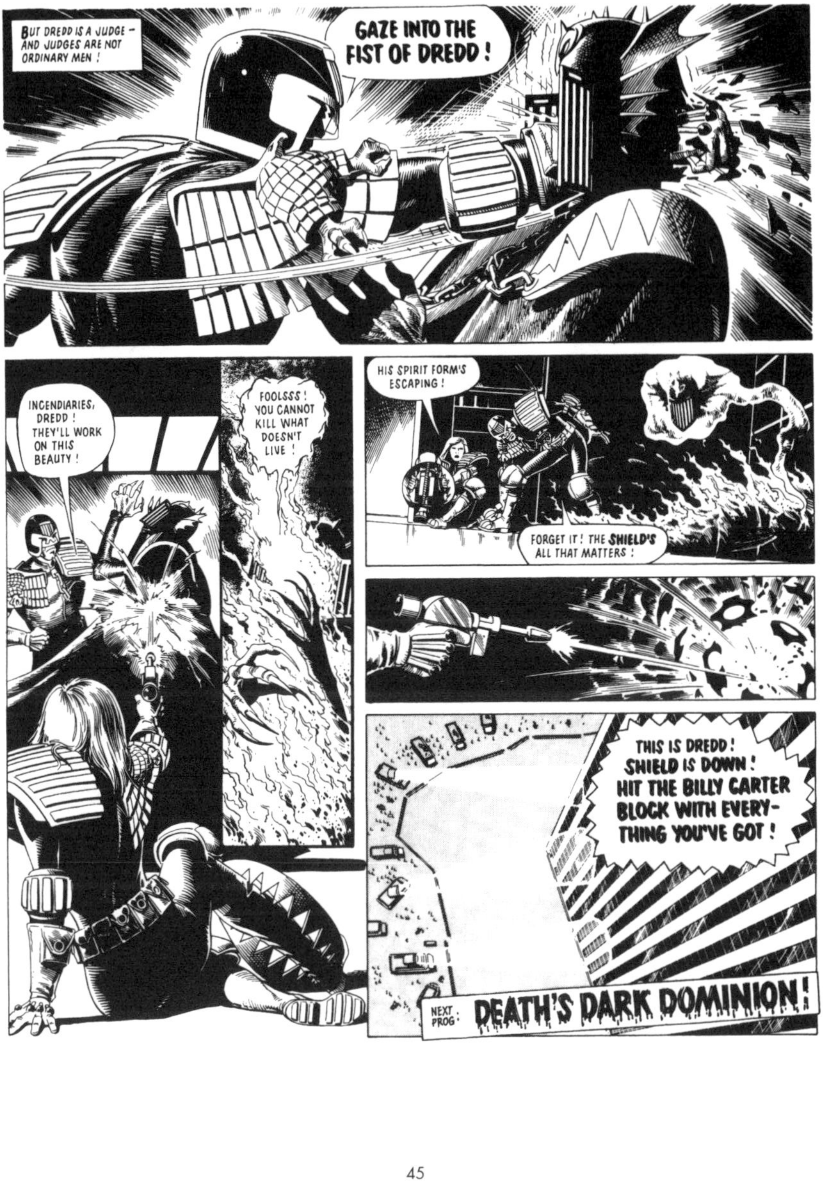
BUT DREDD IS A JUDGE - AND JUDGES ARE NOT ORDINARY MEN !
GAZE INTO THE FIST OF DREDD !
INCENDIARIES, DREDD ! THEY'LL WORK ON THIS BEAUTY !
FOOLSSS ! YOU CANNOT KILL WHAT DOESN'T LIVE !
HIS SPIRIT FORM'S ESCAPING !
FORGET IT ! THE SHIELD'S ALL THAT MATTERS !
THIS IS DREDD ! SHIELD IS DOWN ! HIT THE BILLY CARTER BLOCK WITH EVERY-THING YOU'VE GOT !
NEXT PROG: DEATH'S DARK DOMINION!

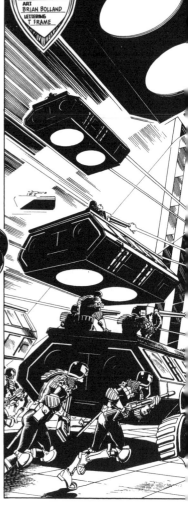

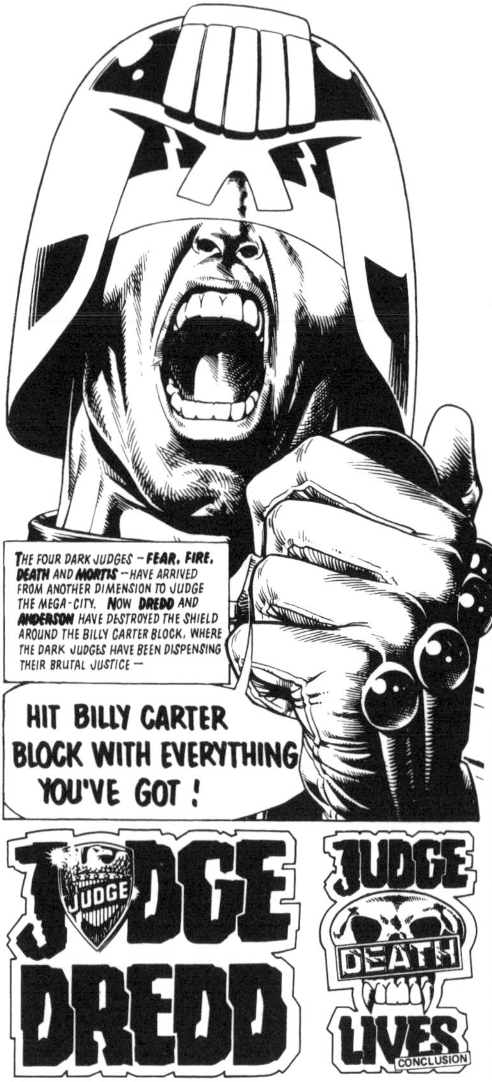
THE FOUR DARK JUDGES – FEAR, FIRE, DEATH AND MORTIS – HAVE ARRIVED FROM ANOTHER DIMENSION TO JUDGE THE MEGA-CITY. NOW DREDD AND ANDERSON HAVE DESTROYED THE SHIELD AROUND THE BILLY CARTER BLOCK, WHERE THE DARK JUDGES HAVE BEEN DISPENSING THEIR BRUTAL JUSTICE –
HIT BILLY CARTER BLOCK WITH EVERYTHING YOU'VE GOT !
JUDGE
DREDD
JUDGE DEATH LIVES
CONCLUSION

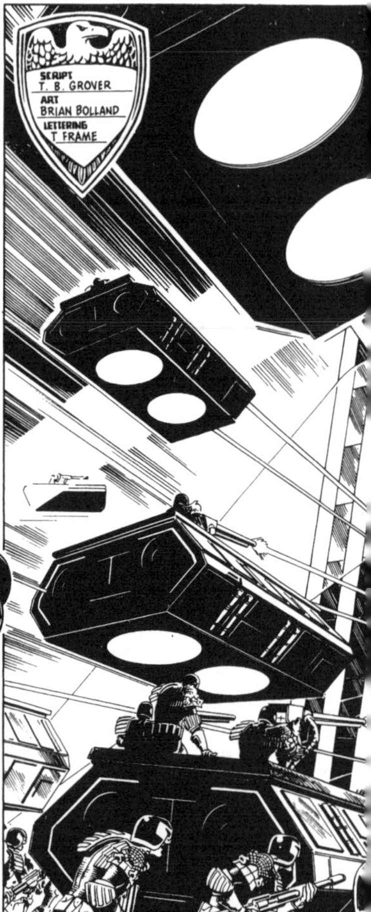
SCRIPT T. B. GROVER
ART BRIAN BOLLAND
LETTERING T FRAME

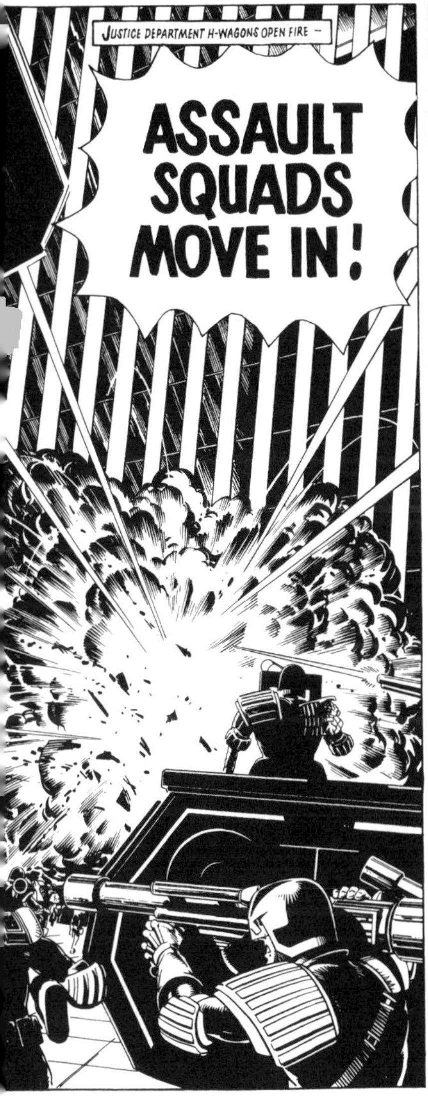
JUSTICE DEPARTMENT H-WAGONS OPEN FIRE –
ASSAULT SQUADS MOVE IN!

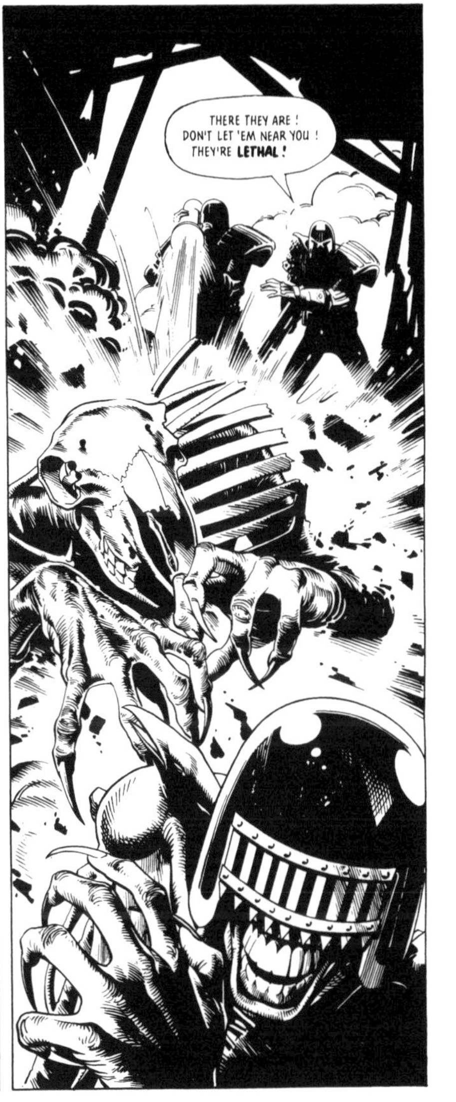
THERE THEY ARE! DON'T LET 'EM NEAR YOU! THEY'RE LETHAL!

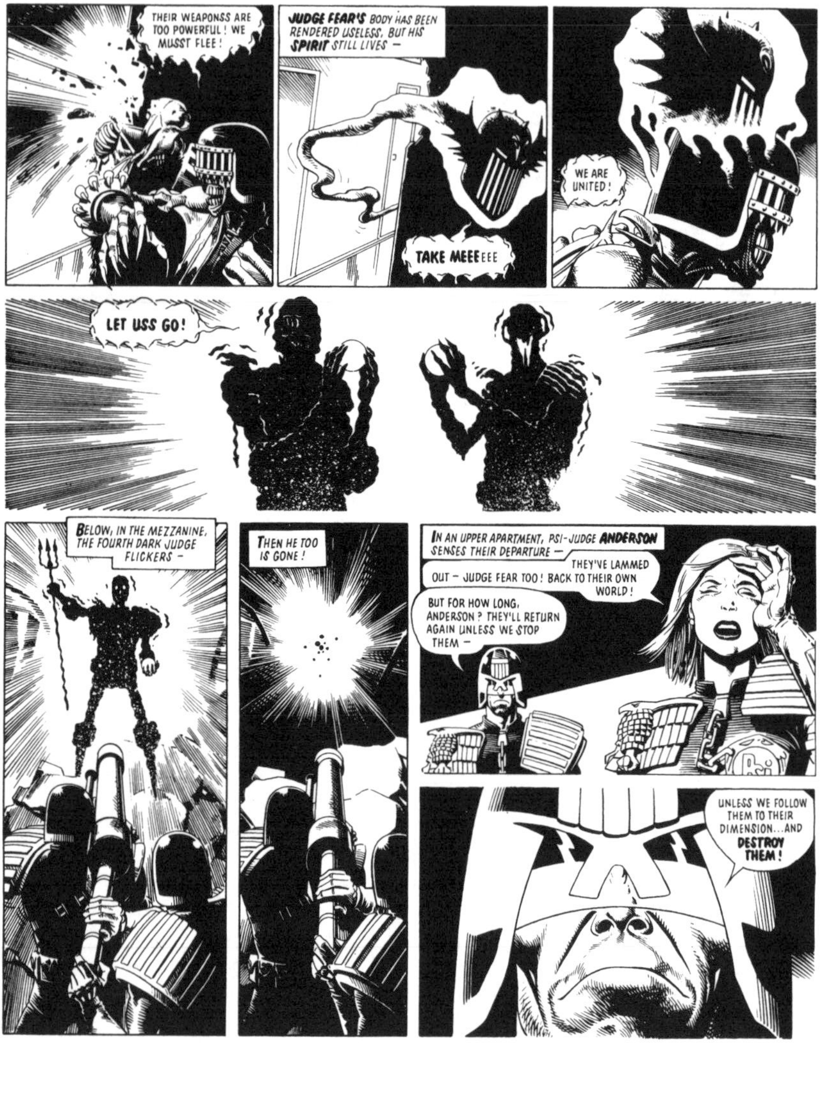
THEIR WEAPONSS ARE TOO POWERFUL! WE MUSST FLEE!
JUDGE FEAR'S BODY HAS BEEN RENDERED USELESS, BUT HIS SPIRIT STILL LIVES –
TAKE MEEEEEE
WE ARE UNITED!
LET USS GO!
BELOW, IN THE MEZZANINE, THE FOURTH DARK JUDGE FLICKERS –
THEN HE TOO IS GONE!
IN AN UPPER APARTMENT, PSI-JUDGE ANDERSON SENSES THEIR DEPARTURE –
THEY'VE LAMMED OUT – JUDGE FEAR TOO! BACK TO THEIR OWN WORLD!
BUT FOR HOW LONG, ANDERSON? THEY'LL RETURN AGAIN UNLESS WE STOP THEM –
UNLESS WE FOLLOW THEM TO THEIR DIMENSION...AND DESTROY THEM!

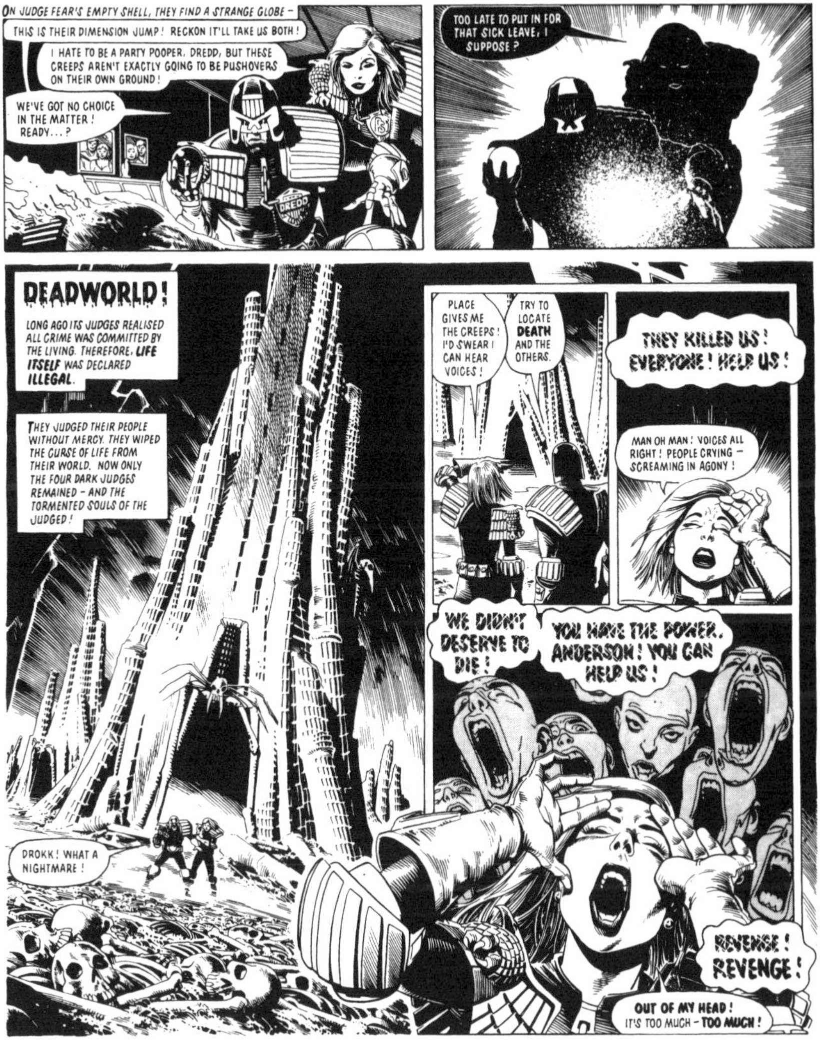
ON JUDGE FEAR'S EMPTY SHELL, THEY FIND A STRANGE GLOBE –
THIS IS THEIR DIMENSION JUMP! RECKON IT'LL TAKE US BOTH!
I HATE TO BE A PARTY POOPER, DREDD, BUT THESE CREEPS AREN'T EXACTLY GOING TO BE PUSHOVERS ON THEIR OWN GROUND!
WE'VE GOT NO CHOICE IN THE MATTER! READY...?
DREDD
TOO LATE TO PUT IN FOR THAT SICK LEAVE, I SUPPOSE?
DEADWORLD!
LONG AGO ITS JUDGES REALISED ALL CRIME WAS COMMITTED BY THE LIVING. THEREFORE, LIFE ITSELF WAS DECLARED ILLEGAL.
THEY JUDGED THEIR PEOPLE WITHOUT MERCY. THEY WIPED THE CURSE OF LIFE FROM THEIR WORLD. NOW ONLY THE FOUR DARK JUDGES REMAINED – AND THE TORMENTED SOULS OF THE JUDGED!
DROKK! WHAT A NIGHTMARE!
PLACE GIVES ME THE CREEPS! I'D SWEAR I CAN HEAR VOICES!
TRY TO LOCATE DEATH AND THE OTHERS.
THEY KILLED US! EVERYONE! HELP US!
MAN OH MAN! VOICES ALL RIGHT! PEOPLE CRYING – SCREAMING IN AGONY!
WE DIDN'T DESERVE TO DIE!
YOU HAVE THE POWER, ANDERSON! YOU CAN HELP US!
REVENGE! REVENGE!
OUT OF MY HEAD! IT'S TOO MUCH – TOO MUCH!

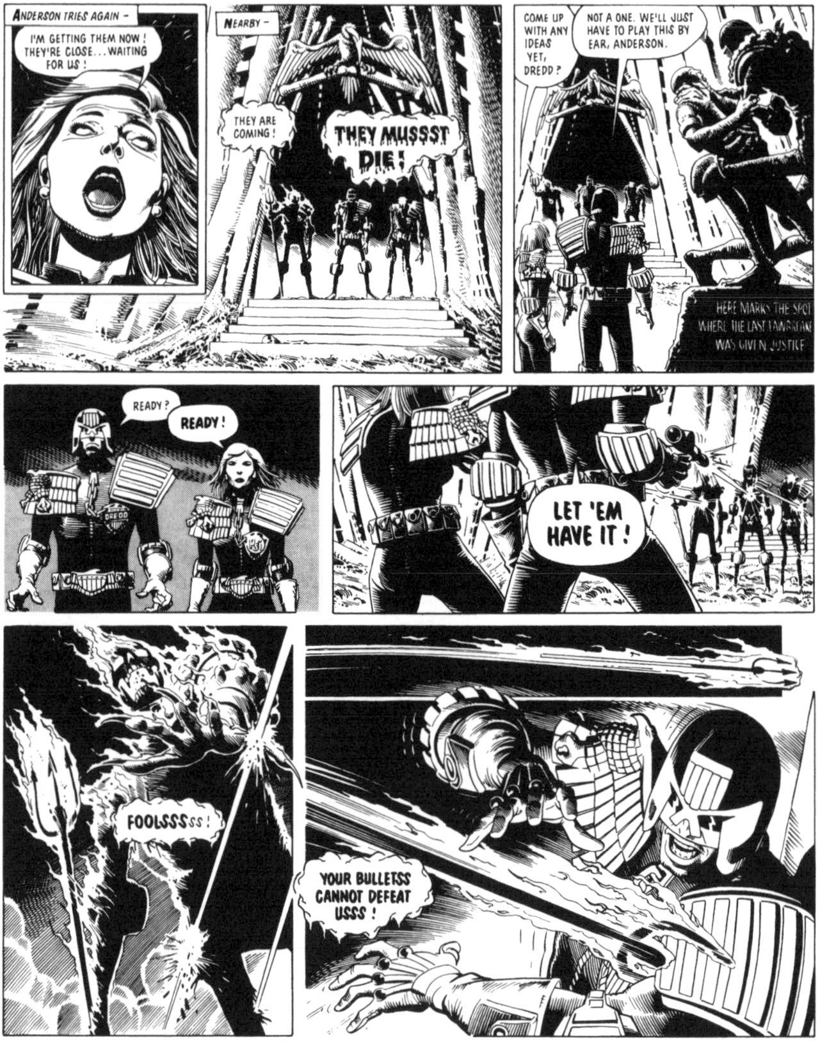
ANDERSON TRIES AGAIN –
I'M GETTING THEM NOW! THEY'RE CLOSE... WAITING FOR US!
NEARBY –
THEY ARE COMING!
THEY MUSSST DIE!
COME UP WITH ANY IDEAS YET, DREDD?
NOT A ONE. WE'LL JUST HAVE TO PLAY THIS BY EAR, ANDERSON.
READY?
READY!
LET 'EM HAVE IT!
FOOLSSSss!
YOUR BULLETSS CANNOT DEFEAT USSS!

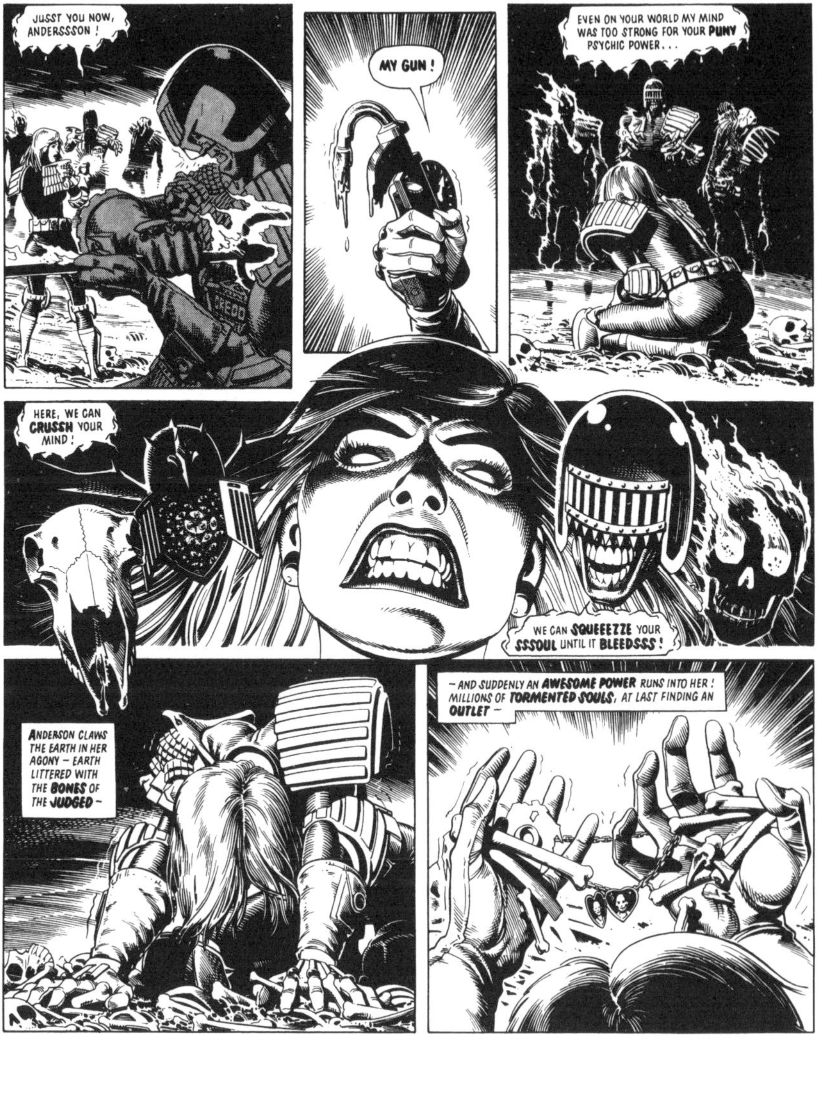
JUSST YOU NOW, ANDERSSSON!
MY GUN!
EVEN ON YOUR WORLD MY MIND WAS TOO STRONG FOR YOUR PUNY PSYCHIC POWER...
HERE, WE CAN CRUSSH YOUR MIND!
WE CAN SQUEEEZZE YOUR SSSOUL UNTIL IT BLEEDSSS!
ANDERSON CLAWS THE EARTH IN HER AGONY – EARTH LITTERED WITH THE BONES OF THE JUDGED –
– AND SUDDENLY AN AWESOME POWER RUNS INTO HER! MILLIONS OF TORMENTED SOULS, AT LAST FINDING AN OUTLET –

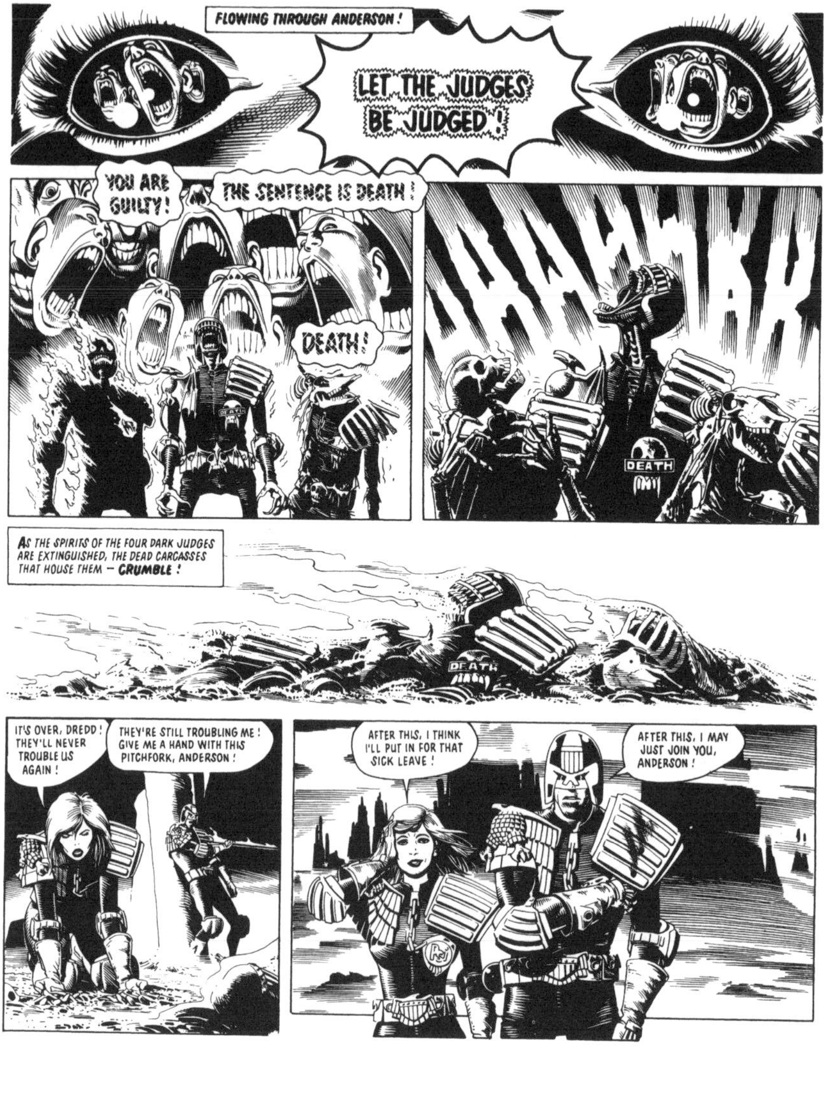
FLOWING THROUGH ANDERSON!
LET THE JUDGES BE JUDGED!
YOU ARE GUILTY!
THE SENTENCE IS DEATH!
DEATH!
AAAAAAAAAAAR
DEATH
AS THE SPIRITS OF THE FOUR DARK JUDGES ARE EXTINGUISHED, THE DEAD CARCASSES THAT HOUSE THEM – CRUMBLE!
DEATH
IT'S OVER, DREDD! THEY'LL NEVER TROUBLE US AGAIN!
THEY'RE STILL TROUBLING ME! GIVE ME A HAND WITH THIS PITCHFORK, ANDERSON!
AFTER THIS, I THINK I'LL PUT IN FOR THAT SICK LEAVE!
AFTER THIS, I MAY JUST JOIN YOU, ANDERSON!

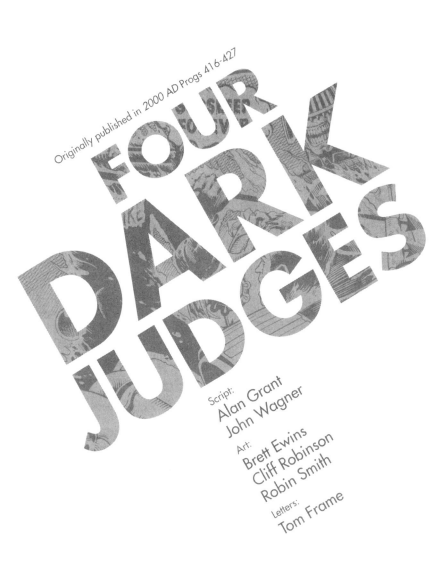

Originally published in 2000 AD Progs 416-427

FOUR DARK JUDGES

Script:
Alan Grant
John Wagner

Art:
Brett Ewins
Cliff Robinson
Robin Smith

Letters:
Tom Frame

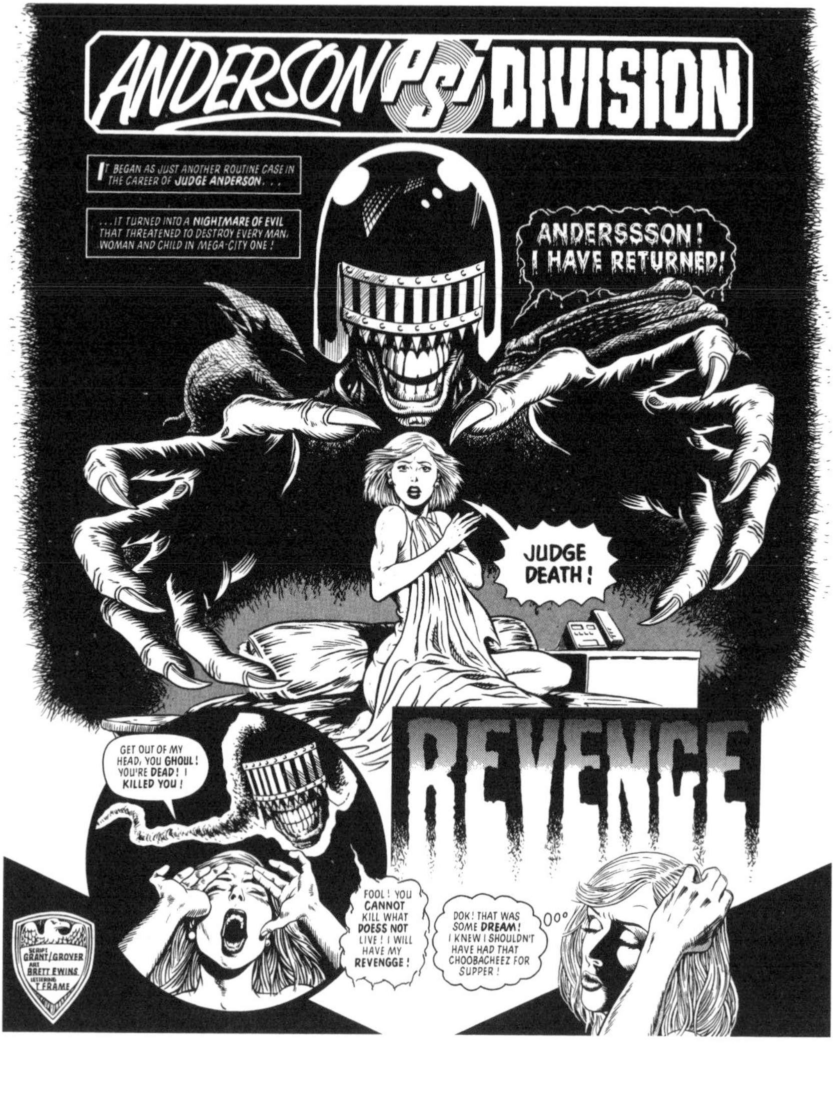
ANDERSON PSI DIVISION
IT BEGAN AS JUST ANOTHER ROUTINE CASE IN THE CAREER OF JUDGE ANDERSON . . .
. . . IT TURNED INTO A NIGHTMARE OF EVIL THAT THREATENED TO DESTROY EVERY MAN, WOMAN AND CHILD IN MEGA-CITY ONE !
ANDERSSSON ! I HAVE RETURNED!
JUDGE DEATH !
REVENGE
GET OUT OF MY HEAD, YOU GHOUL! YOU'RE DEAD! I KILLED YOU!
FOOL! YOU CANNOT KILL WHAT DOESS NOT LIVE! I WILL HAVE MY REVENGGE!
DOK! THAT WAS SOME DREAM! I KNEW I SHOULDN'T HAVE HAD THAT CHOOBACHEEZ FOR SUPPER!
OOO
SCRIPT GRANT/GROVER
ART BRETT EWINS
LETTERING T FRAME

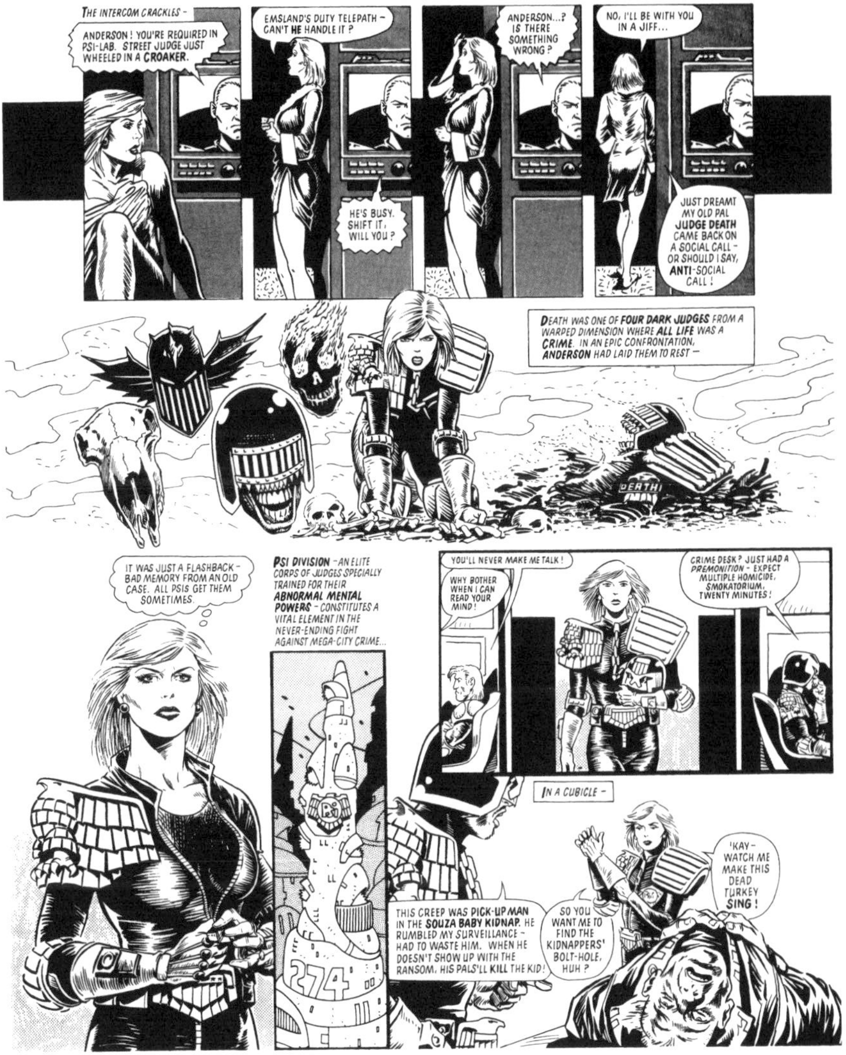
THE INTERCOM CRACKLES –
ANDERSON! YOU'RE REQUIRED IN PSI-LAB. STREET JUDGE JUST WHEELED IN A CROAKER.
EMSLAND'S DUTY TELEPATH – CAN'T HE HANDLE IT?
HE'S BUSY. SHIFT IT, WILL YOU?
ANDERSON...? IS THERE SOMETHING WRONG?
NO, I'LL BE WITH YOU IN A JIFF...
JUST DREAMT MY OLD PAL JUDGE DEATH CAME BACK ON A SOCIAL CALL – OR SHOULD I SAY, ANTI-SOCIAL CALL!
DEATH WAS ONE OF FOUR DARK JUDGES FROM A WARPED DIMENSION WHERE ALL LIFE WAS A CRIME. IN AN EPIC CONFRONTATION, ANDERSON HAD LAID THEM TO REST –
DEATH
IT WAS JUST A FLASHBACK – BAD MEMORY FROM AN OLD CASE. ALL PSIS GET THEM SOMETIMES.
PSI DIVISION – AN ELITE CORPS OF JUDGES SPECIALLY TRAINED FOR THEIR ABNORMAL MENTAL POWERS – CONSTITUTES A VITAL ELEMENT IN THE NEVER-ENDING FIGHT AGAINST MEGA-CITY CRIME...
274
YOU'LL NEVER MAKE ME TALK!
WHY BOTHER WHEN I CAN READ YOUR MIND!
CRIME DESK? JUST HAD A PREMONITION – EXPECT MULTIPLE HOMICIDE, SMOKATORIUM, TWENTY MINUTES!
IN A CUBICLE –
THIS CREEP WAS PICK-UP MAN IN THE SOUZA BABY KIDNAP. HE RUMBLED MY SURVEILLANCE – HAD TO WASTE HIM. WHEN HE DOESN'T SHOW UP WITH THE RANSOM, HIS PALS'LL KILL THE KID!
SO YOU WANT ME TO FIND THE KIDNAPPERS' BOLT-HOLE, HUH?
'KAY – WATCH ME MAKE THIS DEAD TURKEY SING!

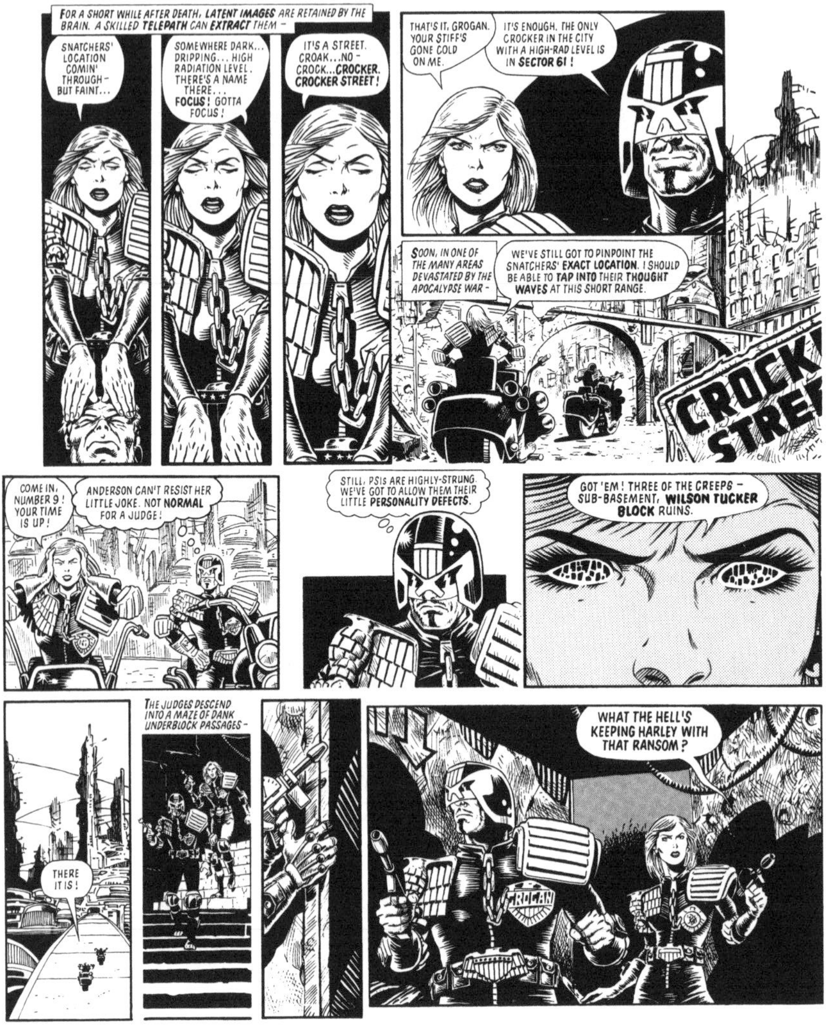
FOR A SHORT WHILE AFTER DEATH, LATENT IMAGES ARE RETAINED BY THE BRAIN. A SKILLED TELEPATH CAN EXTRACT THEM –
SNATCHERS' LOCATION COMIN' THROUGH– BUT FAINT...
SOMEWHERE DARK... DRIPPING... HIGH RADIATION LEVEL. THERE'S A NAME THERE... FOCUS! GOTTA FOCUS!
IT'S A STREET. CROAK...NO– CROCK...CROCKER. CROCKER STREET!
THAT'S IT, GROGAN. YOUR STIFF'S GONE COLD ON ME.
IT'S ENOUGH. THE ONLY CROCKER IN THE CITY WITH A HIGH-RAD LEVEL IS IN SECTOR 61!
SOON, IN ONE OF THE MANY AREAS DEVASTATED BY THE APOCALYPSE WAR –
WE'VE STILL GOT TO PINPOINT THE SNATCHERS' EXACT LOCATION. I SHOULD BE ABLE TO TAP INTO THEIR THOUGHT WAVES AT THIS SHORT RANGE.
CROCK STREE
COME IN, NUMBER 9! YOUR TIME IS UP!
ANDERSON CAN'T RESIST HER LITTLE JOKE. NOT NORMAL FOR A JUDGE!
STILL, PSIS ARE HIGHLY-STRUNG. WE'VE GOT TO ALLOW THEM THEIR LITTLE PERSONALITY DEFECTS.
GOT 'EM! THREE OF THE CREEPS – SUB-BASEMENT, WILSON TUCKER BLOCK RUINS.
THERE IT IS!
THE JUDGES DESCEND INTO A MAZE OF DANK UNDERBLOCK PASSAGES –
WHAT THE HELL'S KEEPING HARLEY WITH THAT RANSOM?
GROGAN

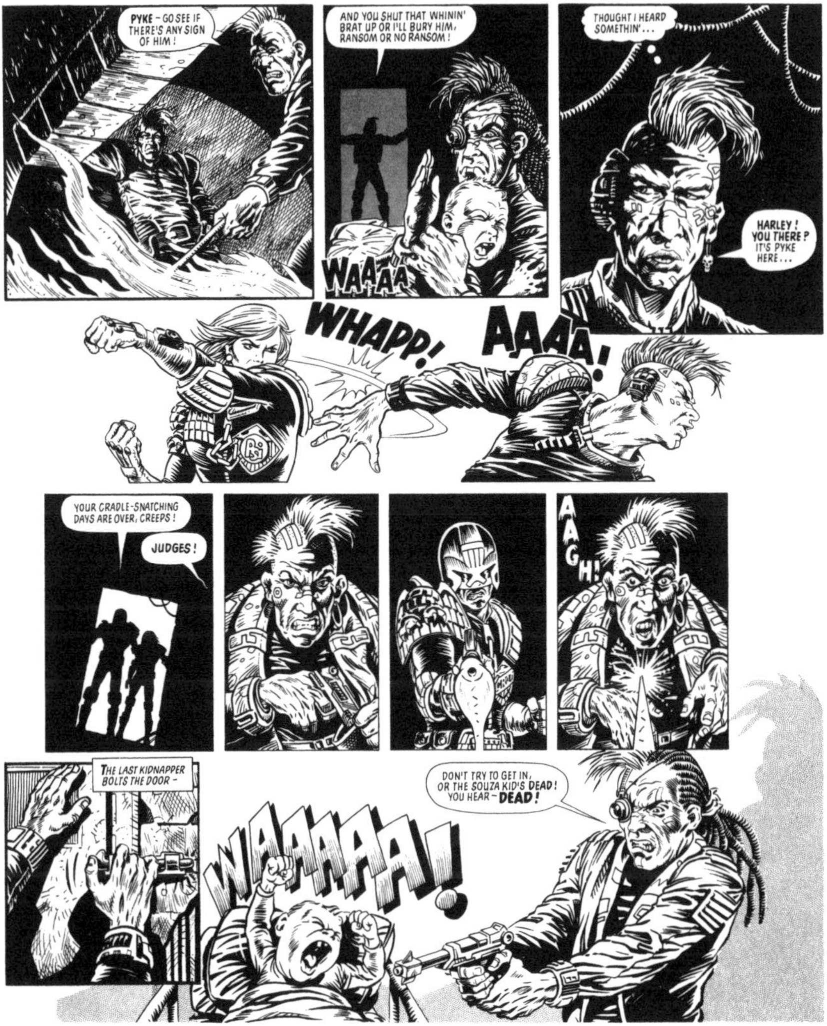
PYKE – GO SEE IF THERE'S ANY SIGN OF HIM !
AND YOU SHUT THAT WHININ' BRAT UP OR I'LL BURY HIM, RANSOM OR NO RANSOM !
WAAAA
THOUGHT I HEARD SOMETHIN'...
HARLEY ! YOU THERE ? IT'S PYKE HERE...
WHAPP!
AAAA!
YOUR CRADLE-SNATCHING DAYS ARE OVER, CREEPS !
JUDGES !
AAGH!
THE LAST KIDNAPPER BOLTS THE DOOR –
WAAAAA!
DON'T TRY TO GET IN, OR THE SOUZA KID'S DEAD ! YOU HEAR – DEAD !

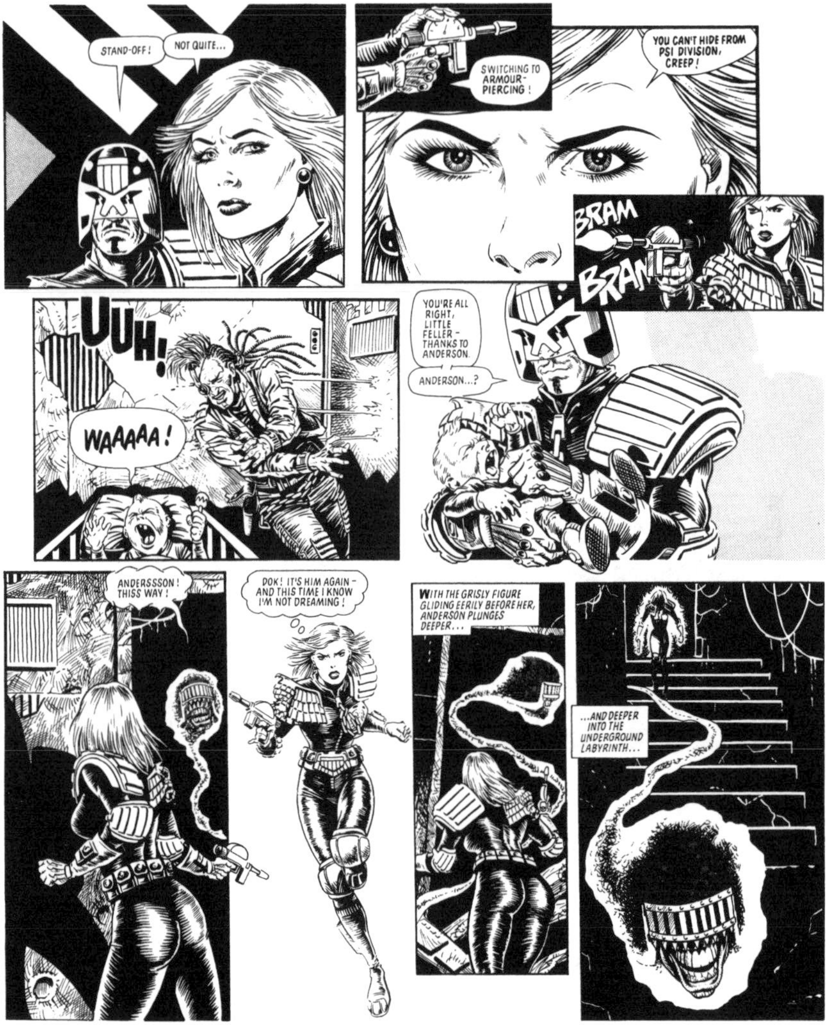
STAND-OFF!
NOT QUITE...
SWITCHING TO ARMOUR-PIERCING!
YOU CAN'T HIDE FROM PSI DIVISION, CREEP!
BRAM
BRAM
UUH!
WAAAAA!
YOU'RE ALL RIGHT, LITTLE FELLER - THANKS TO ANDERSON.
ANDERSON...?
ANDERSSSON! THISS WAY!
DOK! IT'S HIM AGAIN - AND THIS TIME I KNOW I'M NOT DREAMING!
WITH THE GRISLY FIGURE GLIDING EERILY BEFORE HER, ANDERSON PLUNGES DEEPER...
...AND DEEPER INTO THE UNDERGROUND LABYRINTH...

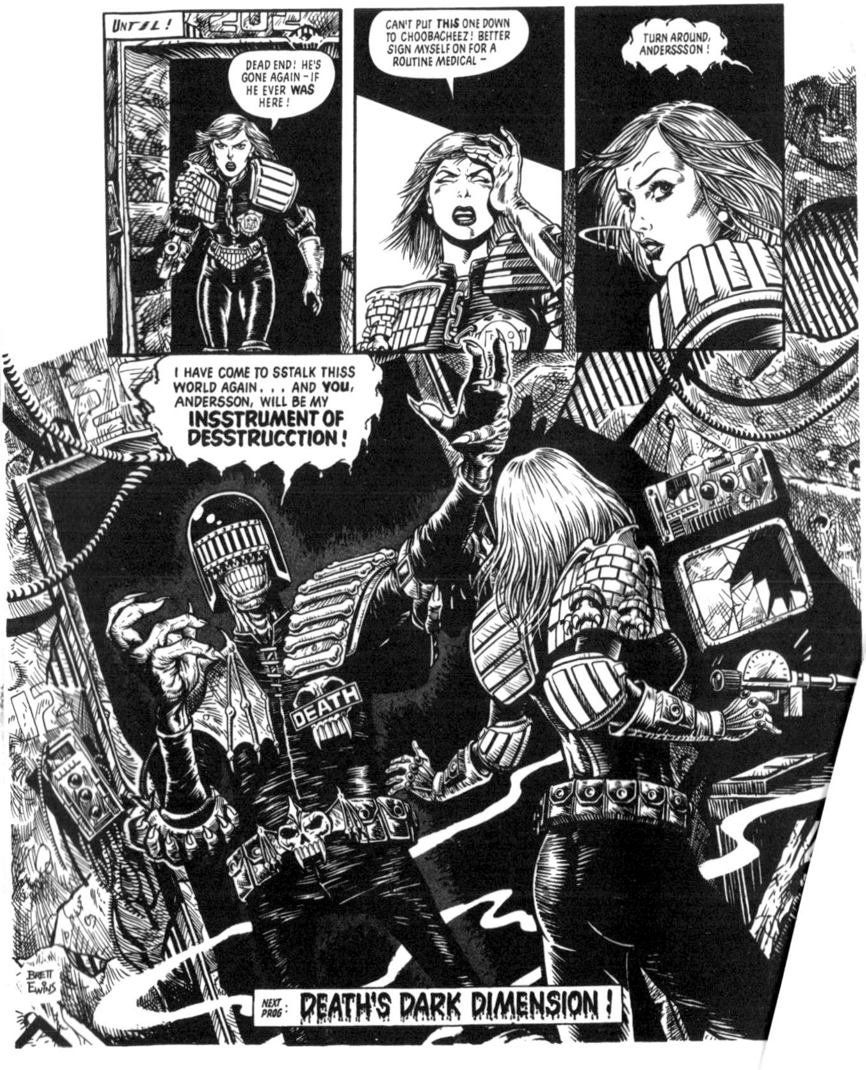
UNTIL!
DEAD END! HE'S GONE AGAIN – IF HE EVER WAS HERE!
CAN'T PUT THIS ONE DOWN TO CHOOBACHEEZ! BETTER SIGN MYSELF ON FOR A ROUTINE MEDICAL –
TURN AROUND, ANDERSSSON!
I HAVE COME TO SSTALK THISS WORLD AGAIN. . . AND YOU, ANDERSSON, WILL BE MY INSSTRUMENT OF DESSTRUCCTION!
DEATH
BRETT EWINS
NEXT PROG: DEATH'S DARK DIMENSION!

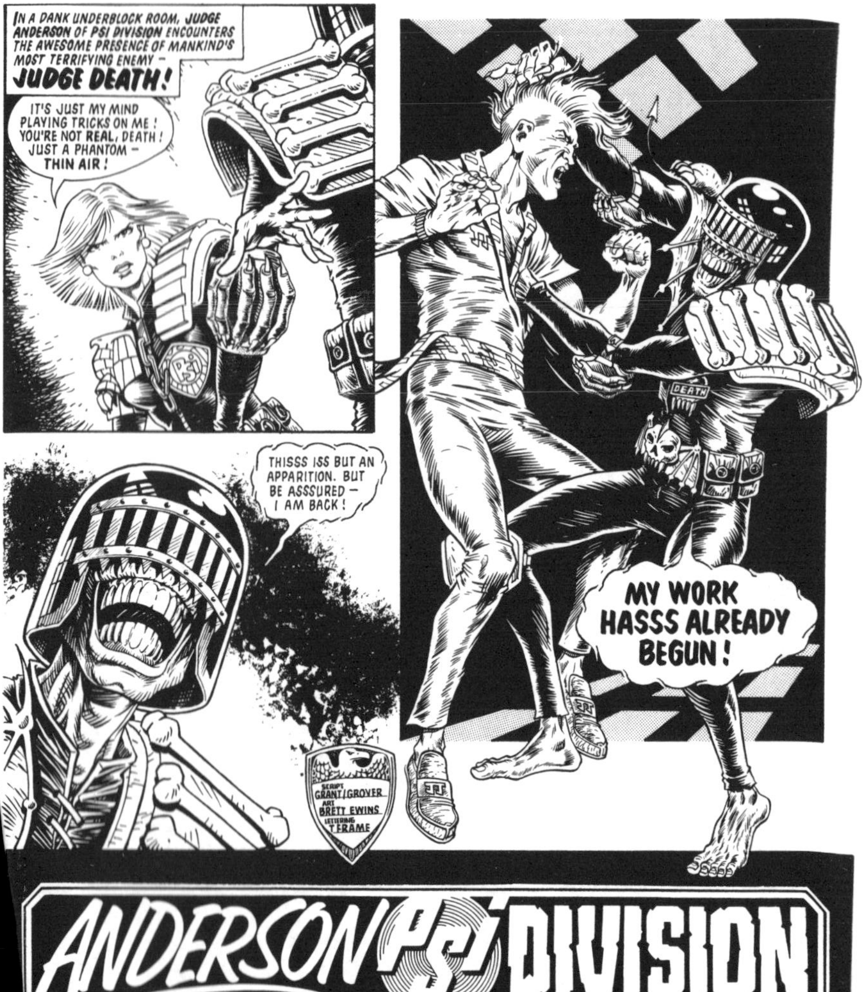
IN A DANK UNDERBLOCK ROOM, JUDGE ANDERSON OF PSI DIVISION ENCOUNTERS THE AWESOME PRESENCE OF MANKIND'S MOST TERRIFYING ENEMY – JUDGE DEATH!
IT'S JUST MY MIND PLAYING TRICKS ON ME! YOU'RE NOT REAL, DEATH! JUST A PHANTOM – THIN AIR!
THISSS ISS BUT AN APPARITION. BUT BE ASSSURED – I AM BACK!
MY WORK HASSS ALREADY BEGUN!
SCRIPT GRANT/GROVER
ART BRETT EWINS
LETTERING T FRAME
ANDERSON PSI DIVISION

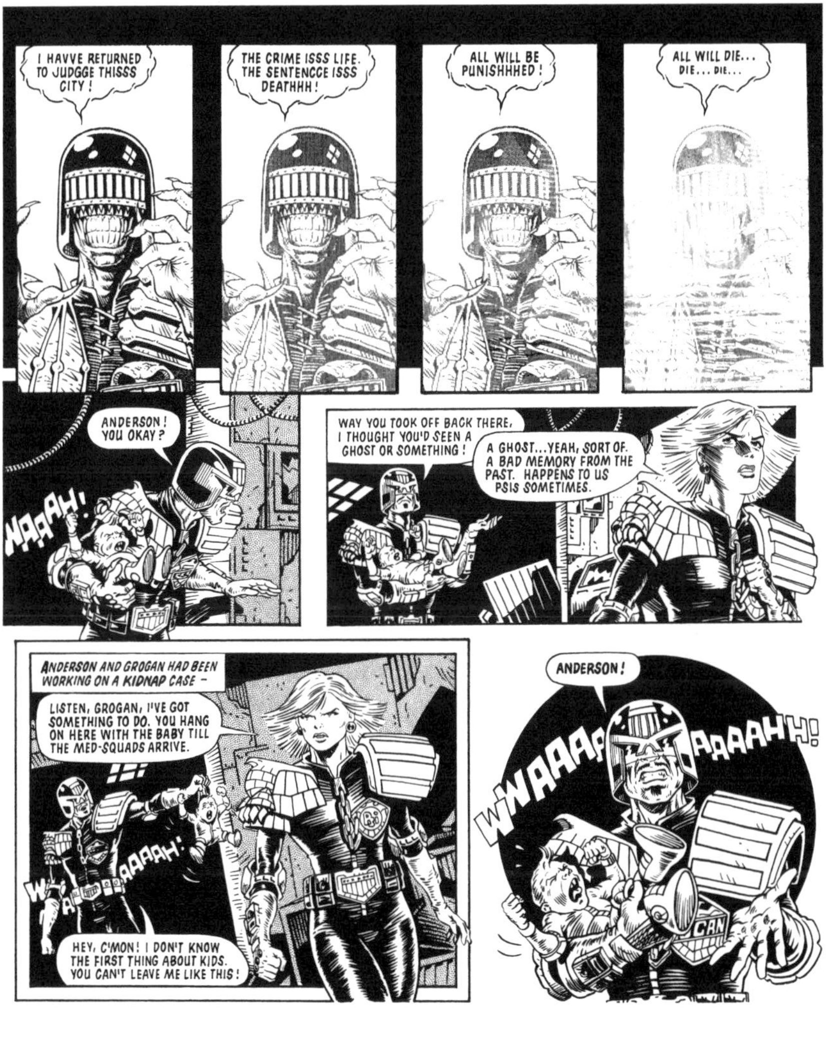
I HAVVE RETURNED TO JUDGGE THISSS CITY!
THE CRIME ISSS LIFE. THE SENTENCCE ISSS DEATHHH!
ALL WILL BE PUNISHHHED!
ALL WILL DIE... DIE... DIE...
ANDERSON! YOU OKAY?
WAAAH!
WAY YOU TOOK OFF BACK THERE, I THOUGHT YOU'D SEEN A GHOST OR SOMETHING!
A GHOST...YEAH, SORT OF. A BAD MEMORY FROM THE PAST. HAPPENS TO US PSIS SOMETIMES.
ANDERSON AND GROGAN HAD BEEN WORKING ON A KIDNAP CASE –
LISTEN, GROGAN, I'VE GOT SOMETHING TO DO. YOU HANG ON HERE WITH THE BABY TILL THE MED-SQUADS ARRIVE.
WAAAAH!
HEY, C'MON! I DON'T KNOW THE FIRST THING ABOUT KIDS. YOU CAN'T LEAVE ME LIKE THIS!
ANDERSON!
WWAAAAAAAAHH!

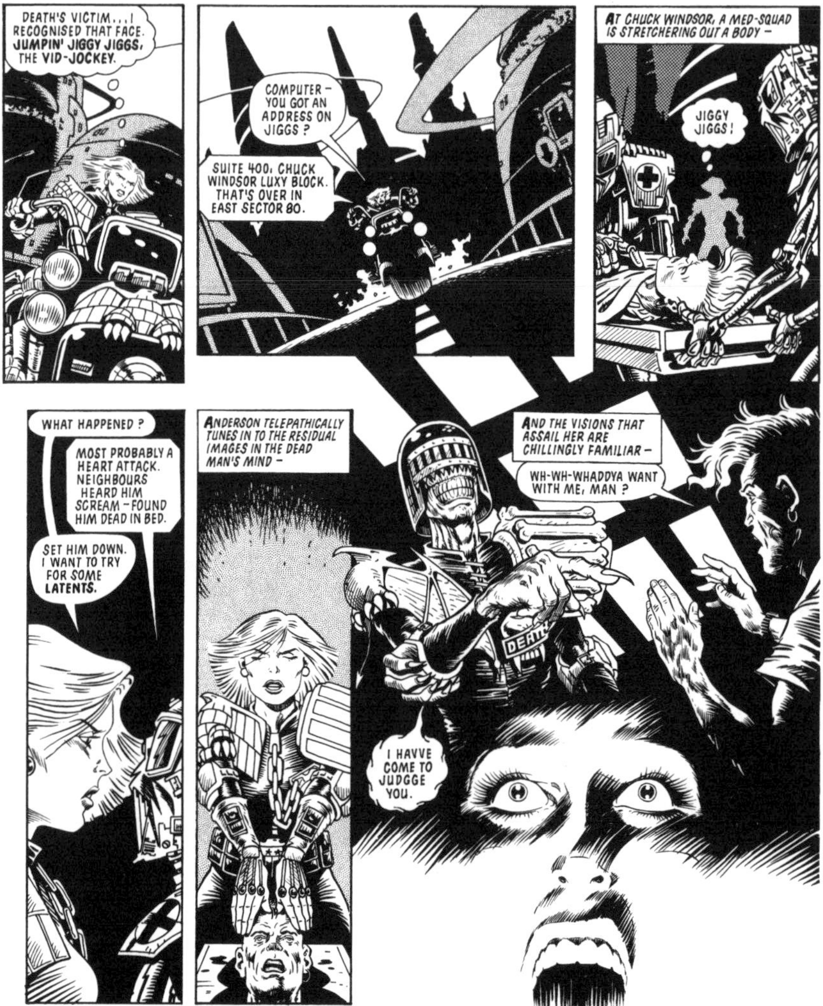
DEATH'S VICTIM... I RECOGNISED THAT FACE. JUMPIN' JIGGY JIGGS, THE VID-JOCKEY.
COMPUTER – YOU GOT AN ADDRESS ON JIGGS ?
SUITE 400, CHUCK WINDSOR LUXY BLOCK. THAT'S OVER IN EAST SECTOR 80.
AT CHUCK WINDSOR, A MED-SQUAD IS STRETCHERING OUT A BODY –
JIGGY JIGGS !
WHAT HAPPENED ?
MOST PROBABLY A HEART ATTACK. NEIGHBOURS HEARD HIM SCREAM – FOUND HIM DEAD IN BED.
SET HIM DOWN. I WANT TO TRY FOR SOME LATENTS.
ANDERSON TELEPATHICALLY TUNES IN TO THE RESIDUAL IMAGES IN THE DEAD MAN'S MIND –
AND THE VISIONS THAT ASSAIL HER ARE CHILLINGLY FAMILIAR –
WH-WH-WHADDYA WANT WITH ME, MAN ?
I HAVVE COME TO JUDGGE YOU.
DEATH

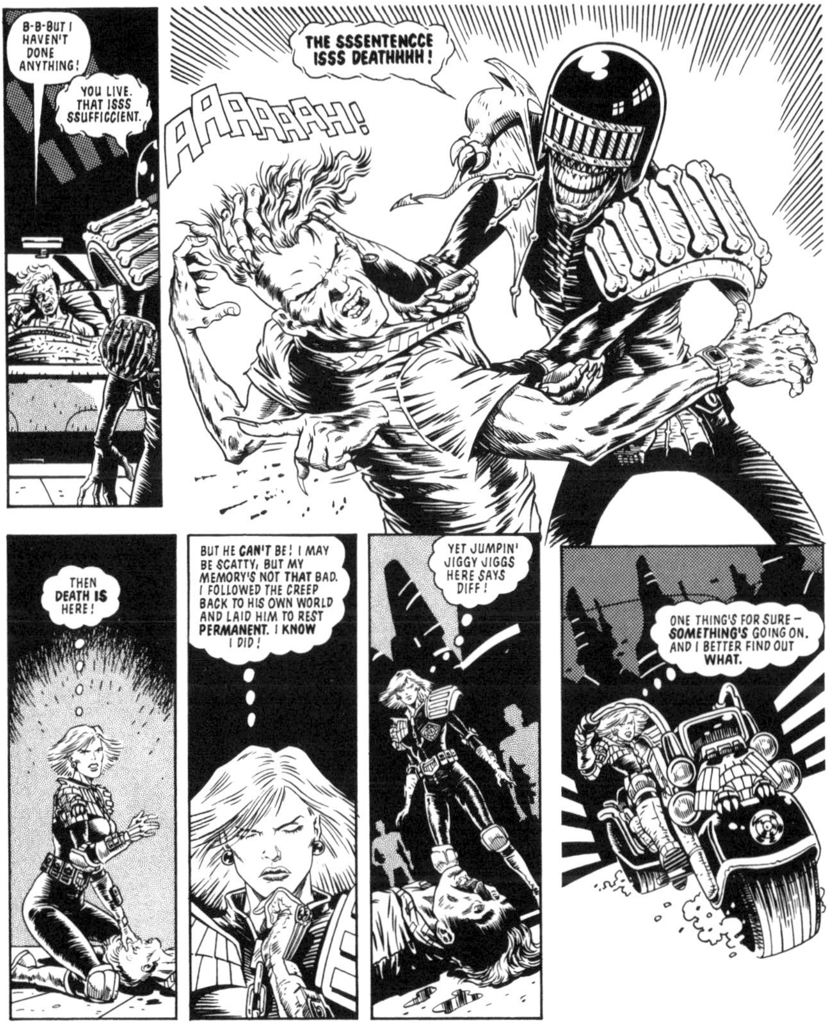
B-B-BUT I HAVEN'T DONE ANYTHING!
YOU LIVE. THAT ISSS SSUFFICCIENT.
THE SSSENTENCCE ISSS DEATHHHH!
AAAAAAAH!
THEN DEATH IS HERE!
BUT HE CAN'T BE! I MAY BE SCATTY, BUT MY MEMORY'S NOT THAT BAD. I FOLLOWED THE CREEP BACK TO HIS OWN WORLD AND LAID HIM TO REST PERMANENT. I KNOW I DID!
YET JUMPIN' JIGGY JIGGS HERE SAYS DIFF!
ONE THING'S FOR SURE — SOMETHING'S GOING ON. AND I BETTER FIND OUT WHAT.

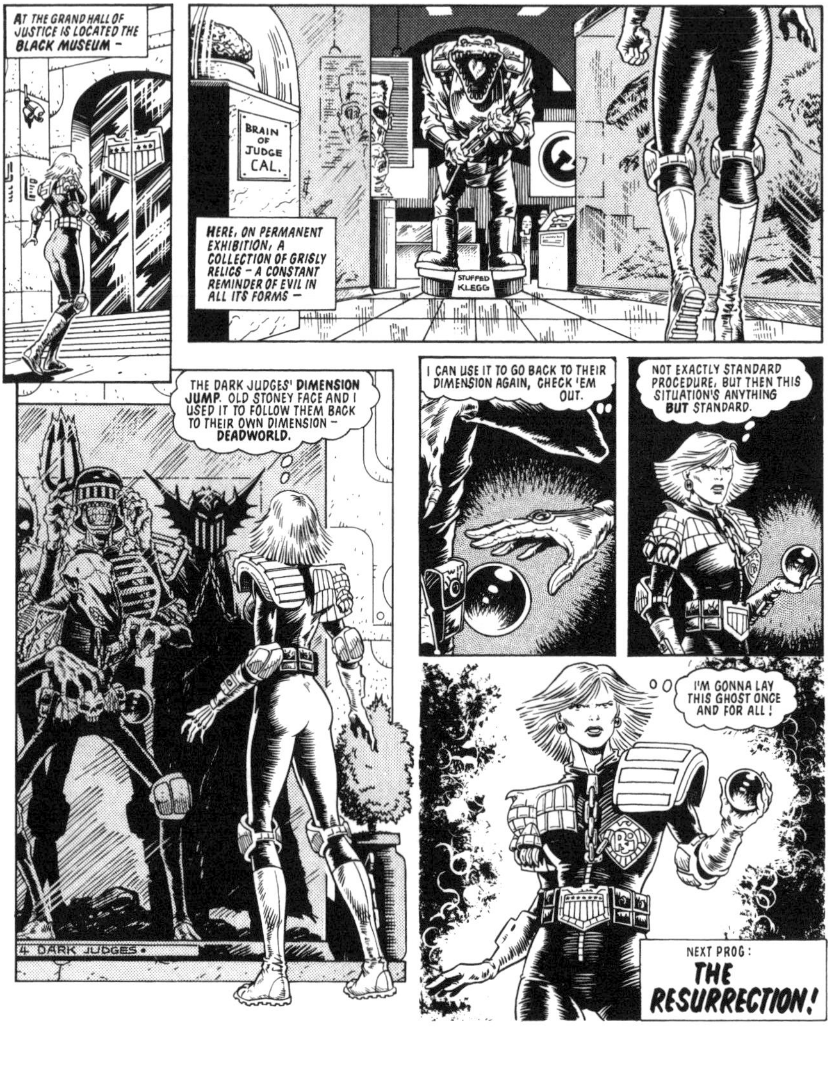
AT THE GRAND HALL OF JUSTICE IS LOCATED THE BLACK MUSEUM –
BRAIN OF JUDGE CAL.
HERE, ON PERMANENT EXHIBITION, A COLLECTION OF GRISLY RELICS – A CONSTANT REMINDER OF EVIL IN ALL ITS FORMS –
STUFFED KLEGG
THE DARK JUDGES' DIMENSION JUMP. OLD STONEY FACE AND I USED IT TO FOLLOW THEM BACK TO THEIR OWN DIMENSION – DEADWORLD.
4 DARK JUDGES
I CAN USE IT TO GO BACK TO THEIR DIMENSION AGAIN, CHECK 'EM OUT.
NOT EXACTLY STANDARD PROCEDURE, BUT THEN THIS SITUATION'S ANYTHING BUT STANDARD.
I'M GONNA LAY THIS GHOST ONCE AND FOR ALL!
NEXT PROG:
THE RESURRECTION!

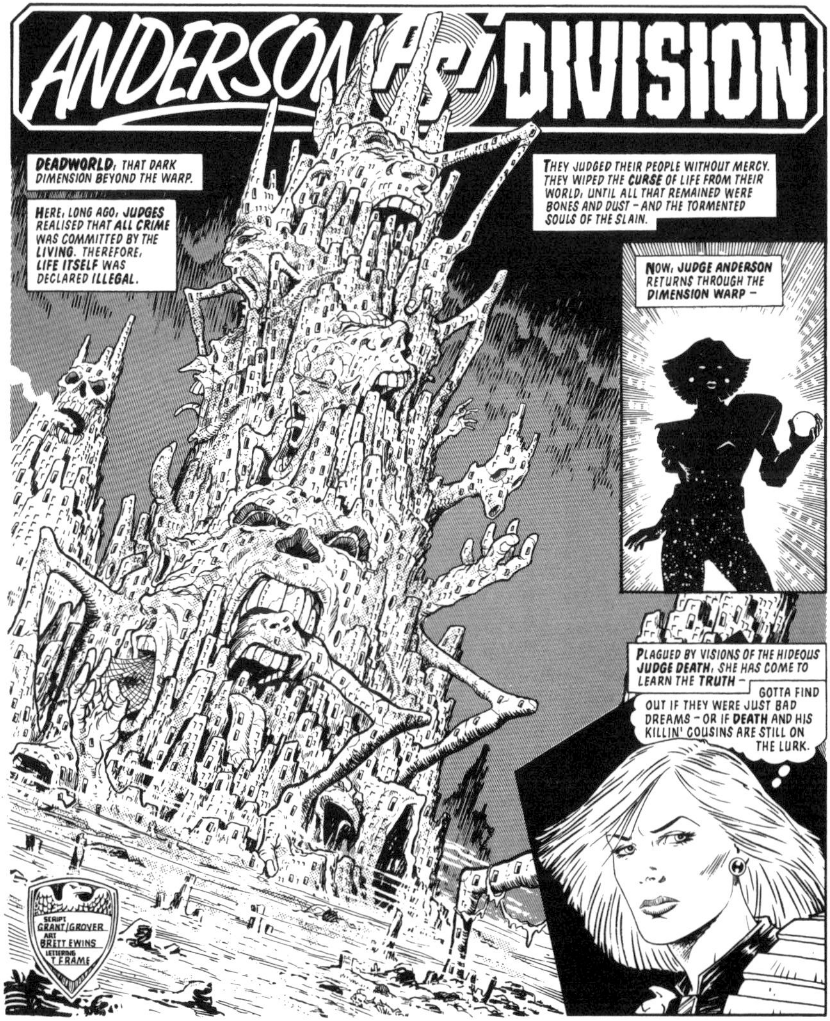
ANDERSON PSI DIVISION
DEADWORLD, THAT DARK DIMENSION BEYOND THE WARP.
HERE, LONG AGO, JUDGES REALISED THAT ALL CRIME WAS COMMITTED BY THE LIVING. THEREFORE, LIFE ITSELF WAS DECLARED ILLEGAL.
THEY JUDGED THEIR PEOPLE WITHOUT MERCY. THEY WIPED THE CURSE OF LIFE FROM THEIR WORLD, UNTIL ALL THAT REMAINED WERE BONES AND DUST – AND THE TORMENTED SOULS OF THE SLAIN.
NOW, JUDGE ANDERSON RETURNS THROUGH THE DIMENSION WARP –
PLAGUED BY VISIONS OF THE HIDEOUS JUDGE DEATH, SHE HAS COME TO LEARN THE TRUTH –
GOTTA FIND OUT IF THEY WERE JUST BAD DREAMS – OR IF DEATH AND HIS KILLIN' COUSINS ARE STILL ON THE LURK.
SCRIPT GRANT/GROVER
ART BRETT EWINS
LETTERING T FRAME

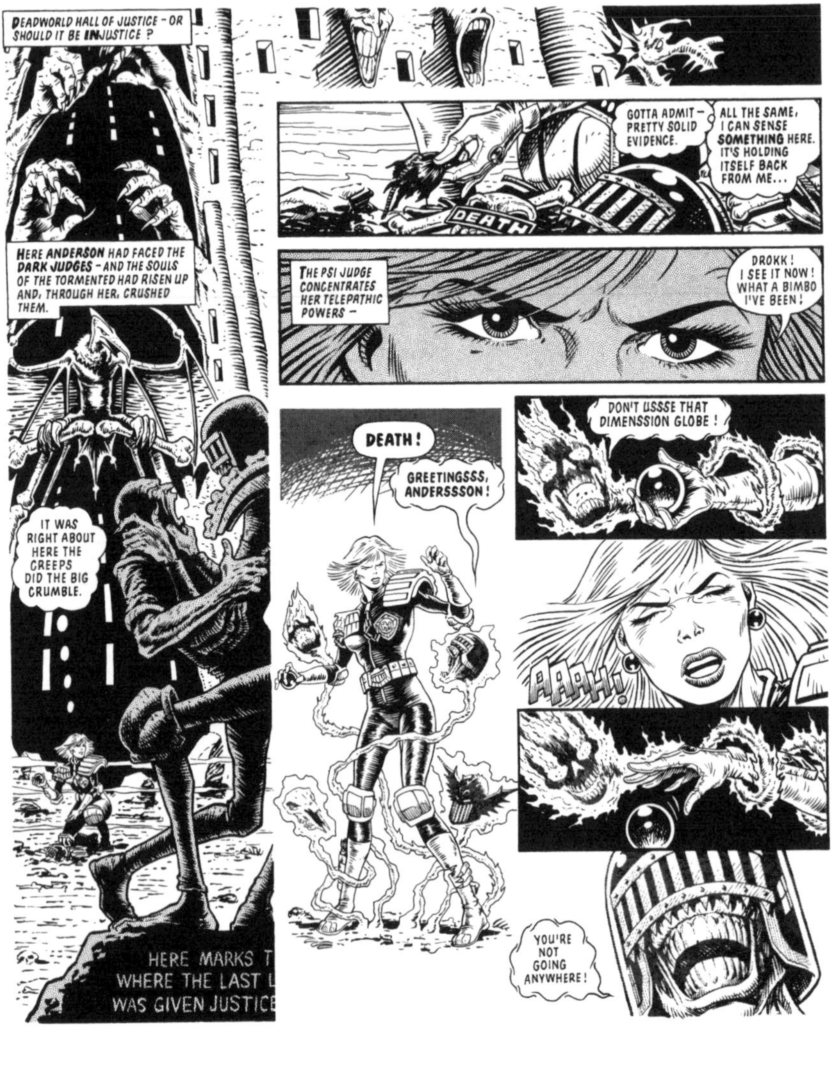
DEADWORLD HALL OF JUSTICE - OR SHOULD IT BE INJUSTICE ?
HERE ANDERSON HAD FACED THE DARK JUDGES - AND THE SOULS OF THE TORMENTED HAD RISEN UP AND, THROUGH HER, CRUSHED THEM.
IT WAS RIGHT ABOUT HERE THE CREEPS DID THE BIG CRUMBLE.
HERE MARKS T
WHERE THE LAST L
WAS GIVEN JUSTICE
DEATH
GOTTA ADMIT - PRETTY SOLID EVIDENCE.
ALL THE SAME, I CAN SENSE SOMETHING HERE. IT'S HOLDING ITSELF BACK FROM ME...
THE PSI JUDGE CONCENTRATES HER TELEPATHIC POWERS -
DROKK! I SEE IT NOW! WHAT A BIMBO I'VE BEEN!
DEATH!
GREETINGSSS, ANDERSSSON!
DON'T USSSE THAT DIMENSSION GLOBE!
AAAH!
YOU'RE NOT GOING ANYWHERE!

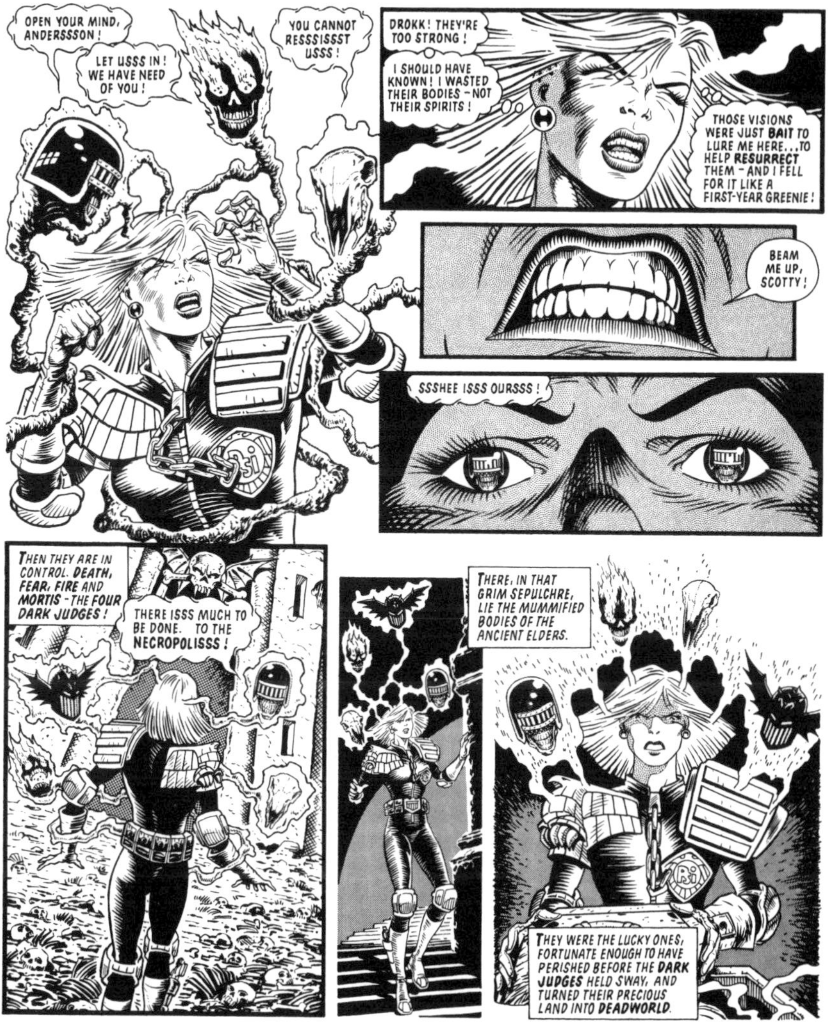
OPEN YOUR MIND, ANDERSSSON!
LET USSS IN! WE HAVE NEED OF YOU!
YOU CANNOT RESSSISSST USSS!
DROKK! THEY'RE TOO STRONG!
I SHOULD HAVE KNOWN! I WASTED THEIR BODIES – NOT THEIR SPIRITS!
THOSE VISIONS WERE JUST BAIT TO LURE ME HERE... TO HELP RESURRECT THEM – AND I FELL FOR IT LIKE A FIRST-YEAR GREENIE!
BEAM ME UP, SCOTTY!
SSSHEE ISSS OURSSS!
THEN THEY ARE IN CONTROL. DEATH, FEAR, FIRE AND MORTIS – THE FOUR DARK JUDGES!
THERE ISSS MUCH TO BE DONE. TO THE NECROPOLISSS!
THERE, IN THAT GRIM SEPULCHRE, LIE THE MUMMIFIED BODIES OF THE ANCIENT ELDERS.
THEY WERE THE LUCKY ONES, FORTUNATE ENOUGH TO HAVE PERISHED BEFORE THE DARK JUDGES HELD SWAY, AND TURNED THEIR PRECIOUS LAND INTO DEADWORLD.

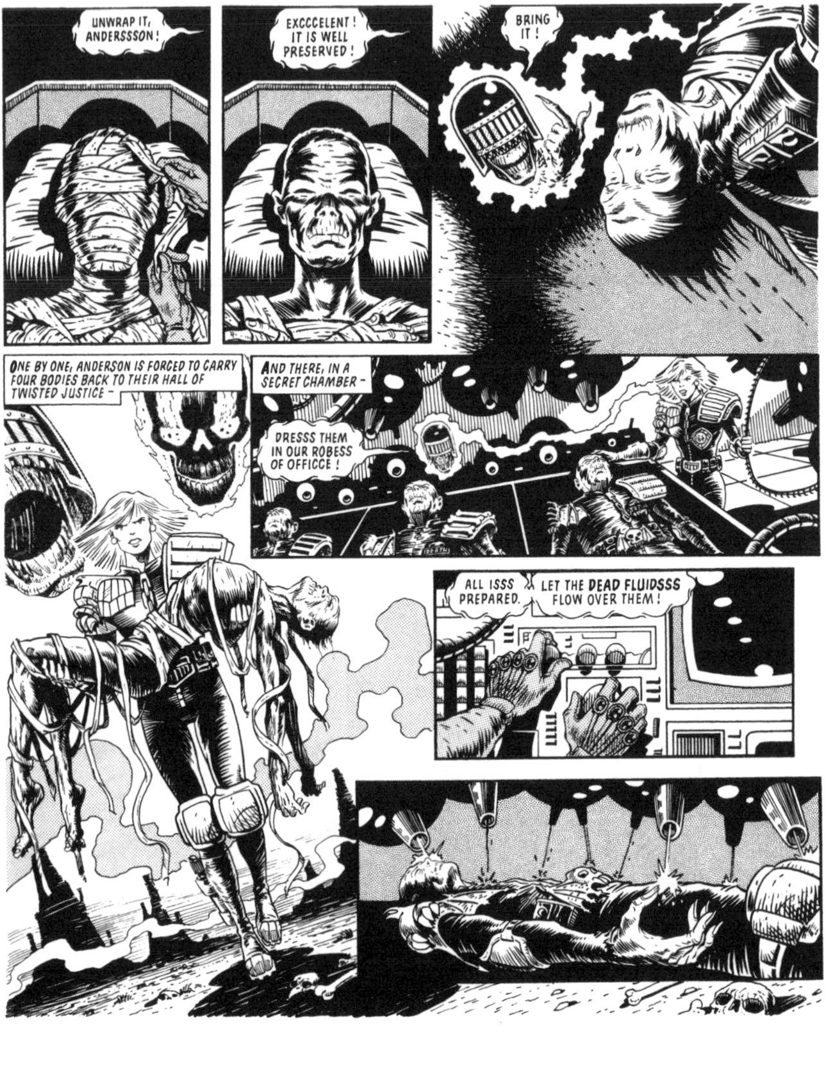
UNWRAP IT, ANDERSSSON!
EXCCCELENT! IT IS WELL PRESERVED!
BRING IT!
ONE BY ONE, ANDERSON IS FORCED TO CARRY FOUR BODIES BACK TO THEIR HALL OF TWISTED JUSTICE -
AND THERE, IN A SECRET CHAMBER -
DRESSS THEM IN OUR ROBESS OF OFFICCE!
ALL ISSS PREPARED.
LET THE DEAD FLUIDSSS FLOW OVER THEM!

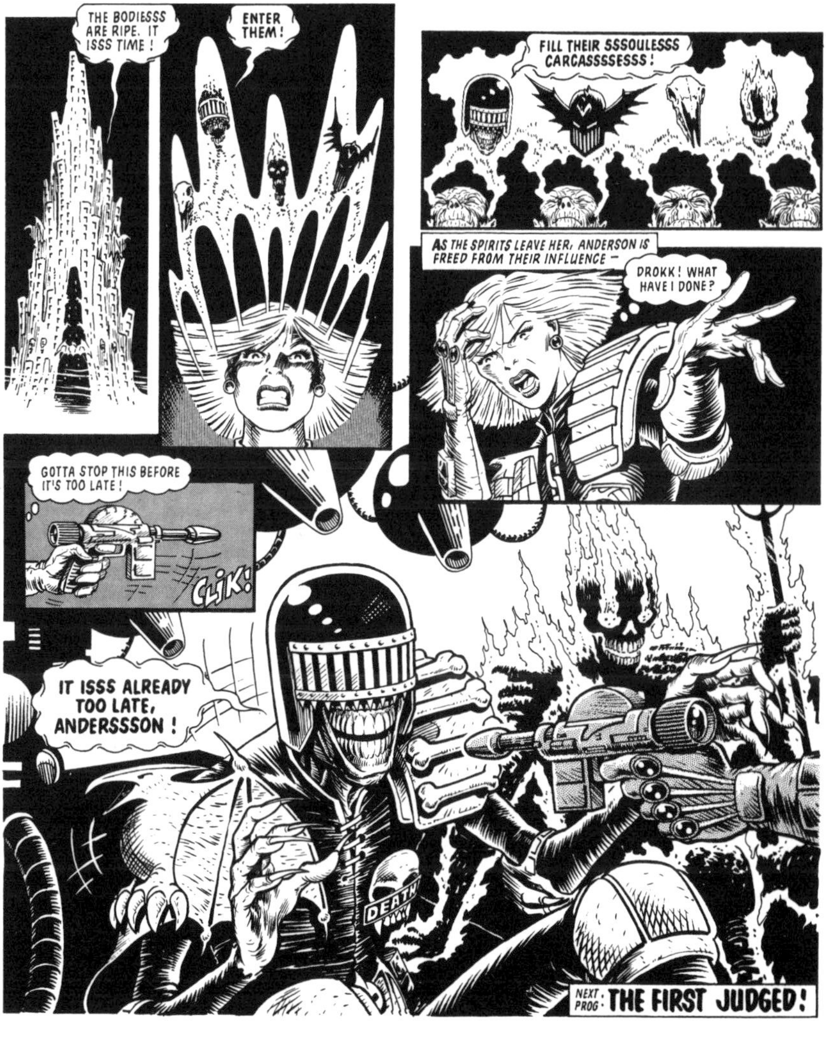
THE BODIESSS ARE RIPE. IT ISSS TIME!
ENTER THEM!
FILL THEIR SSSOULESSS CARCASSSSESSS!
AS THE SPIRITS LEAVE HER, ANDERSON IS FREED FROM THEIR INFLUENCE —
DROKK! WHAT HAVE I DONE?
GOTTA STOP THIS BEFORE IT'S TOO LATE!
CLIK!
IT ISSS ALREADY TOO LATE, ANDERSSSON!
DEATH
NEXT PROG: THE FIRST JUDGED!

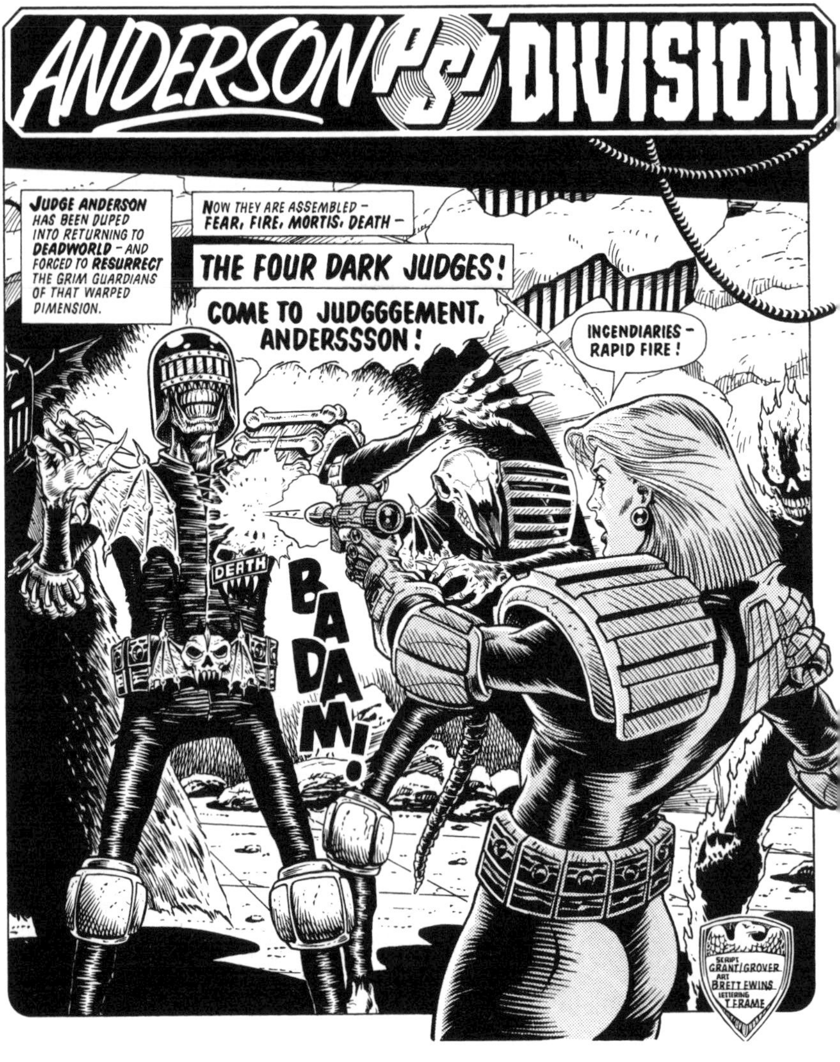
ANDERSON PSI DIVISION
JUDGE ANDERSON HAS BEEN DUPED INTO RETURNING TO DEADWORLD – AND FORCED TO RESURRECT THE GRIM GUARDIANS OF THAT WARPED DIMENSION.
NOW THEY ARE ASSEMBLED – FEAR, FIRE, MORTIS, DEATH –
THE FOUR DARK JUDGES!
COME TO JUDGGGEMENT, ANDERSSSON!
INCENDIARIES – RAPID FIRE!
DEATH
BADAM!
SCRIPT GRANT/GROVER
ART BRETT EWINS
LETTERING T. FRAME

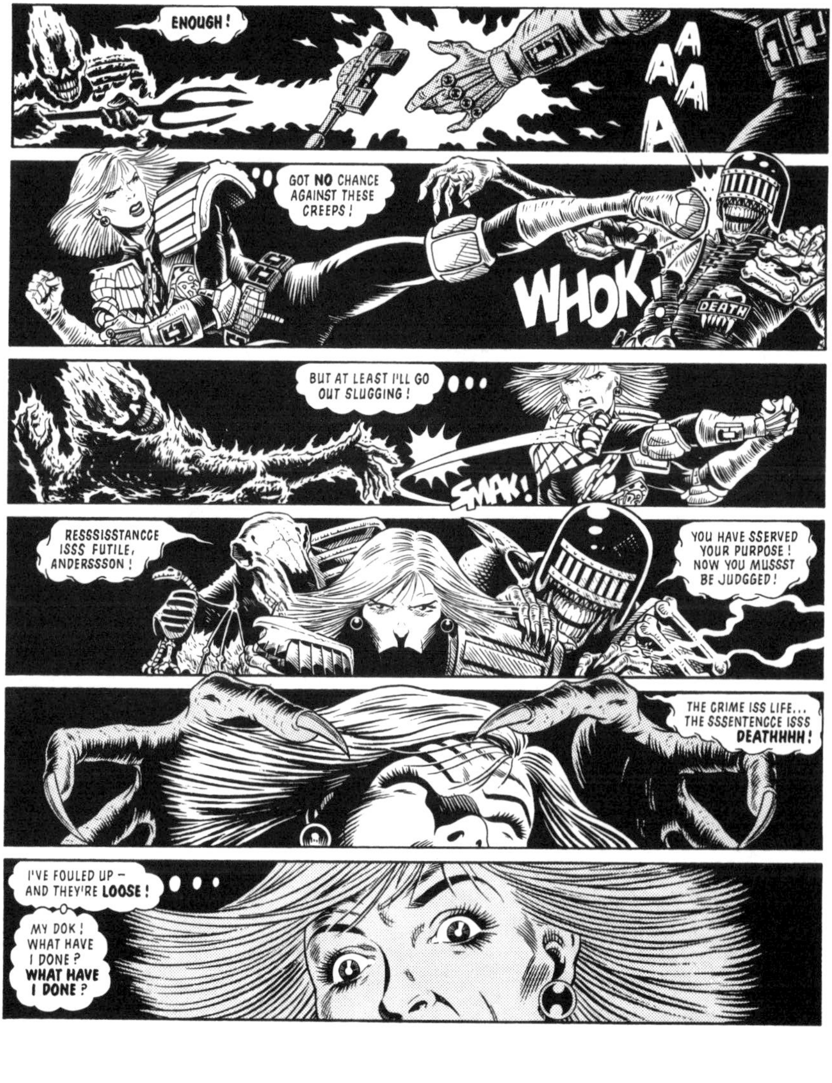
ENOUGH!
AAAAA
GOT NO CHANCE AGAINST THESE CREEPS!
WHOK!
DEATH
BUT AT LEAST I'LL GO OUT SLUGGING!
SMAK!
RESSSISSTANCCE ISSS FUTILE, ANDERSSSON!
YOU HAVE SSERVED YOUR PURPOSE! NOW YOU MUSSST BE JUDGGED!
THE CRIME ISS LIFE... THE SSSENTENCCE ISSS DEATHHHH!
I'VE FOULED UP – AND THEY'RE LOOSE!
MY DOK! WHAT HAVE I DONE? WHAT HAVE I DONE?

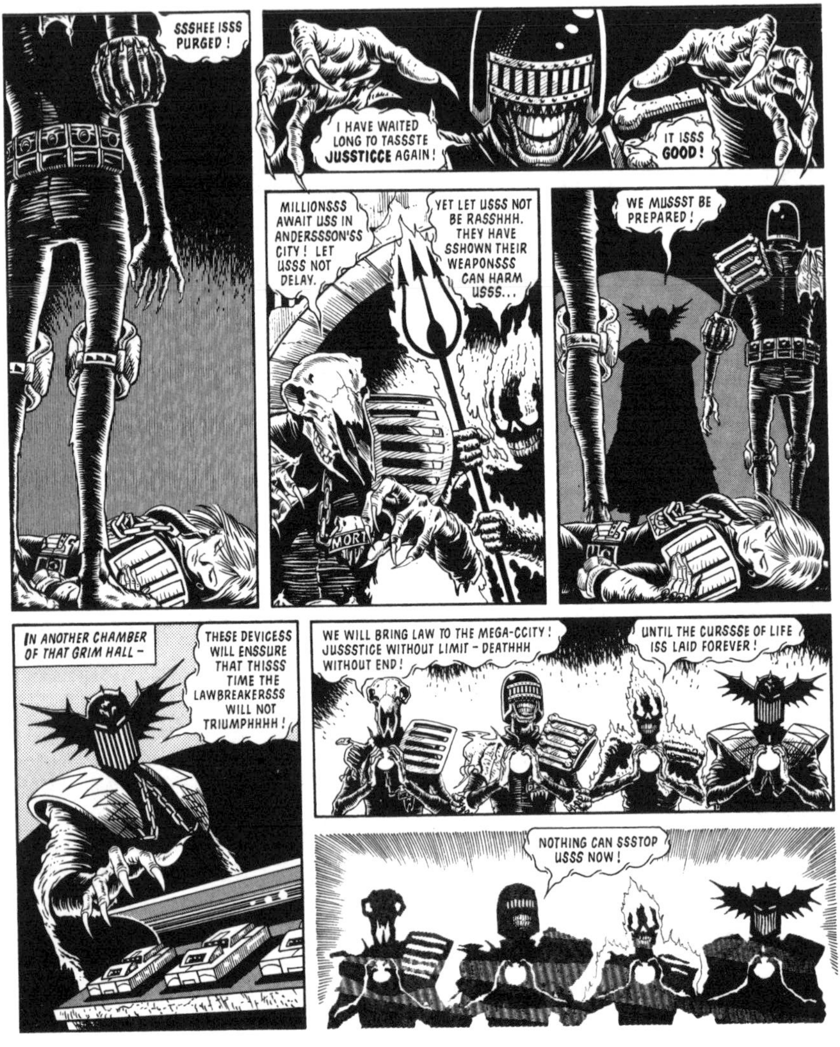
SSSHEE ISSS PURGED!
I HAVE WAITED LONG TO TASSSTE JUSSTICCE AGAIN!
IT ISSS GOOD!
MILLIONSSS AWAIT USS IN ANDERSSSON'SS CITY! LET USSS NOT DELAY.
YET LET USSS NOT BE RASSHHH. THEY HAVE SSHOWN THEIR WEAPONSSS CAN HARM USSS...
MORT
WE MUSSST BE PREPARED!
IN ANOTHER CHAMBER OF THAT GRIM HALL–
THESE DEVICESS WILL ENSSURE THAT THISSS TIME THE LAWBREAKERSSS WILL NOT TRIUMPHHHH!
WE WILL BRING LAW TO THE MEGA-CCITY! JUSSSTICE WITHOUT LIMIT – DEATHHH WITHOUT END!
UNTIL THE CURSSSE OF LIFE ISS LAID FOREVER!
NOTHING CAN SSSTOP USSS NOW!

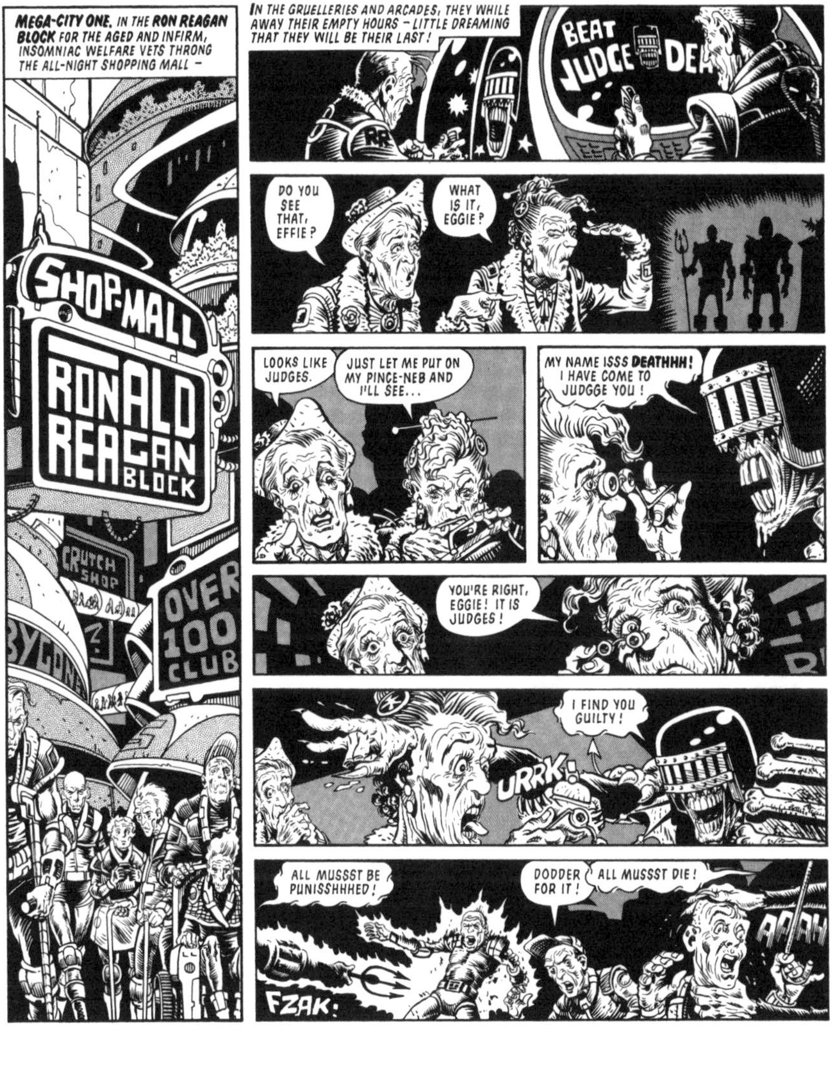
MEGA-CITY ONE. IN THE RON REAGAN BLOCK FOR THE AGED AND INFIRM, INSOMNIAC WELFARE VETS THRONG THE ALL-NIGHT SHOPPING MALL –
SHOP-MALL
RONALD REAGAN BLOCK
CRUTCH SHOP
OVER 100 CLUB
IN THE GRUELLERIES AND ARCADES, THEY WHILE AWAY THEIR EMPTY HOURS – LITTLE DREAMING THAT THEY WILL BE THEIR LAST!
BEAT JUDGE DEA
DO YOU SEE THAT, EFFIE?
WHAT IS IT, EGGIE?
LOOKS LIKE JUDGES.
JUST LET ME PUT ON MY PINCE-NEB AND I'LL SEE...
MY NAME ISSS DEATHHH! I HAVE COME TO JUDGGE YOU!
YOU'RE RIGHT, EGGIE! IT IS JUDGES!
I FIND YOU GUILTY!
URRK!
ALL MUSSST BE PUNISSHHHED!
DODDER FOR IT!
ALL MUSSST DIE!
AAAH
FZAK!

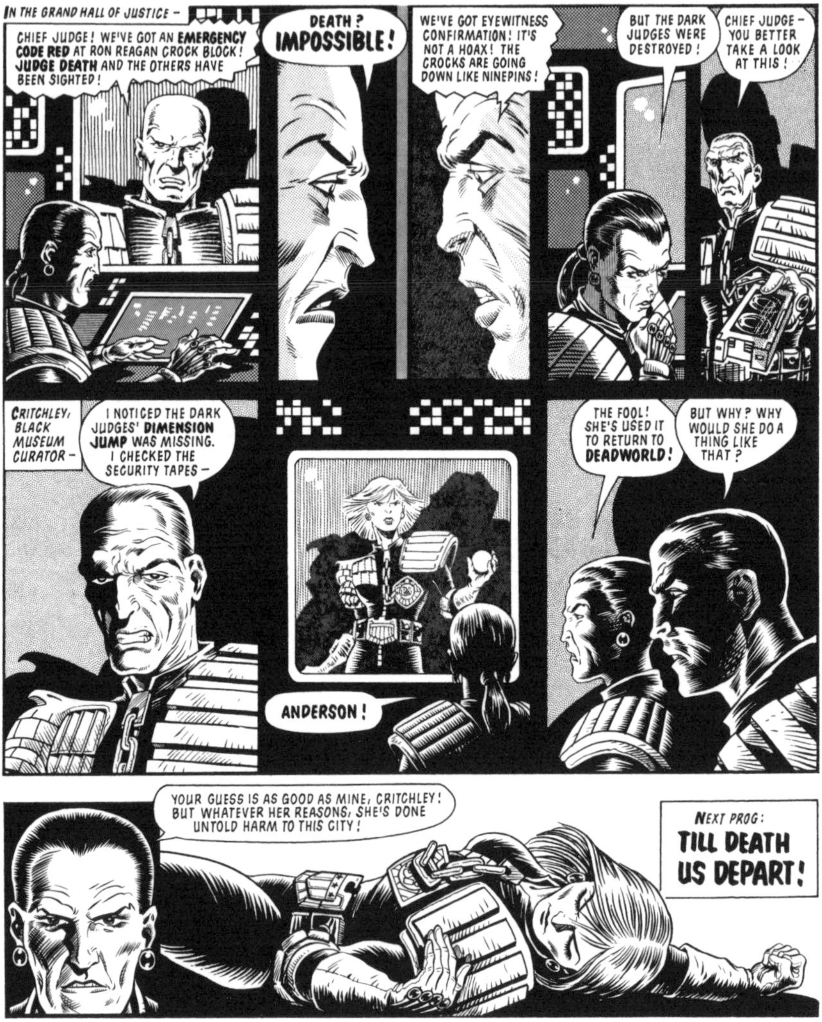
IN THE GRAND HALL OF JUSTICE –
CHIEF JUDGE! WE'VE GOT AN EMERGENCY CODE RED AT RON REAGAN CROCK BLOCK! JUDGE DEATH AND THE OTHERS HAVE BEEN SIGHTED!
DEATH? IMPOSSIBLE!
WE'VE GOT EYEWITNESS CONFIRMATION! IT'S NOT A HOAX! THE CROCKS ARE GOING DOWN LIKE NINEPINS!
BUT THE DARK JUDGES WERE DESTROYED!
CHIEF JUDGE – YOU BETTER TAKE A LOOK AT THIS!
CRITCHLEY, BLACK MUSEUM CURATOR –
I NOTICED THE DARK JUDGES' DIMENSION JUMP WAS MISSING. I CHECKED THE SECURITY TAPES –
ANDERSON!
THE FOOL! SHE'S USED IT TO RETURN TO DEADWORLD!
BUT WHY? WHY WOULD SHE DO A THING LIKE THAT?
YOUR GUESS IS AS GOOD AS MINE, CRITCHLEY! BUT WHATEVER HER REASONS, SHE'S DONE UNTOLD HARM TO THIS CITY!
NEXT PROG: TILL DEATH US DEPART!

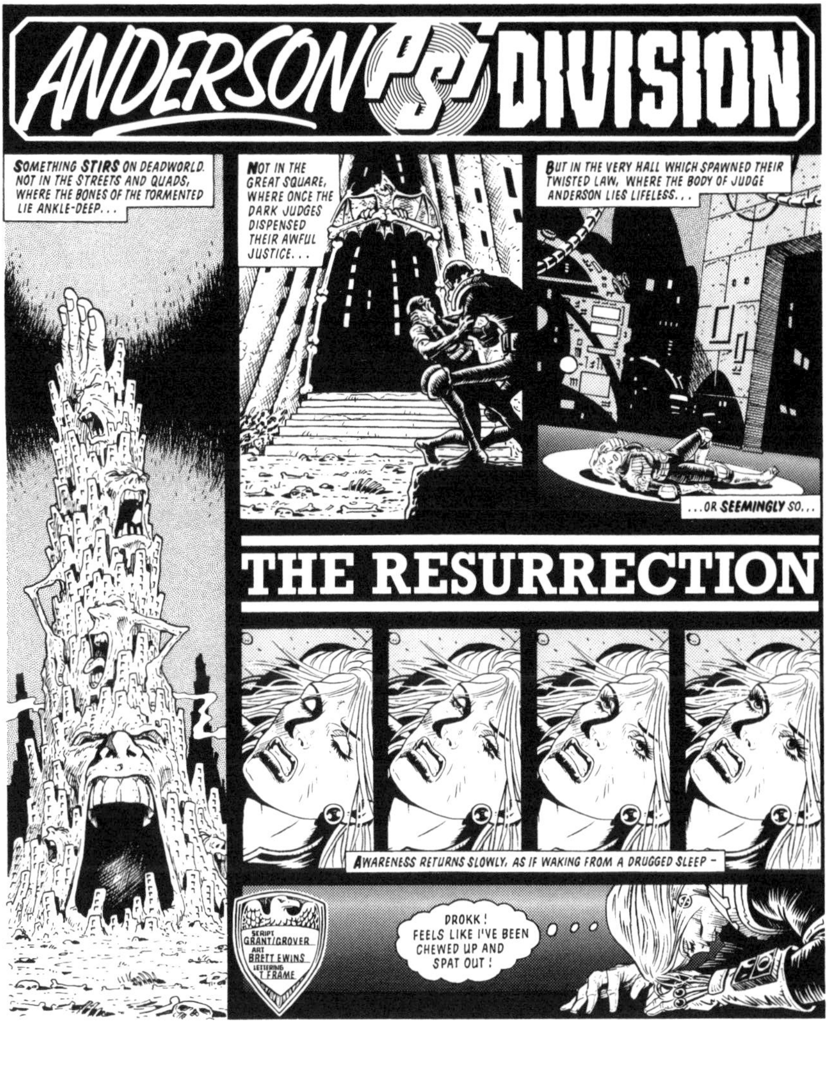
ANDERSON PSI DIVISION
SOMETHING STIRS ON DEADWORLD. NOT IN THE STREETS AND QUADS, WHERE THE BONES OF THE TORMENTED LIE ANKLE-DEEP...
NOT IN THE GREAT SQUARE, WHERE ONCE THE DARK JUDGES DISPENSED THEIR AWFUL JUSTICE...
BUT IN THE VERY HALL WHICH SPAWNED THEIR TWISTED LAW, WHERE THE BODY OF JUDGE ANDERSON LIES LIFELESS...
...OR SEEMINGLY SO...
THE RESURRECTION
AWARENESS RETURNS SLOWLY, AS IF WAKING FROM A DRUGGED SLEEP –
SCRIPT GRANT/GROVER
ART BRETT EWINS
LETTERING T FRAME
DROKK! FEELS LIKE I'VE BEEN CHEWED UP AND SPAT OUT!

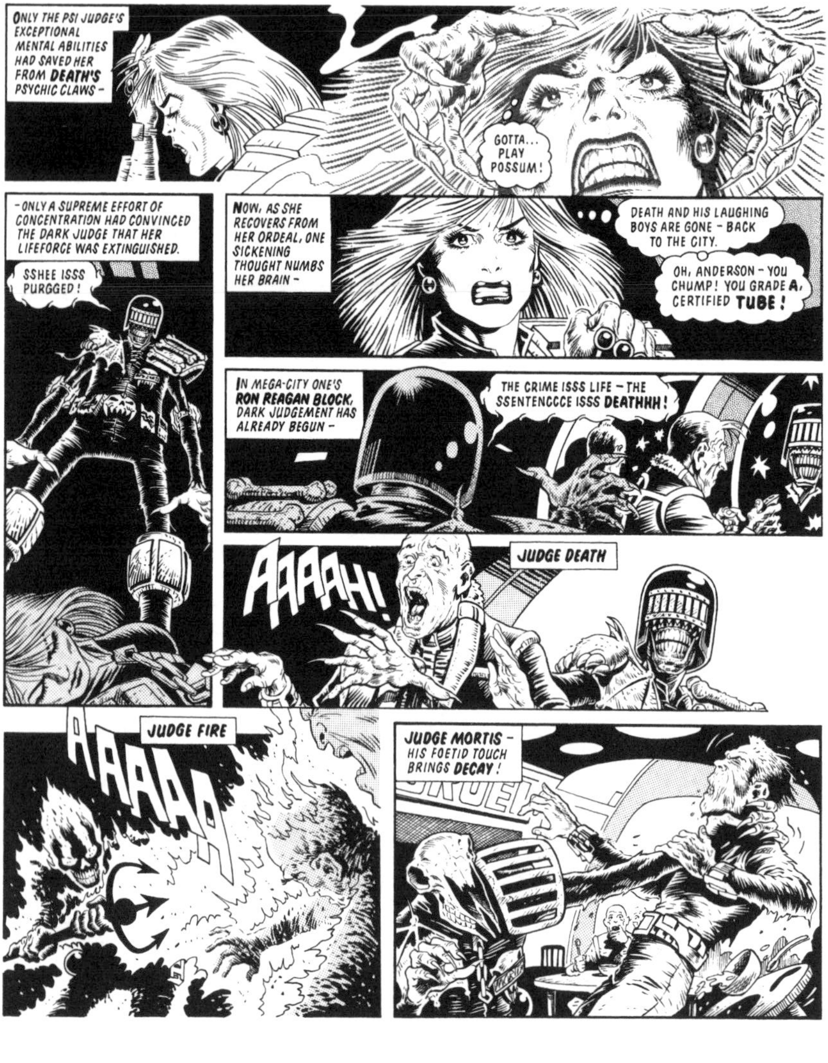
ONLY THE PSI JUDGE'S EXCEPTIONAL MENTAL ABILITIES HAD SAVED HER FROM DEATH'S PSYCHIC CLAWS -
GOTTA... PLAY POSSUM!
- ONLY A SUPREME EFFORT OF CONCENTRATION HAD CONVINCED THE DARK JUDGE THAT HER LIFEFORCE WAS EXTINGUISHED.
SSHEE ISSS PURGGED!
NOW, AS SHE RECOVERS FROM HER ORDEAL, ONE SICKENING THOUGHT NUMBS HER BRAIN -
DEATH AND HIS LAUGHING BOYS ARE GONE - BACK TO THE CITY.
OH, ANDERSON - YOU CHUMP! YOU GRADE A, CERTIFIED TUBE!
IN MEGA-CITY ONE'S RON REAGAN BLOCK, DARK JUDGEMENT HAS ALREADY BEGUN -
THE CRIME ISSS LIFE - THE SSENTENCCCE ISSS DEATHHH!
AAAAH!
JUDGE DEATH
AAAAA
JUDGE FIRE
JUDGE MORTIS - HIS FOETID TOUCH BRINGS DECAY!

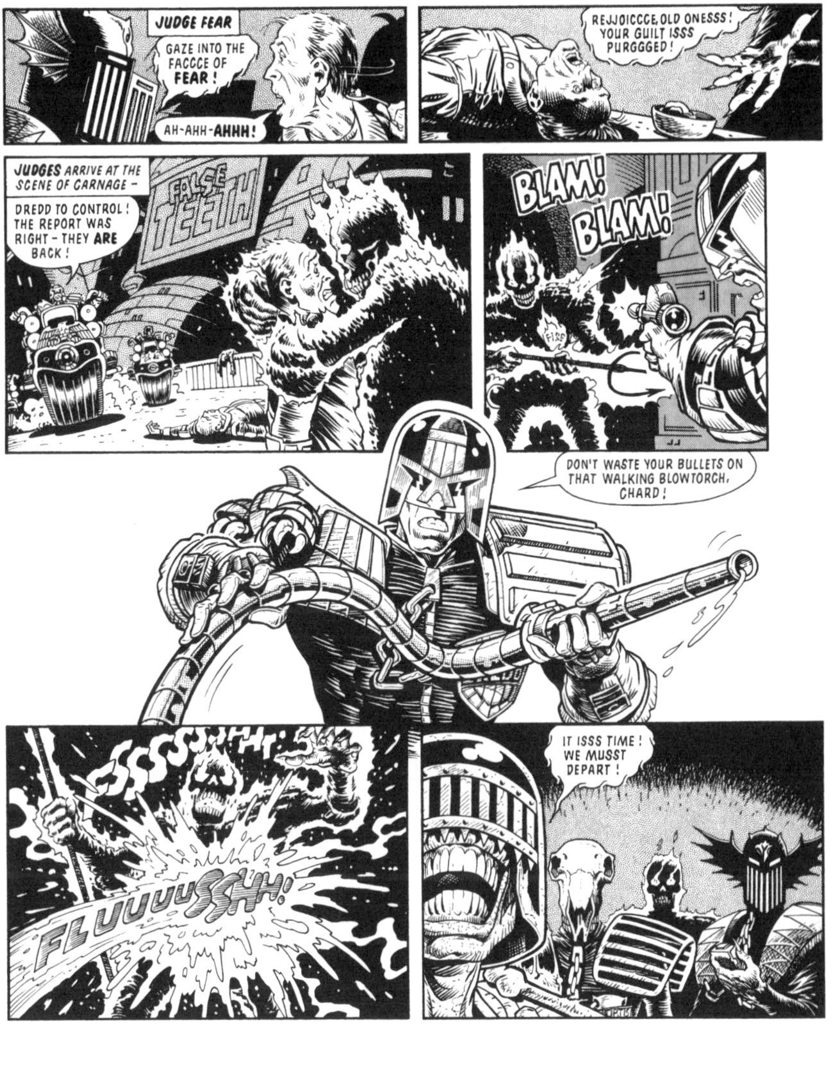
JUDGE FEAR
GAZE INTO THE FACCCE OF FEAR!
AH-AHH-AHHH!
REJJOICCCE, OLD ONESSS! YOUR GUILT ISSS PURGGGED!
JUDGES ARRIVE AT THE SCENE OF CARNAGE -
DREDD TO CONTROL! THE REPORT WAS RIGHT - THEY ARE BACK!
FALSE TEETH
BLAM! BLAM!
DON'T WASTE YOUR BULLETS ON THAT WALKING BLOWTORCH, CHARD!
FLUUUUSSHH!
IT ISSS TIME! WE MUSST DEPART!

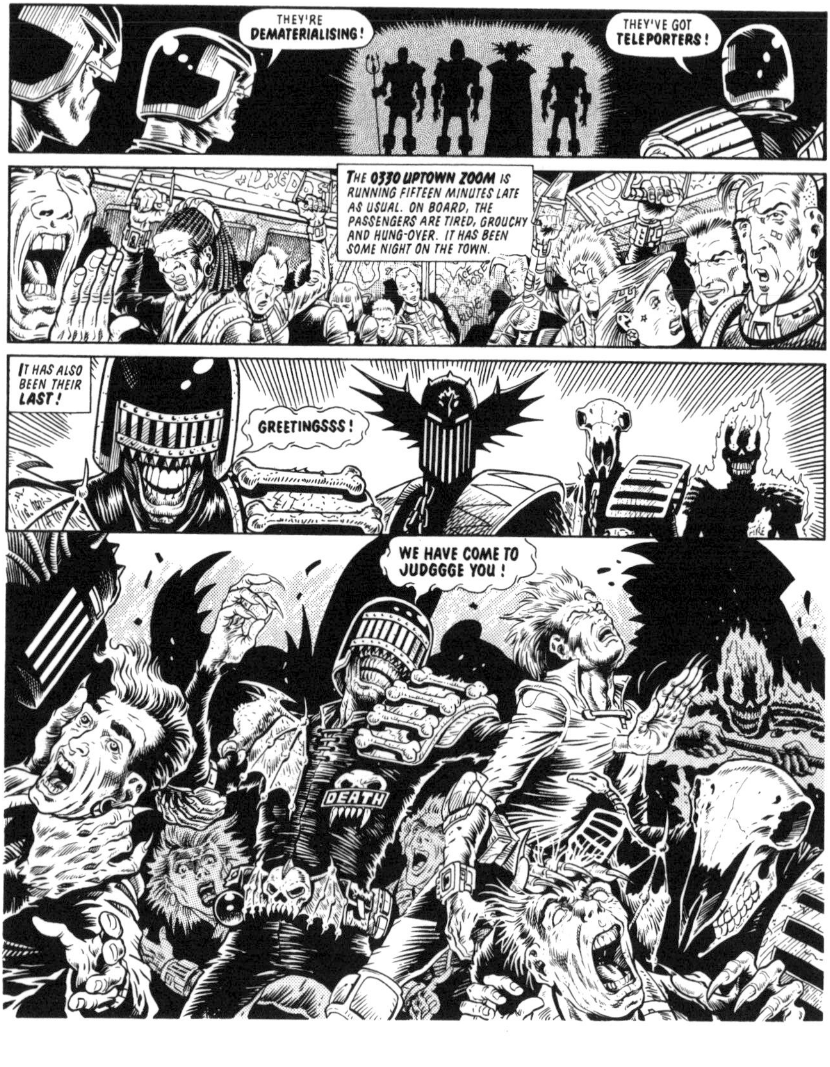
THEY'RE DEMATERIALISING!
THEY'VE GOT TELEPORTERS!
THE 0330 UPTOWN ZOOM IS RUNNING FIFTEEN MINUTES LATE AS USUAL. ON BOARD, THE PASSENGERS ARE TIRED, GROUCHY AND HUNG-OVER. IT HAS BEEN SOME NIGHT ON THE TOWN.
IT HAS ALSO BEEN THEIR LAST!
GREETINGSSS!
WE HAVE COME TO JUDGGGE YOU!
DEATH

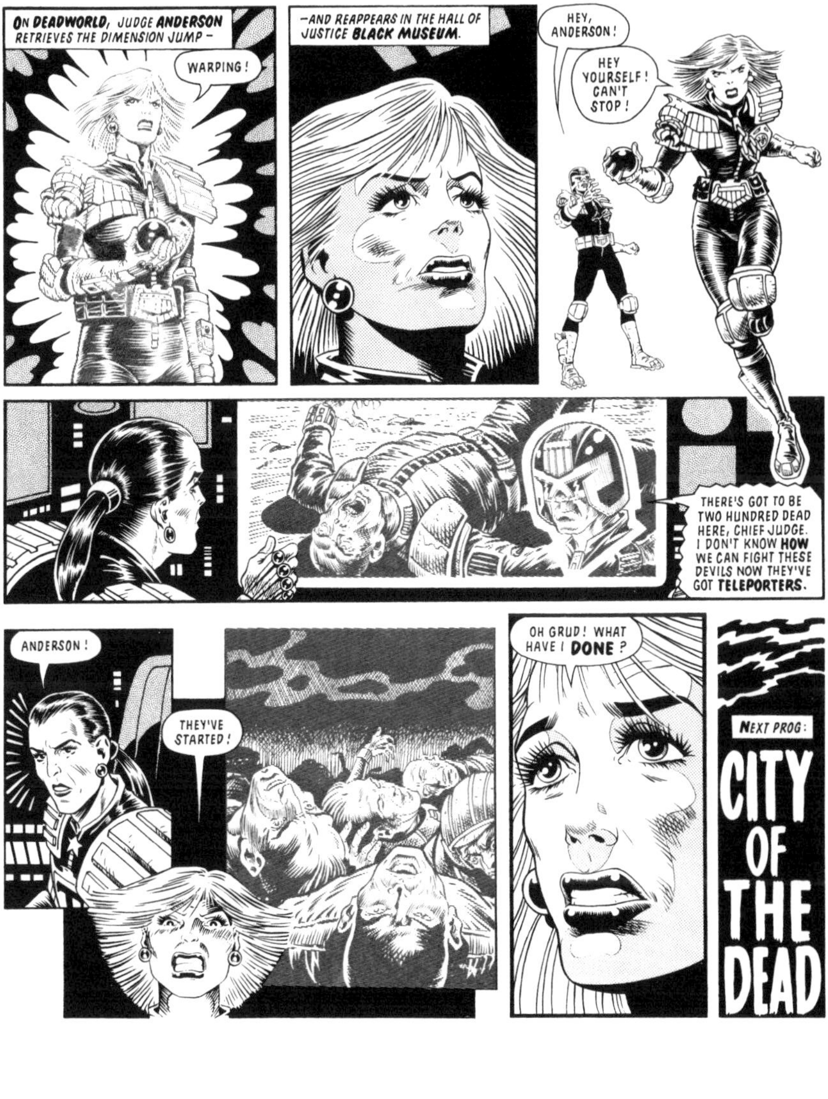
ON DEADWORLD, JUDGE ANDERSON RETRIEVES THE DIMENSION JUMP –
WARPING!
–AND REAPPEARS IN THE HALL OF JUSTICE BLACK MUSEUM.
HEY, ANDERSON!
HEY YOURSELF! CAN'T STOP!
THERE'S GOT TO BE TWO HUNDRED DEAD HERE, CHIEF JUDGE. I DON'T KNOW HOW WE CAN FIGHT THESE DEVILS NOW THEY'VE GOT TELEPORTERS.
ANDERSON!
THEY'VE STARTED!
OH GRUD! WHAT HAVE I DONE?
NEXT PROG:
CITY OF THE DEAD

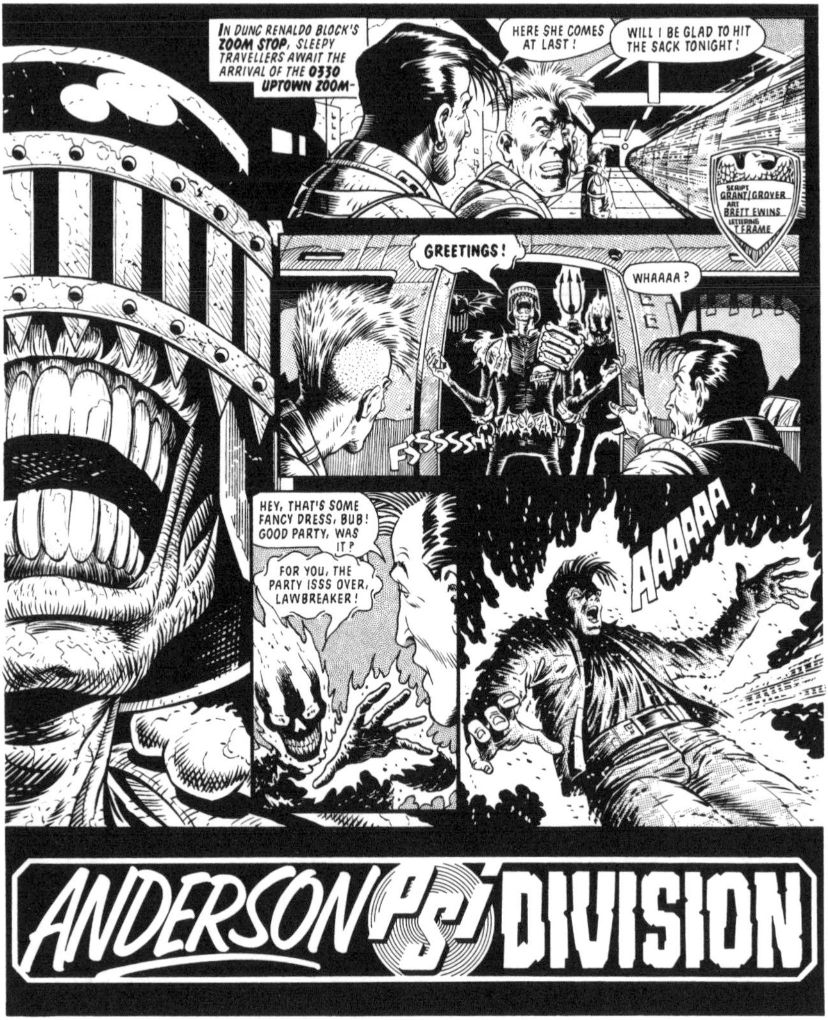
IN DUNC RENALDO BLOCK'S ZOOM STOP, SLEEPY TRAVELLERS AWAIT THE ARRIVAL OF THE 0330 UPTOWN ZOOM-
HERE SHE COMES AT LAST!
WILL I BE GLAD TO HIT THE SACK TONIGHT!
SCRIPT GRANT/GROVER
ART BRETT EWINS
LETTERING T FRAME
GREETINGS!
WHAAAA?
FSSSSSH
HEY, THAT'S SOME FANCY DRESS, BUB! GOOD PARTY, WAS IT?
FOR YOU, THE PARTY ISSS OVER, LAWBREAKER!
AAAAAA
ANDERSON PSI DIVISION

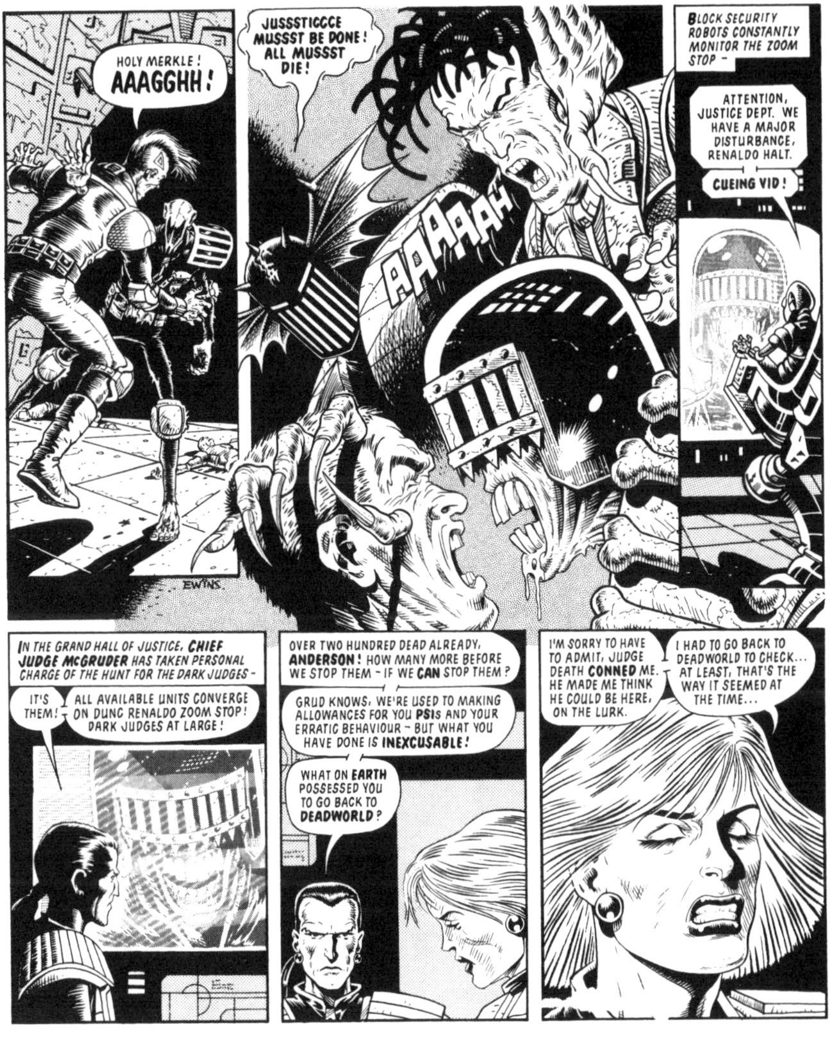
HOLY MERKLE! AAAGGHH!
JUSSSTICCCE MUSSST BE DONE! ALL MUSSST DIE!
AAAAAAH
BLOCK SECURITY ROBOTS CONSTANTLY MONITOR THE ZOOM STOP -
ATTENTION, JUSTICE DEPT. WE HAVE A MAJOR DISTURBANCE, RENALDO HALT.
CUEING VID!
EWINS
IN THE GRAND HALL OF JUSTICE, CHIEF JUDGE MCGRUDER HAS TAKEN PERSONAL CHARGE OF THE HUNT FOR THE DARK JUDGES -
IT'S THEM!
ALL AVAILABLE UNITS CONVERGE ON DUNC RENALDO ZOOM STOP! DARK JUDGES AT LARGE!
OVER TWO HUNDRED DEAD ALREADY, ANDERSON! HOW MANY MORE BEFORE WE STOP THEM - IF WE CAN STOP THEM?
GRUD KNOWS, WE'RE USED TO MAKING ALLOWANCES FOR YOU PSIs AND YOUR ERRATIC BEHAVIOUR - BUT WHAT YOU HAVE DONE IS INEXCUSABLE!
WHAT ON EARTH POSSESSED YOU TO GO BACK TO DEADWORLD?
I'M SORRY TO HAVE TO ADMIT, JUDGE DEATH CONNED ME. HE MADE ME THINK HE COULD BE HERE, ON THE LURK.
I HAD TO GO BACK TO DEADWORLD TO CHECK... AT LEAST, THAT'S THE WAY IT SEEMED AT THE TIME...

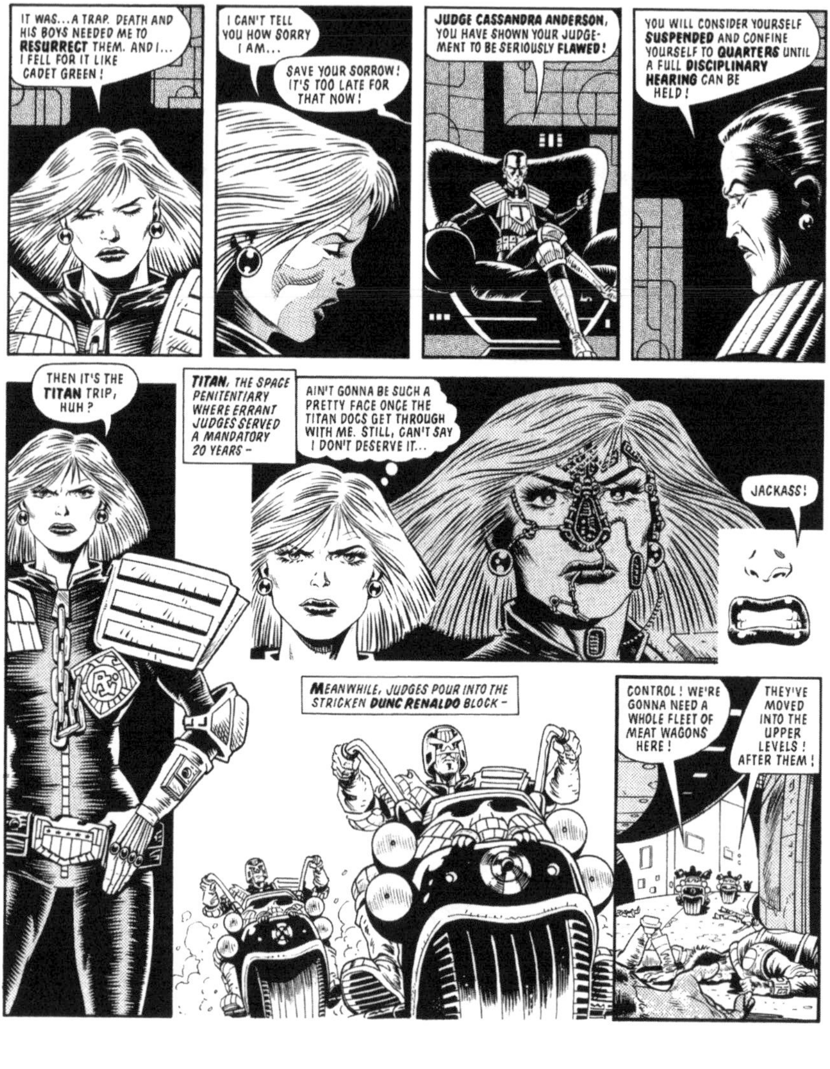
IT WAS... A TRAP. DEATH AND HIS BOYS NEEDED ME TO RESURRECT THEM. AND I... I FELL FOR IT LIKE CADET GREEN!
I CAN'T TELL YOU HOW SORRY I AM...
SAVE YOUR SORROW! IT'S TOO LATE FOR THAT NOW!
JUDGE CASSANDRA ANDERSON, YOU HAVE SHOWN YOUR JUDGEMENT TO BE SERIOUSLY FLAWED!
YOU WILL CONSIDER YOURSELF SUSPENDED AND CONFINE YOURSELF TO QUARTERS UNTIL A FULL DISCIPLINARY HEARING CAN BE HELD!
THEN IT'S THE TITAN TRIP, HUH?
TITAN, THE SPACE PENITENTIARY WHERE ERRANT JUDGES SERVED A MANDATORY 20 YEARS –
AIN'T GONNA BE SUCH A PRETTY FACE ONCE THE TITAN DOCS GET THROUGH WITH ME. STILL, CAN'T SAY I DON'T DESERVE IT...
JACKASS!
MEANWHILE, JUDGES POUR INTO THE STRICKEN DUNC RENALDO BLOCK –
CONTROL! WE'RE GONNA NEED A WHOLE FLEET OF MEAT WAGONS HERE!
THEY'VE MOVED INTO THE UPPER LEVELS! AFTER THEM!

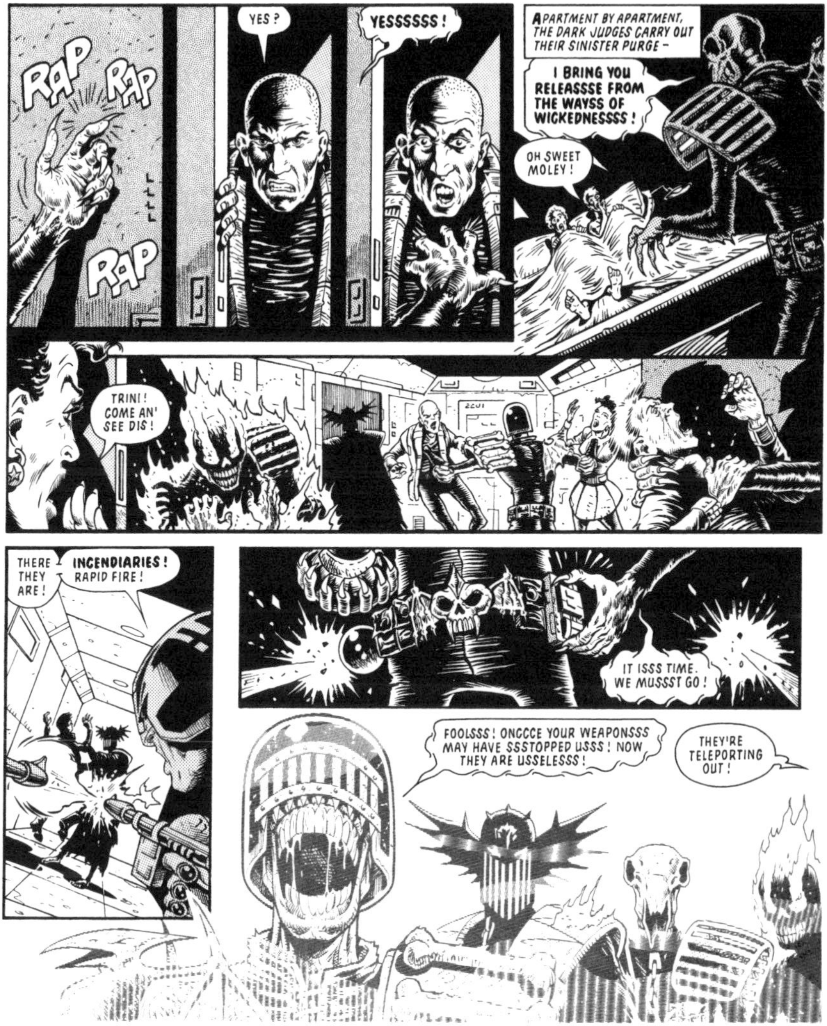
RAP RAP
RAP
YES?
YESSSSSS!
APARTMENT BY APARTMENT, THE DARK JUDGES CARRY OUT THEIR SINISTER PURGE –
I BRING YOU RELEASSSE FROM THE WAYSS OF WICKEDNESSSS!
OH SWEET MOLEY!
TRINI! COME AN' SEE DIS!
THERE THEY ARE!
INCENDIARIES! RAPID FIRE!
IT ISSS TIME. WE MUSSST GO!
FOOLSSS! ONCCCE YOUR WEAPONSSS MAY HAVE SSSTOPPED USSS! NOW THEY ARE USSELESSS!
THEY'RE TELEPORTING OUT!

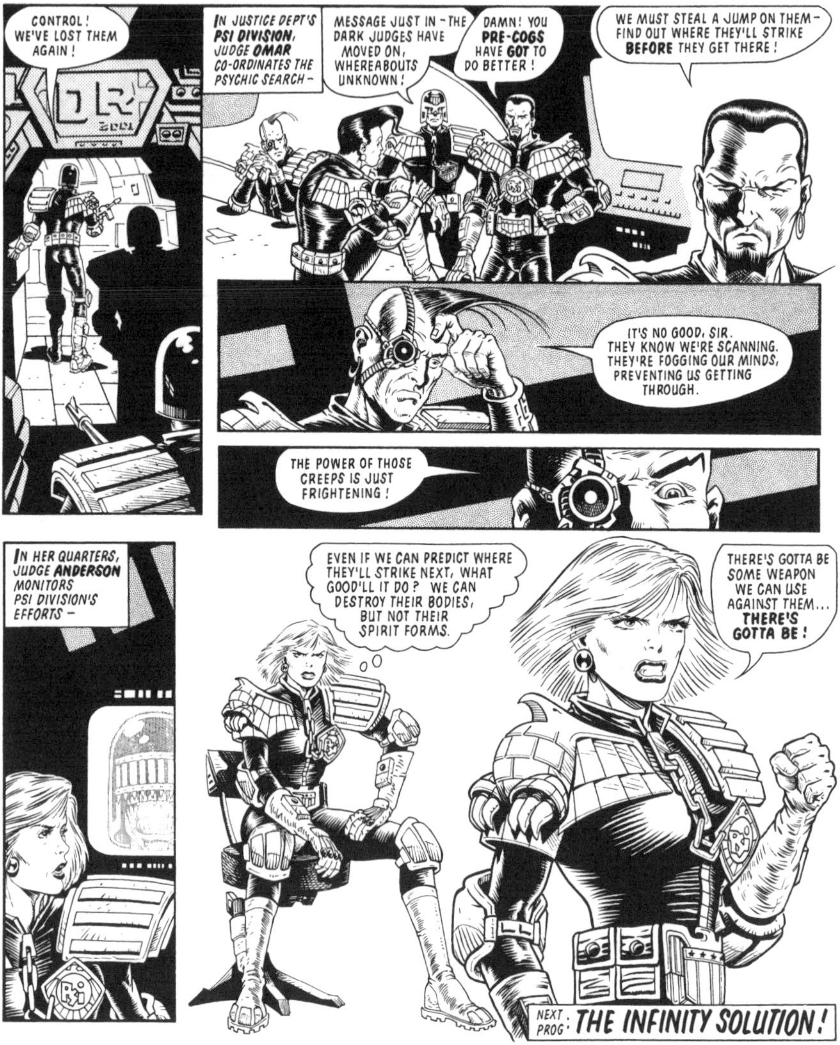
CONTROL! WE'VE LOST THEM AGAIN!
IN JUSTICE DEPT'S PSI DIVISION, JUDGE OMAR CO-ORDINATES THE PSYCHIC SEARCH –
MESSAGE JUST IN – THE DARK JUDGES HAVE MOVED ON, WHEREABOUTS UNKNOWN!
DAMN! YOU PRE-COGS HAVE GOT TO DO BETTER!
WE MUST STEAL A JUMP ON THEM – FIND OUT WHERE THEY'LL STRIKE BEFORE THEY GET THERE!
IT'S NO GOOD, SIR. THEY KNOW WE'RE SCANNING. THEY'RE FOGGING OUR MINDS, PREVENTING US GETTING THROUGH.
THE POWER OF THOSE CREEPS IS JUST FRIGHTENING!
IN HER QUARTERS, JUDGE ANDERSON MONITORS PSI DIVISION'S EFFORTS –
EVEN IF WE CAN PREDICT WHERE THEY'LL STRIKE NEXT, WHAT GOOD'LL IT DO? WE CAN DESTROY THEIR BODIES, BUT NOT THEIR SPIRIT FORMS.
THERE'S GOTTA BE SOME WEAPON WE CAN USE AGAINST THEM... THERE'S GOTTA BE!
NEXT PROG: THE INFINITY SOLUTION!

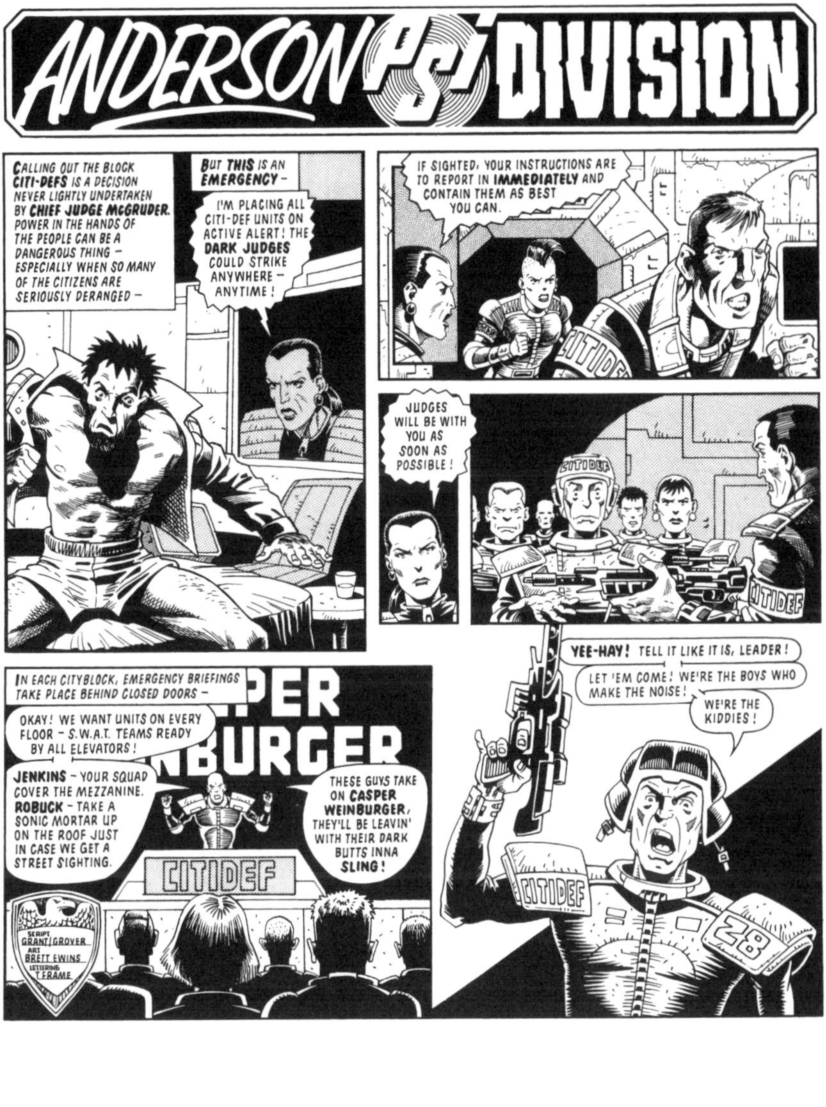
ANDERSON PSI DIVISION
CALLING OUT THE BLOCK CITI-DEFS IS A DECISION NEVER LIGHTLY UNDERTAKEN BY CHIEF JUDGE MCGRUDER. POWER IN THE HANDS OF THE PEOPLE CAN BE A DANGEROUS THING – ESPECIALLY WHEN SO MANY OF THE CITIZENS ARE SERIOUSLY DERANGED –
BUT THIS IS AN EMERGENCY –
I'M PLACING ALL CITI-DEF UNITS ON ACTIVE ALERT! THE DARK JUDGES COULD STRIKE ANYWHERE – ANYTIME!
IF SIGHTED, YOUR INSTRUCTIONS ARE TO REPORT IN IMMEDIATELY AND CONTAIN THEM AS BEST YOU CAN.
CITIDEF
JUDGES WILL BE WITH YOU AS SOON AS POSSIBLE!
CITIDEF
CITIDEF
IN EACH CITYBLOCK, EMERGENCY BRIEFINGS TAKE PLACE BEHIND CLOSED DOORS –
OKAY! WE WANT UNITS ON EVERY FLOOR – S.W.A.T. TEAMS READY BY ALL ELEVATORS!
JENKINS – YOUR SQUAD COVER THE MEZZANINE. ROBUCK – TAKE A SONIC MORTAR UP ON THE ROOF JUST IN CASE WE GET A STREET SIGHTING.
THESE GUYS TAKE ON CASPER WEINBURGER, THEY'LL BE LEAVIN' WITH THEIR DARK BUTTS INNA SLING!
CITIDEF
SCRIPT GRANT/GROVER
ART BRETT EWINS
LETTERING T.FRAME
YEE-HAY! TELL IT LIKE IT IS, LEADER!
LET 'EM COME! WE'RE THE BOYS WHO MAKE THE NOISE!
WE'RE THE KIDDIES!
CITIDEF
28

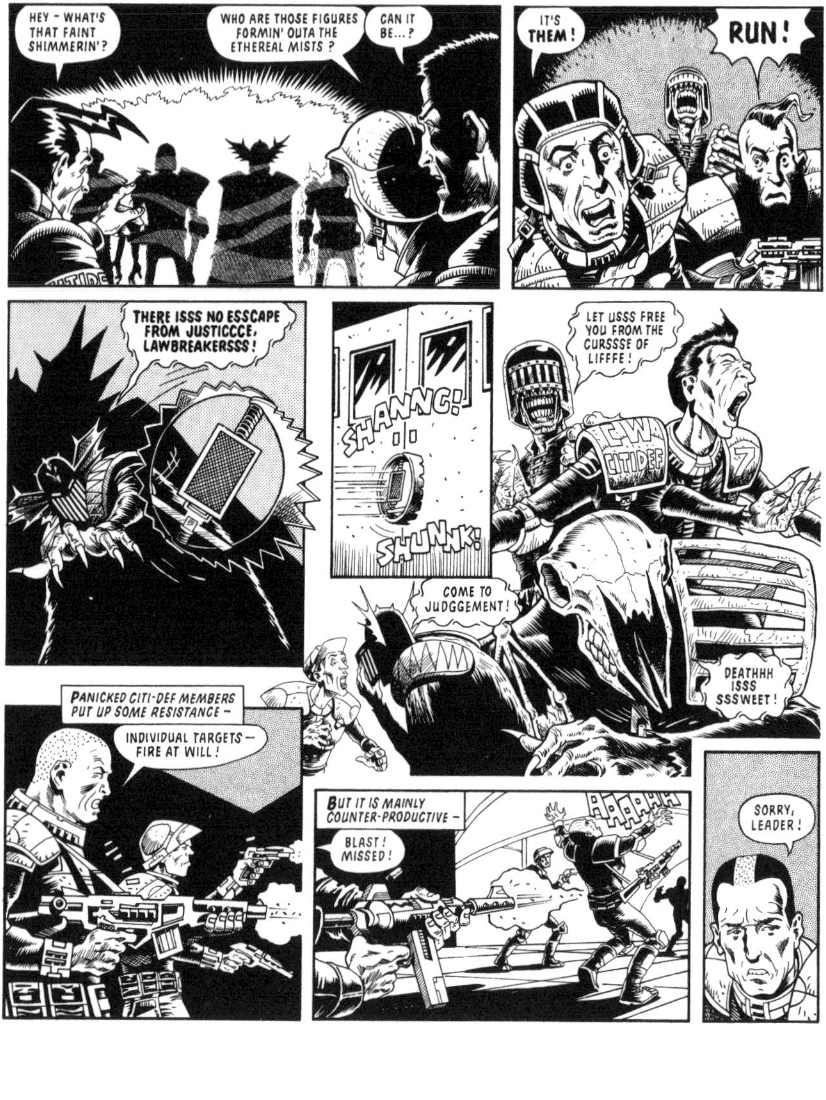
HEY - WHAT'S THAT FAINT SHIMMERIN'?
WHO ARE THOSE FIGURES FORMIN' OUTA THE ETHEREAL MISTS ?
CAN IT BE...?
IT'S THEM!
RUN!
THERE ISSS NO ESSCAPE FROM JUSTICCCE, LAWBREAKERSSS!
SHANNG!
SHUNNK!
LET USSS FREE YOU FROM THE CURSSSE OF LIFFFE!
COME TO JUDGGEMENT!
DEATHHH ISSS SSSWEET!
PANICKED CITI-DEF MEMBERS PUT UP SOME RESISTANCE –
INDIVIDUAL TARGETS – FIRE AT WILL!
BUT IT IS MAINLY COUNTER-PRODUCTIVE –
BLAST! MISSED!
AAAAHH
SORRY, LEADER!

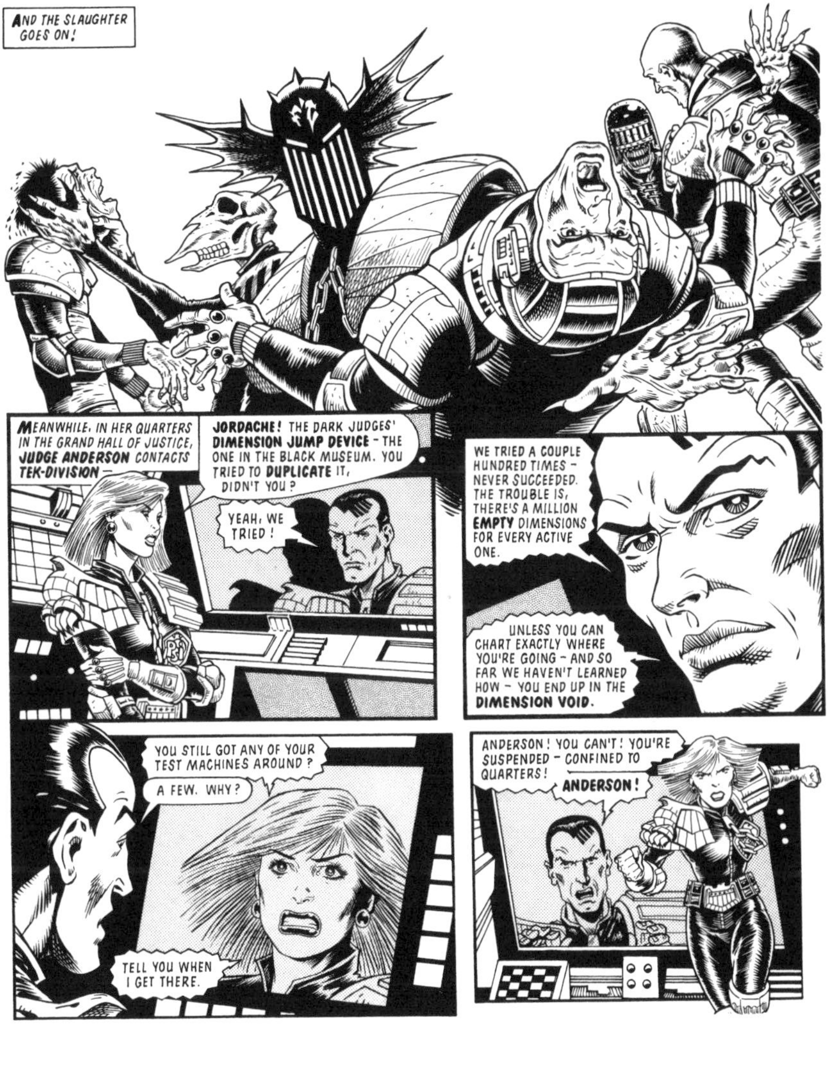
AND THE SLAUGHTER GOES ON!
MEANWHILE, IN HER QUARTERS IN THE GRAND HALL OF JUSTICE, JUDGE ANDERSON CONTACTS TEK-DIVISION —
JORDACHE! THE DARK JUDGES' DIMENSION JUMP DEVICE — THE ONE IN THE BLACK MUSEUM. YOU TRIED TO DUPLICATE IT, DIDN'T YOU?
YEAH, WE TRIED!
WE TRIED A COUPLE HUNDRED TIMES — NEVER SUCCEEDED. THE TROUBLE IS, THERE'S A MILLION EMPTY DIMENSIONS FOR EVERY ACTIVE ONE.
UNLESS YOU CAN CHART EXACTLY WHERE YOU'RE GOING — AND SO FAR WE HAVEN'T LEARNED HOW — YOU END UP IN THE DIMENSION VOID.
YOU STILL GOT ANY OF YOUR TEST MACHINES AROUND?
A FEW. WHY?
TELL YOU WHEN I GET THERE.
ANDERSON! YOU CAN'T! YOU'RE SUSPENDED — CONFINED TO QUARTERS!
ANDERSON!

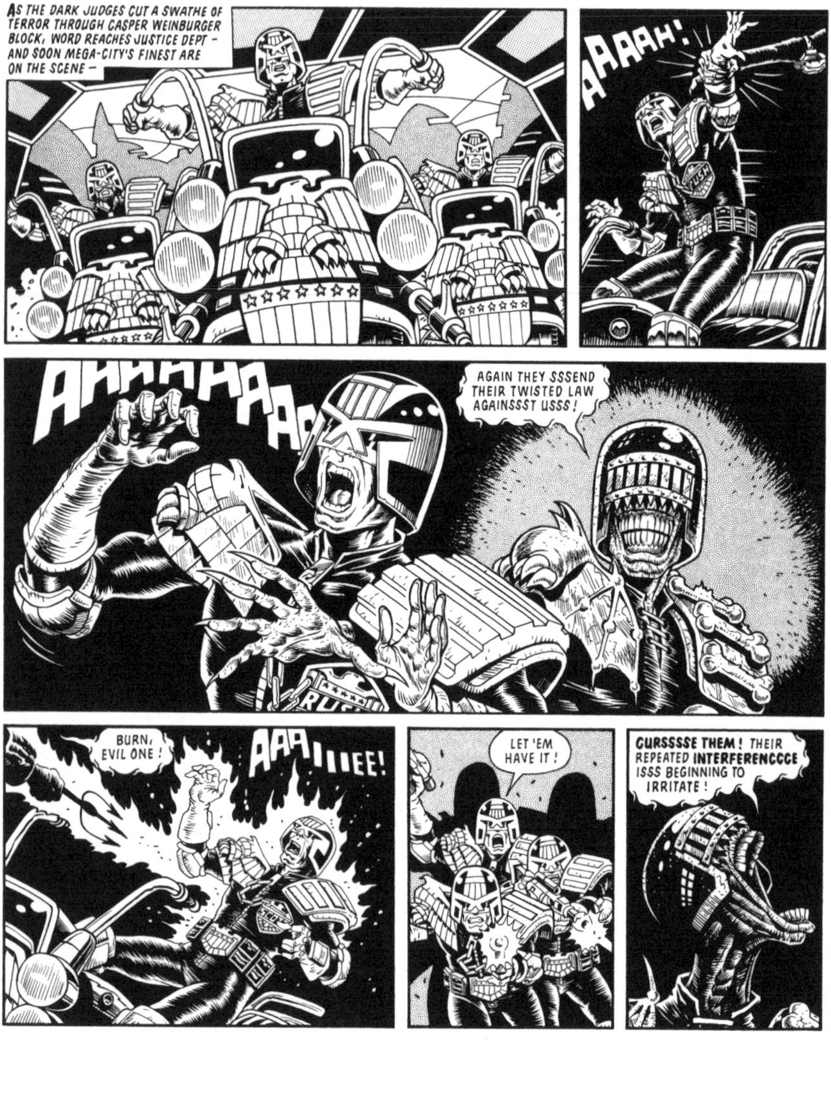
AS THE DARK JUDGES CUT A SWATHE OF TERROR THROUGH CASPER WEINBURGER BLOCK, WORD REACHES JUSTICE DEPT - AND SOON MEGA-CITY'S FINEST ARE ON THE SCENE -
AAAAH!
AGAIN THEY SSSEND THEIR TWISTED LAW AGAINSSST USSS!
BURN, EVIL ONE!
AAAIIIEE!
LET 'EM HAVE IT!
CURSSSSE THEM! THEIR REPEATED INTERFERENCCCE ISSS BEGINNING TO IRRITATE!

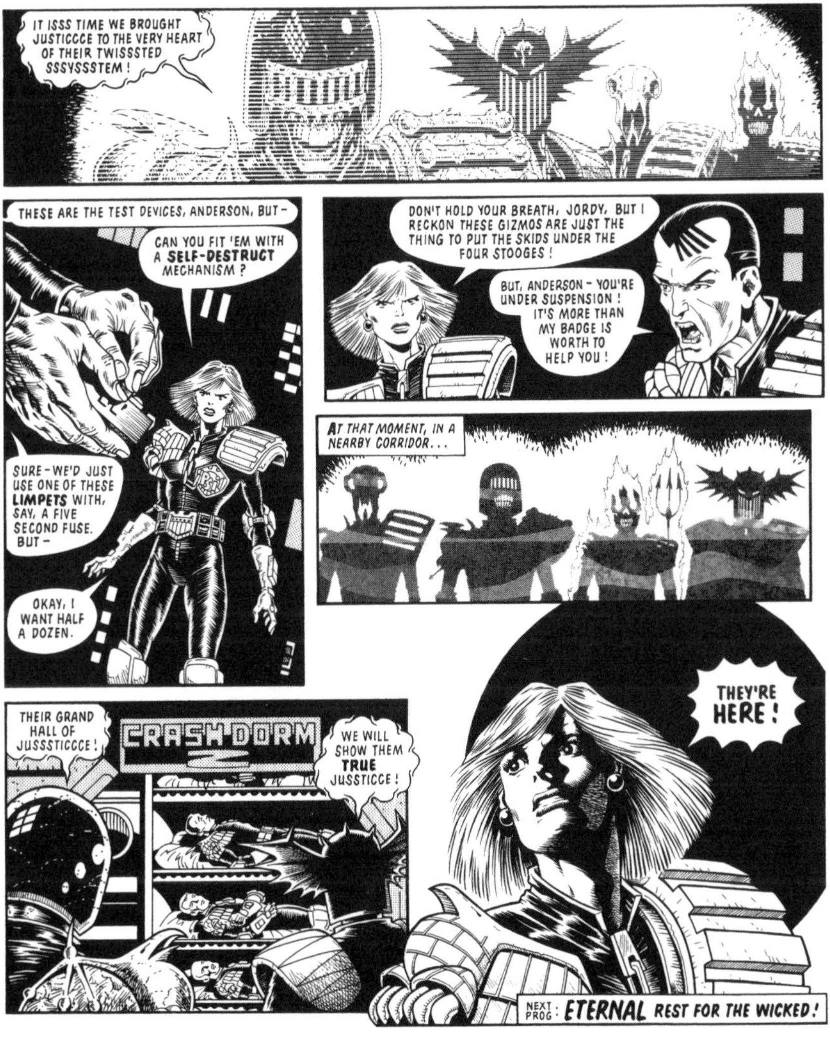
IT ISSS TIME WE BROUGHT JUSTICCCE TO THE VERY HEART OF THEIR TWISSSTED SSSYSSSTEM!
THESE ARE THE TEST DEVICES, ANDERSON, BUT –
CAN YOU FIT 'EM WITH A SELF-DESTRUCT MECHANISM?
SURE – WE'D JUST USE ONE OF THESE LIMPETS WITH, SAY, A FIVE SECOND FUSE. BUT –
OKAY, I WANT HALF A DOZEN.
DON'T HOLD YOUR BREATH, JORDY, BUT I RECKON THESE GIZMOS ARE JUST THE THING TO PUT THE SKIDS UNDER THE FOUR STOOGES!
BUT, ANDERSON – YOU'RE UNDER SUSPENSION! IT'S MORE THAN MY BADGE IS WORTH TO HELP YOU!
AT THAT MOMENT, IN A NEARBY CORRIDOR...
THEIR GRAND HALL OF JUSSSTICCCE!
CRASH DORM
WE WILL SHOW THEM TRUE JUSSTICCE!
THEY'RE HERE!
NEXT PROG: ETERNAL REST FOR THE WICKED!

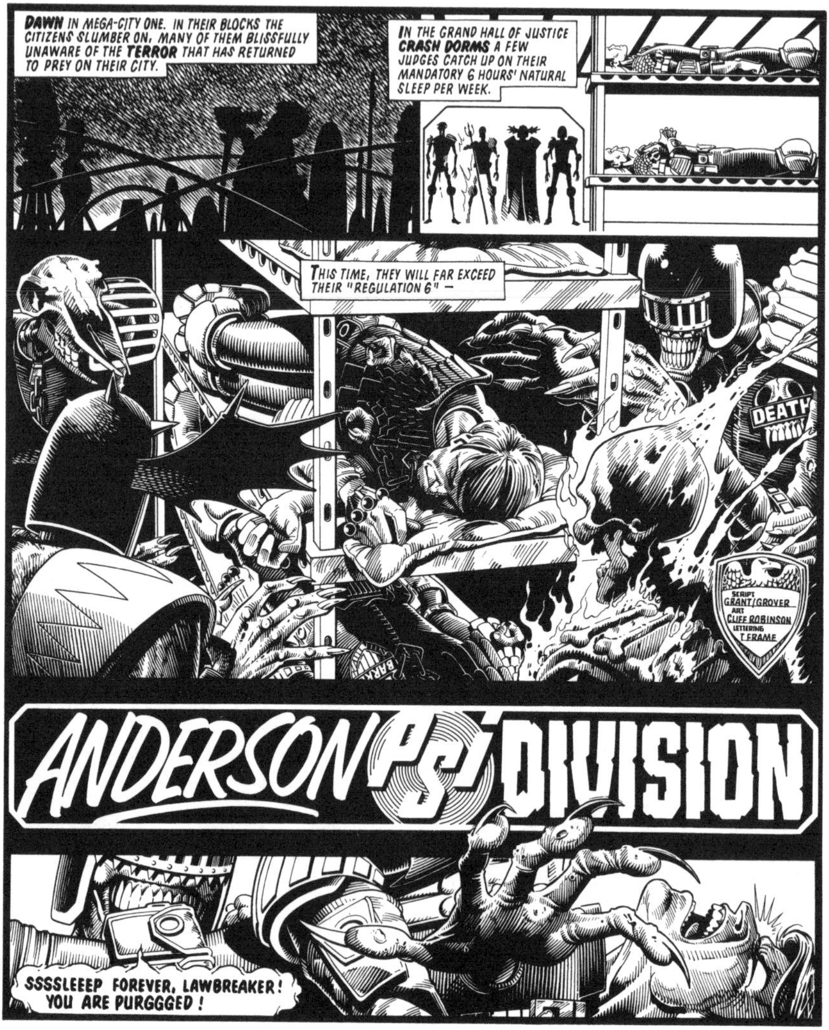
DAWN IN MEGA-CITY ONE. IN THEIR BLOCKS THE CITIZENS SLUMBER ON, MANY OF THEM BLISSFULLY UNAWARE OF THE TERROR THAT HAS RETURNED TO PREY ON THEIR CITY.
IN THE GRAND HALL OF JUSTICE CRASH DORMS A FEW JUDGES CATCH UP ON THEIR MANDATORY 6 HOURS' NATURAL SLEEP PER WEEK.
THIS TIME, THEY WILL FAR EXCEED THEIR "REGULATION 6" —
DEATH
SCRIPT GRANT/GROVER ART CLIFF ROBINSON LETTERING T FRAME
ANDERSON PSI DIVISION
SSSSLEEEP FOREVER, LAWBREAKER! YOU ARE PURGGGED!

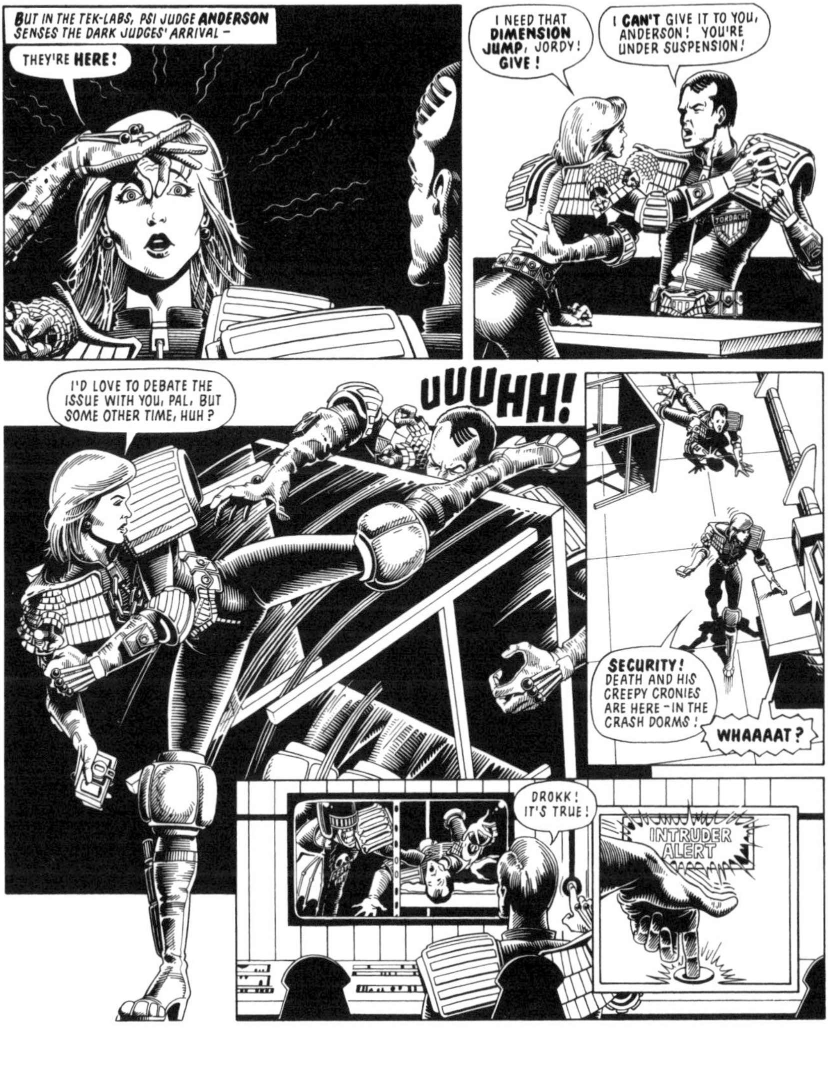
BUT IN THE TEK-LABS, PSI JUDGE ANDERSON SENSES THE DARK JUDGES' ARRIVAL –
THEY'RE HERE!
I NEED THAT DIMENSION JUMP, JORDY! GIVE!
I CAN'T GIVE IT TO YOU, ANDERSON! YOU'RE UNDER SUSPENSION!
JORDACHE
I'D LOVE TO DEBATE THE ISSUE WITH YOU, PAL, BUT SOME OTHER TIME, HUH?
UUUHH!
SECURITY! DEATH AND HIS CREEPY CRONIES ARE HERE – IN THE CRASH DORMS!
WHAAAAT?
DROKK! IT'S TRUE!
INTRUDER ALERT

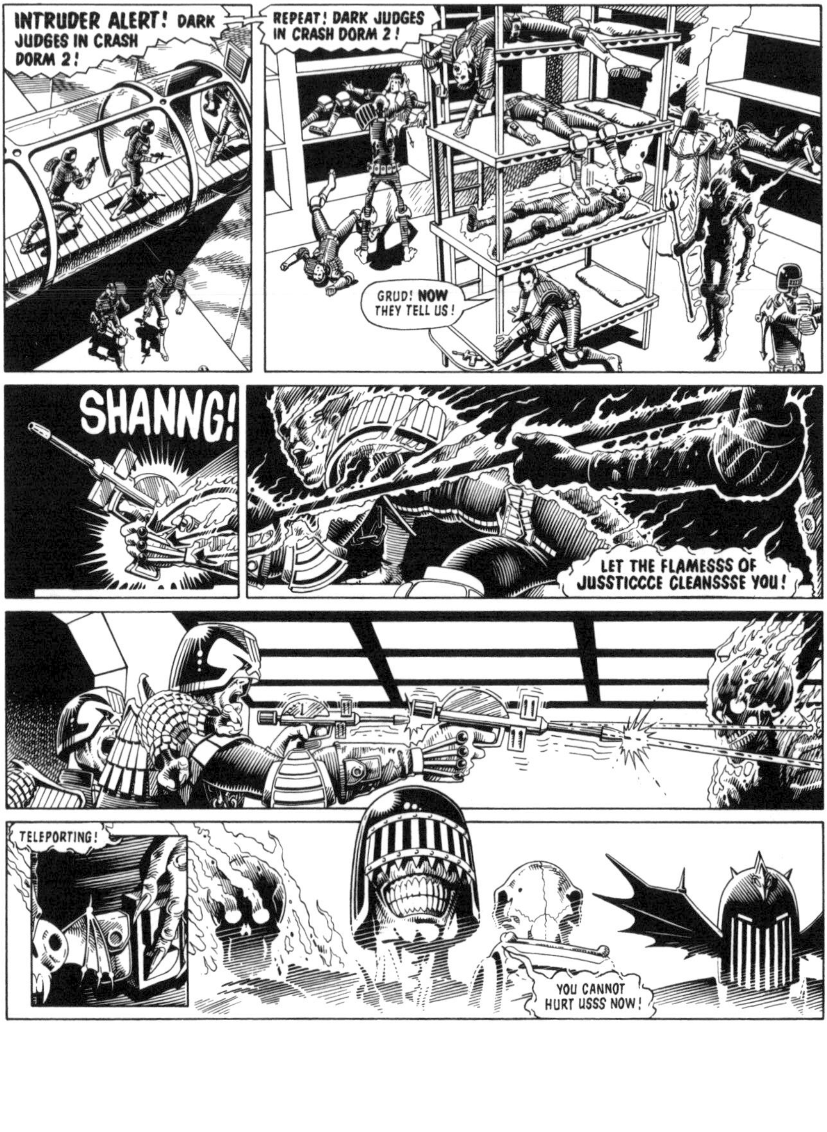
INTRUDER ALERT! DARK JUDGES IN CRASH DORM 2!
REPEAT! DARK JUDGES IN CRASH DORM 2!
GRUD! NOW THEY TELL US!
SHANNG!
LET THE FLAMESSS OF JUSSTICCCE CLEANSSSE YOU!
TELEPORTING!
YOU CANNOT HURT USSS NOW!

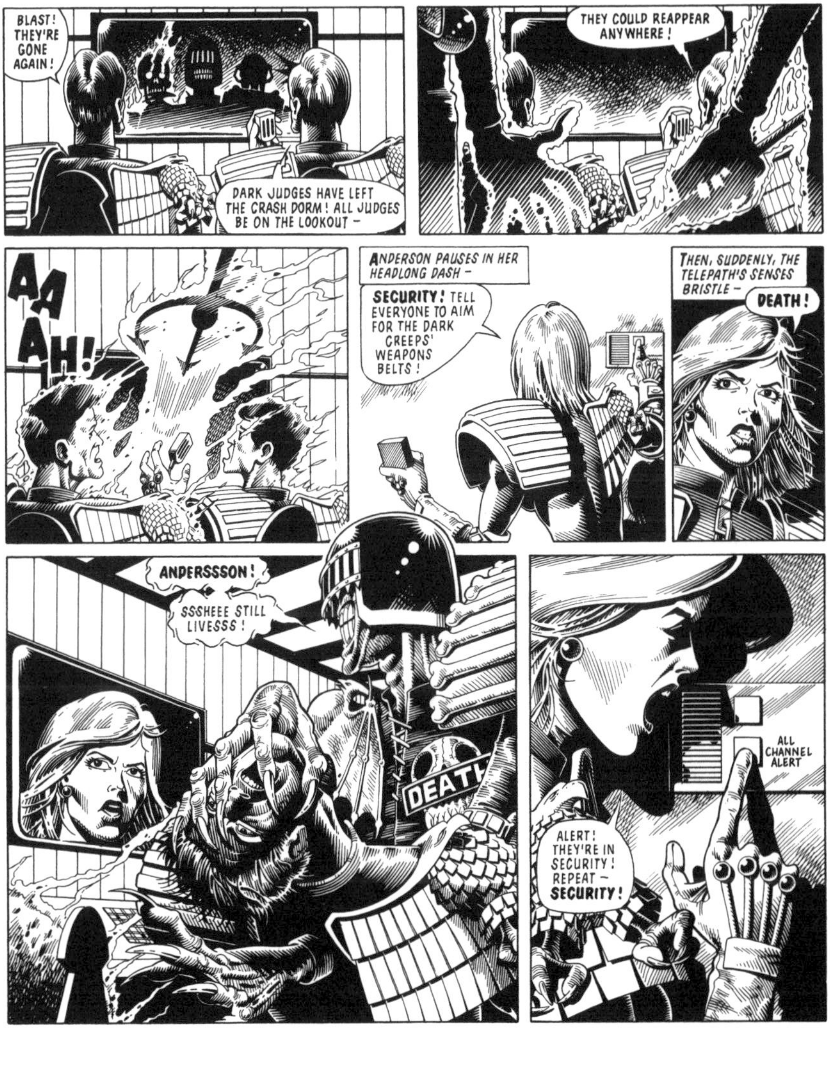
BLAST! THEY'RE GONE AGAIN!
DARK JUDGES HAVE LEFT THE CRASH DORM! ALL JUDGES BE ON THE LOOKOUT –
THEY COULD REAPPEAR ANYWHERE!
AAAH!
ANDERSON PAUSES IN HER HEADLONG DASH –
SECURITY! TELL EVERYONE TO AIM FOR THE DARK CREEPS' WEAPONS BELTS!
THEN, SUDDENLY, THE TELEPATH'S SENSES BRISTLE –
DEATH!
ANDERSSSON!
SSSHEEE STILL LIVESSS!
DEATH
ALL CHANNEL ALERT
ALERT! THEY'RE IN SECURITY! REPEAT – SECURITY!

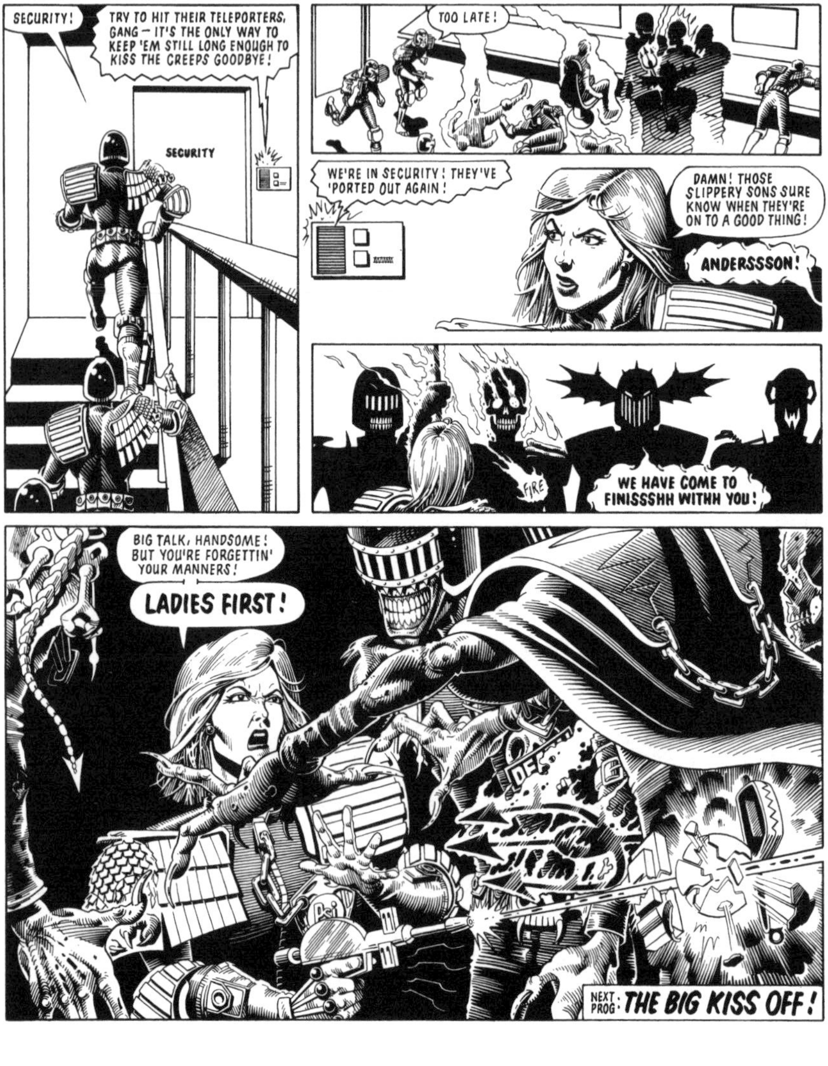
SECURITY!
TRY TO HIT THEIR TELEPORTERS, GANG — IT'S THE ONLY WAY TO KEEP 'EM STILL LONG ENOUGH TO KISS THE CREEPS GOODBYE!
SECURITY
TOO LATE!
WE'RE IN SECURITY! THEY'VE 'PORTED OUT AGAIN!
DAMN! THOSE SLIPPERY SONS SURE KNOW WHEN THEY'RE ON TO A GOOD THING!
ANDERSSSON!
FIRE
WE HAVE COME TO FINISSSHH WITHH YOU!
BIG TALK, HANDSOME! BUT YOU'RE FORGETTIN' YOUR MANNERS!
LADIES FIRST!
NEXT PROG: THE BIG KISS OFF!

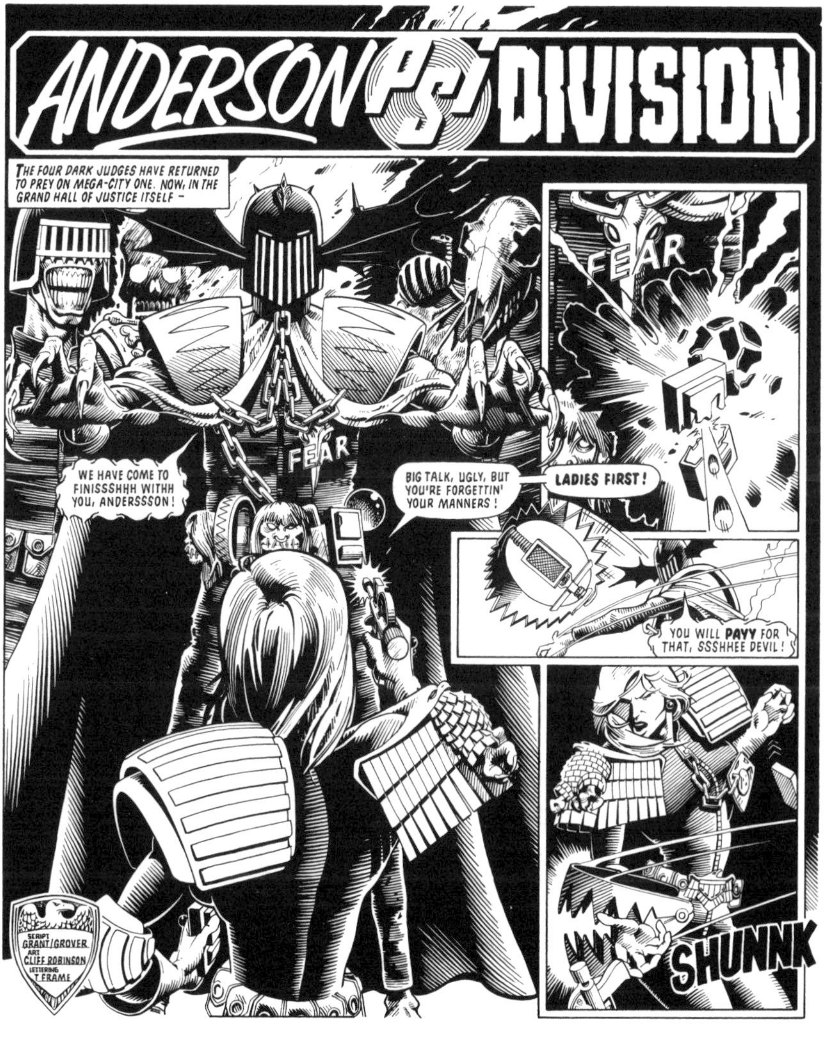
ANDERSON PSI DIVISION
THE FOUR DARK JUDGES HAVE RETURNED TO PREY ON MEGA-CITY ONE. NOW, IN THE GRAND HALL OF JUSTICE ITSELF –
FEAR
FEAR
WE HAVE COME TO FINISSSHHH WITHH YOU, ANDERSSSON!
BIG TALK, UGLY, BUT YOU'RE FORGETTIN' YOUR MANNERS!
LADIES FIRST!
YOU WILL PAYY FOR THAT, SSSHHEE DEVIL!
SHUNNK
SCRIPT GRANT/GROVER
ART CLIFF ROBINSON
LETTERING T FRAME

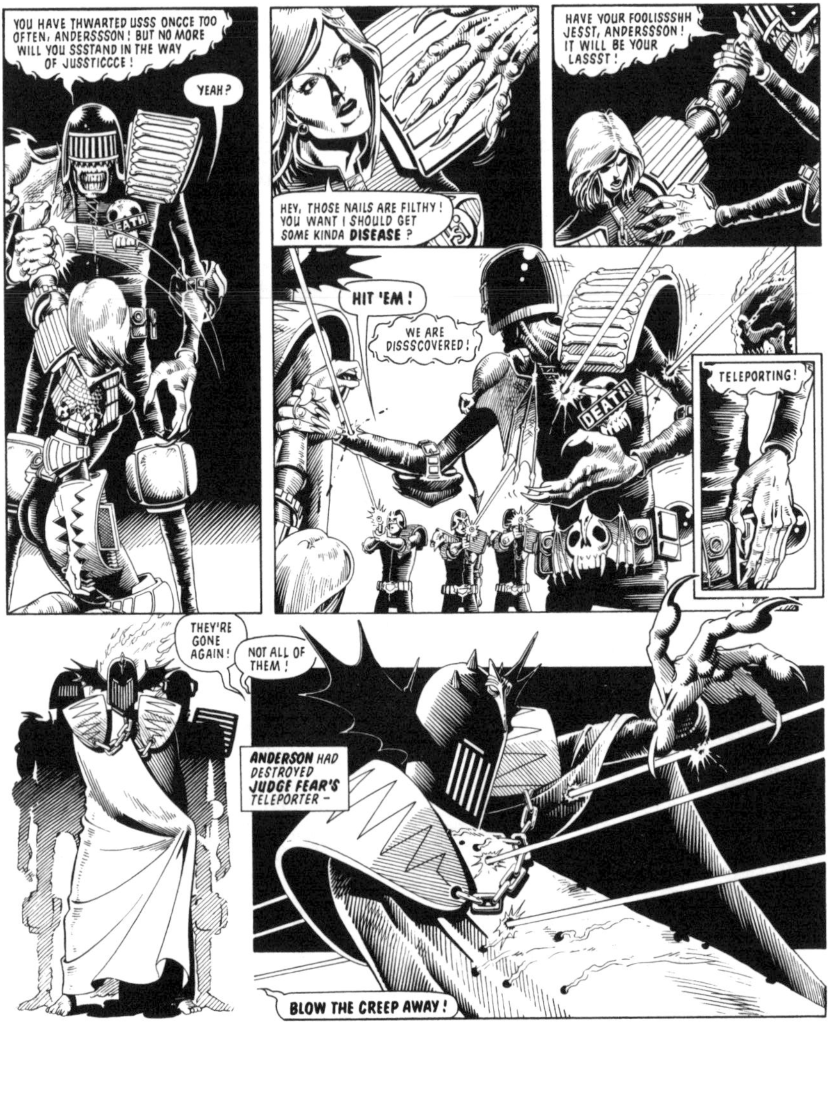
YOU HAVE THWARTED USSS ONCCE TOO OFTEN, ANDERSSSON! BUT NO MORE WILL YOU SSSTAND IN THE WAY OF JUSSTICCCE!
YEAH?
DEATH
HEY, THOSE NAILS ARE FILTHY! YOU WANT I SHOULD GET SOME KINDA DISEASE?
HAVE YOUR FOOLISSSHH JESST, ANDERSSSON! IT WILL BE YOUR LASSST!
HIT 'EM!
WE ARE DISSSCOVERED!
DEATH
TELEPORTING!
THEY'RE GONE AGAIN!
NOT ALL OF THEM!
ANDERSON HAD DESTROYED JUDGE FEAR'S TELEPORTER –
BLOW THE CREEP AWAY!

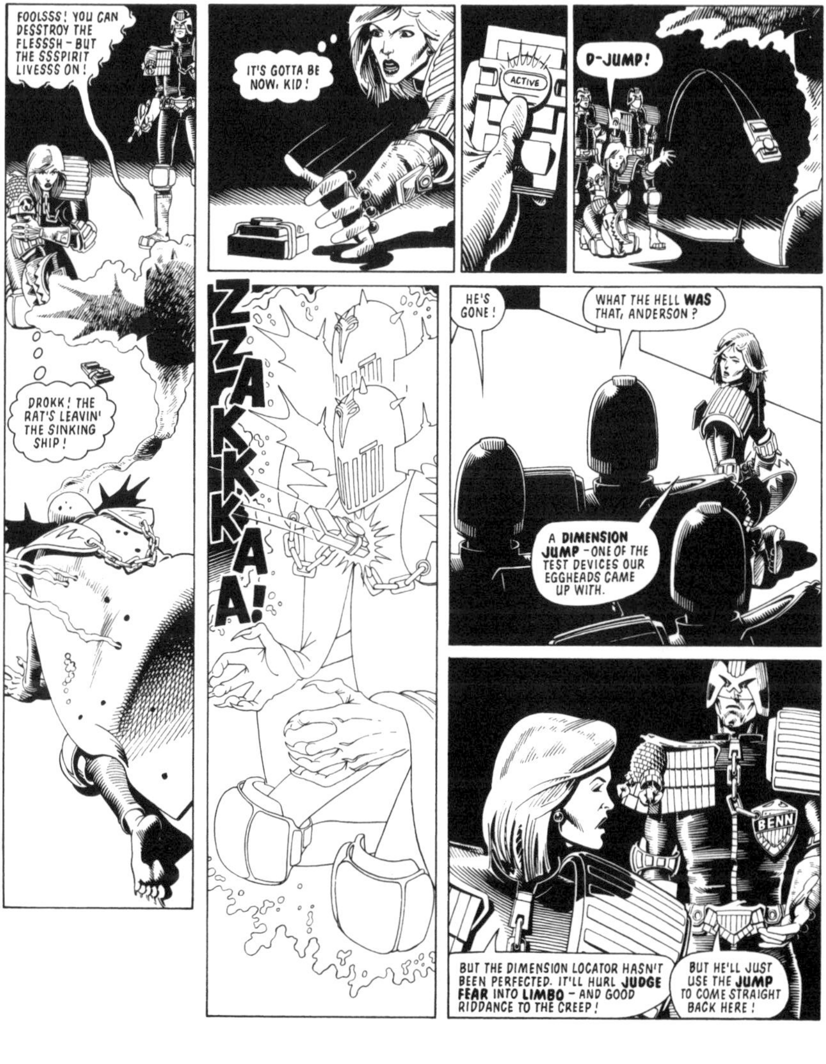
FOOLSSS! YOU CAN DESSTROY THE FLESSSH – BUT THE SSSPIRIT LIVESSS ON!
IT'S GOTTA BE NOW, KID!
ACTIVE
D-JUMP!
DROKK! THE RAT'S LEAVIN' THE SINKING SHIP!
ZZAKKAA!
HE'S GONE!
WHAT THE HELL WAS THAT, ANDERSON?
A DIMENSION JUMP – ONE OF THE TEST DEVICES OUR EGGHEADS CAME UP WITH.
BENN
BUT THE DIMENSION LOCATOR HASN'T BEEN PERFECTED. IT'LL HURL JUDGE FEAR INTO LIMBO – AND GOOD RIDDANCE TO THE CREEP!
BUT HE'LL JUST USE THE JUMP TO COME STRAIGHT BACK HERE!

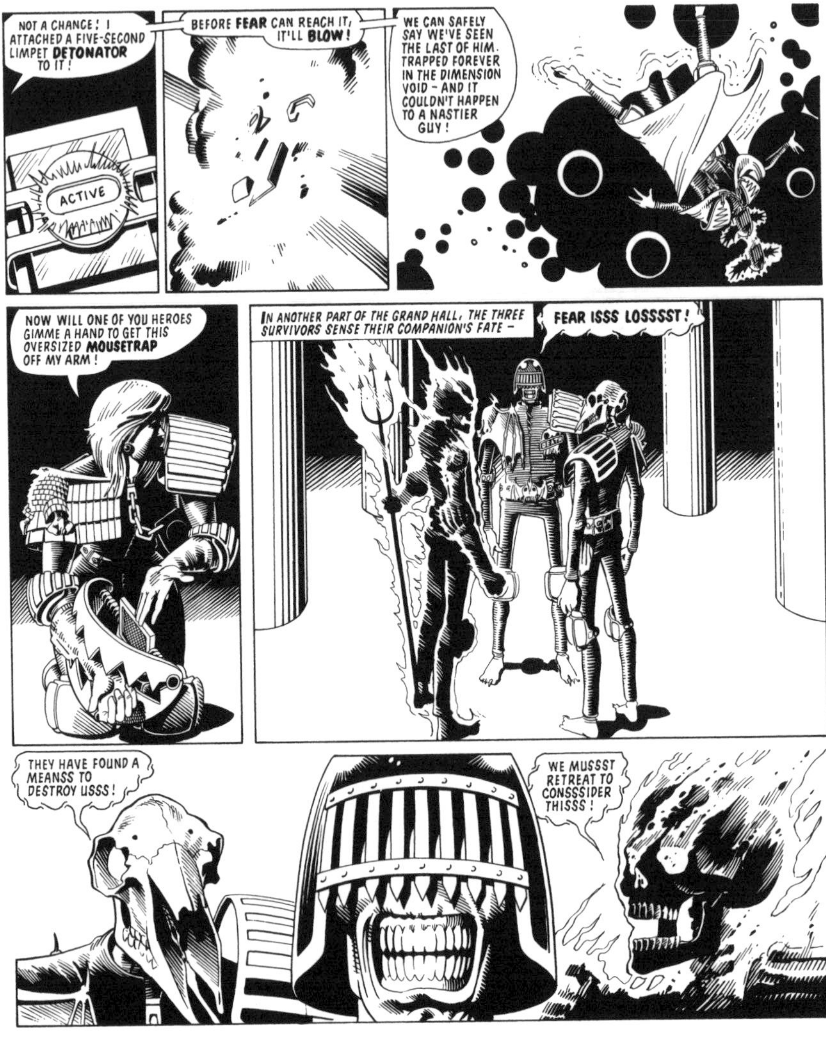
NOT A CHANCE! I ATTACHED A FIVE-SECOND LIMPET DETONATOR TO IT!
ACTIVE
BEFORE FEAR CAN REACH IT, IT'LL BLOW!
WE CAN SAFELY SAY WE'VE SEEN THE LAST OF HIM. TRAPPED FOREVER IN THE DIMENSION VOID – AND IT COULDN'T HAPPEN TO A NASTIER GUY!
NOW WILL ONE OF YOU HEROES GIMME A HAND TO GET THIS OVERSIZED MOUSETRAP OFF MY ARM!
IN ANOTHER PART OF THE GRAND HALL, THE THREE SURVIVORS SENSE THEIR COMPANION'S FATE –
FEAR ISSS LOSSSST!
THEY HAVE FOUND A MEANSS TO DESTROY USSS!
WE MUSSST RETREAT TO CONSSSIDER THISSS!

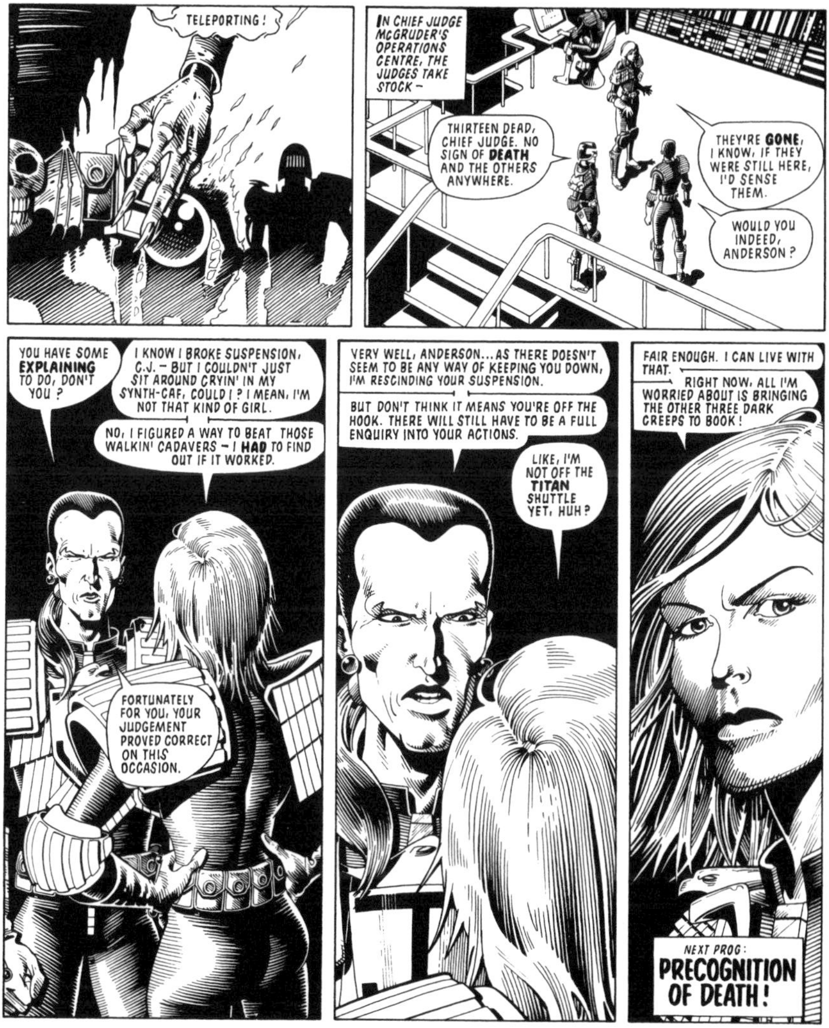
TELEPORTING!
IN CHIEF JUDGE McGRUDER'S OPERATIONS CENTRE, THE JUDGES TAKE STOCK –
THIRTEEN DEAD, CHIEF JUDGE. NO SIGN OF DEATH AND THE OTHERS ANYWHERE.
THEY'RE GONE, I KNOW. IF THEY WERE STILL HERE, I'D SENSE THEM.
WOULD YOU INDEED, ANDERSON?
YOU HAVE SOME EXPLAINING TO DO, DON'T YOU?
I KNOW I BROKE SUSPENSION, C.J. – BUT I COULDN'T JUST SIT AROUND CRYIN' IN MY SYNTH-CAF, COULD I? I MEAN, I'M NOT THAT KIND OF GIRL.
NO, I FIGURED A WAY TO BEAT THOSE WALKIN' CADAVERS – I HAD TO FIND OUT IF IT WORKED.
FORTUNATELY FOR YOU, YOUR JUDGEMENT PROVED CORRECT ON THIS OCCASION.
VERY WELL, ANDERSON... AS THERE DOESN'T SEEM TO BE ANY WAY OF KEEPING YOU DOWN, I'M RESCINDING YOUR SUSPENSION.
BUT DON'T THINK IT MEANS YOU'RE OFF THE HOOK. THERE WILL STILL HAVE TO BE A FULL ENQUIRY INTO YOUR ACTIONS.
LIKE, I'M NOT OFF THE TITAN SHUTTLE YET, HUH?
FAIR ENOUGH. I CAN LIVE WITH THAT.
RIGHT NOW, ALL I'M WORRIED ABOUT IS BRINGING THE OTHER THREE DARK CREEPS TO BOOK!
NEXT PROG:
PRECOGNITION OF DEATH!

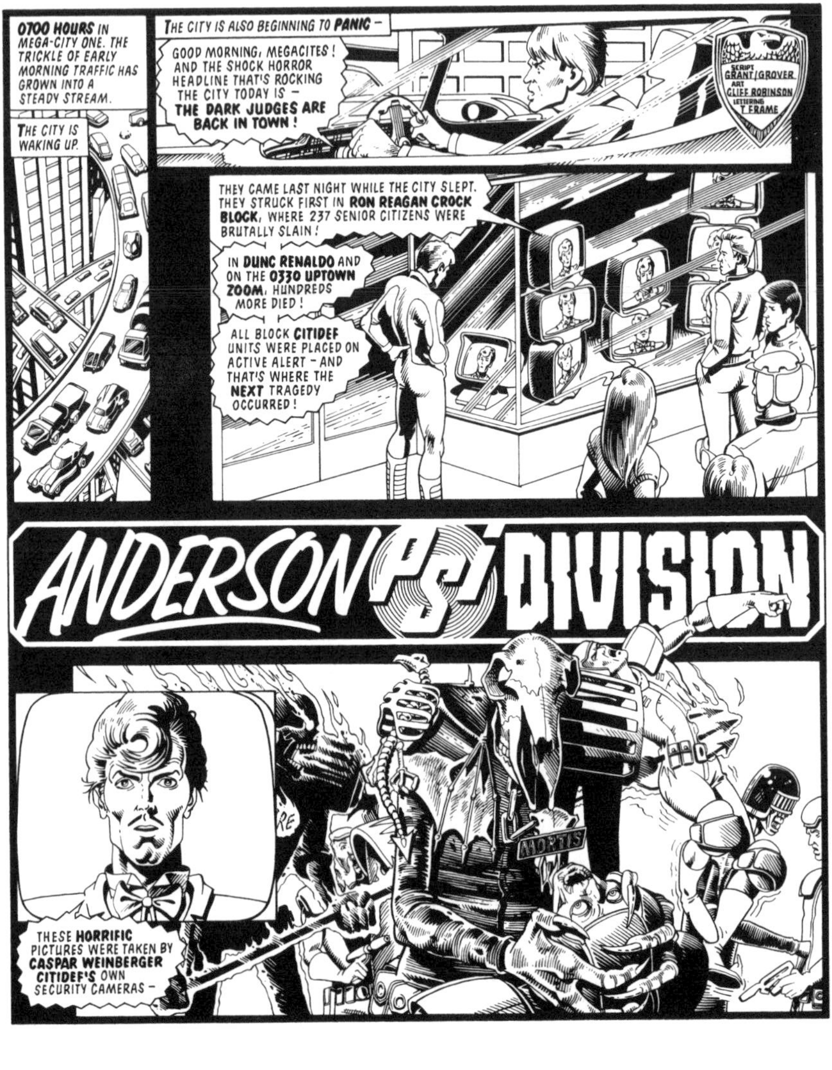
0700 HOURS IN MEGA-CITY ONE. THE TRICKLE OF EARLY MORNING TRAFFIC HAS GROWN INTO A STEADY STREAM.
THE CITY IS WAKING UP.
THE CITY IS ALSO BEGINNING TO PANIC –
GOOD MORNING, MEGACITES! AND THE SHOCK HORROR HEADLINE THAT'S ROCKING THE CITY TODAY IS – THE DARK JUDGES ARE BACK IN TOWN!
SCRIPT GRANT/GROVER
ART CLIFF ROBINSON
LETTERING T FRAME
THEY CAME LAST NIGHT WHILE THE CITY SLEPT. THEY STRUCK FIRST IN RON REAGAN CROCK BLOCK, WHERE 237 SENIOR CITIZENS WERE BRUTALLY SLAIN!
IN DUNC RENALDO AND ON THE 0330 UPTOWN ZOOM, HUNDREDS MORE DIED!
ALL BLOCK CITIDEF UNITS WERE PLACED ON ACTIVE ALERT – AND THAT'S WHERE THE NEXT TRAGEDY OCCURRED!
ANDERSON PSI DIVISION
MORTIS
THESE HORRIFIC PICTURES WERE TAKEN BY CASPAR WEINBERGER CITIDEF'S OWN SECURITY CAMERAS –

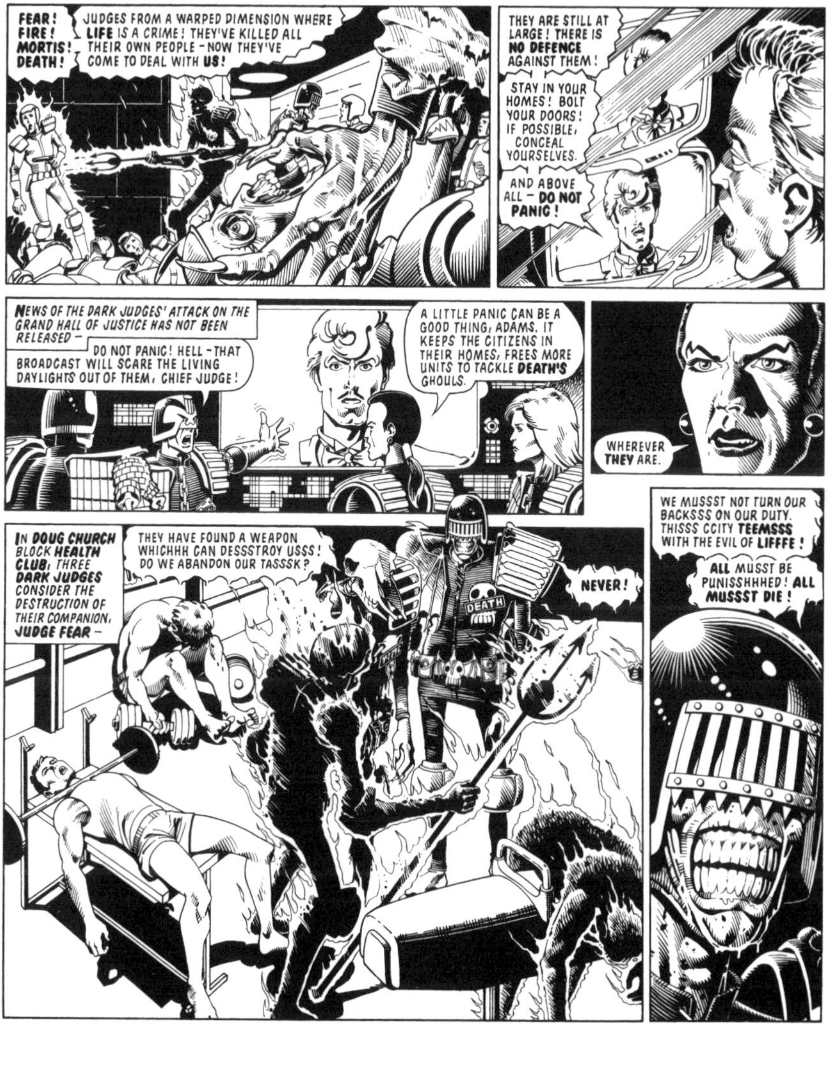
FEAR! FIRE! MORTIS! DEATH!
JUDGES FROM A WARPED DIMENSION WHERE LIFE IS A CRIME! THEY'VE KILLED ALL THEIR OWN PEOPLE – NOW THEY'VE COME TO DEAL WITH US!
THEY ARE STILL AT LARGE! THERE IS NO DEFENCE AGAINST THEM!
STAY IN YOUR HOMES! BOLT YOUR DOORS! IF POSSIBLE, CONCEAL YOURSELVES.
AND ABOVE ALL – DO NOT PANIC!
NEWS OF THE DARK JUDGES' ATTACK ON THE GRAND HALL OF JUSTICE HAS NOT BEEN RELEASED –
DO NOT PANIC! HELL – THAT BROADCAST WILL SCARE THE LIVING DAYLIGHTS OUT OF THEM, CHIEF JUDGE!
A LITTLE PANIC CAN BE A GOOD THING, ADAMS. IT KEEPS THE CITIZENS IN THEIR HOMES, FREES MORE UNITS TO TACKLE DEATH'S GHOULS.
WHEREVER THEY ARE.
IN DOUG CHURCH BLOCK HEALTH CLUB, THREE DARK JUDGES CONSIDER THE DESTRUCTION OF THEIR COMPANION, JUDGE FEAR –
THEY HAVE FOUND A WEAPON WHICHHH CAN DESSSTROY USSS! DO WE ABANDON OUR TASSSK?
NEVER!
DEATH
WE MUSSST NOT TURN OUR BACKSSS ON OUR DUTY. THISSS CCITY TEEMSSS WITH THE EVIL OF LIFFFE!
ALL MUSST BE PUNISSHHHED! ALL MUSSST DIE!

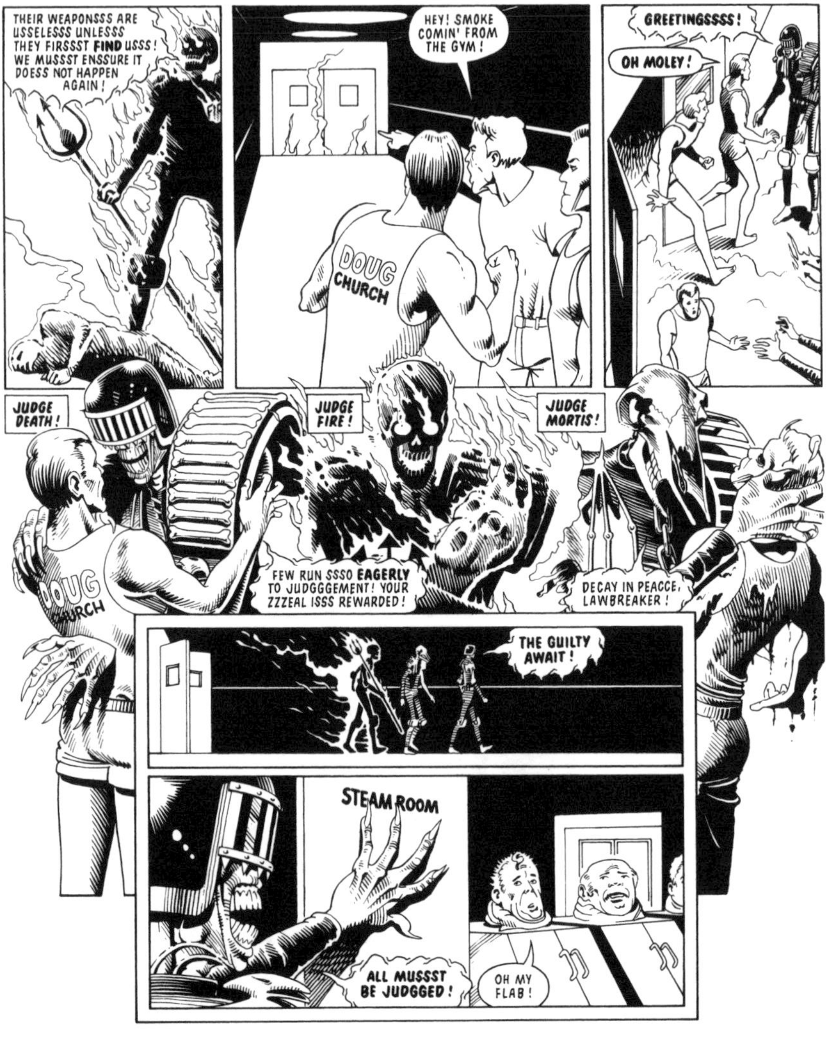
THEIR WEAPONSSS ARE USSELESSS UNLESSS THEY FIRSSST FIND USSS! WE MUSSST ENSSURE IT DOESS NOT HAPPEN AGAIN!
HEY! SMOKE COMIN' FROM THE GYM!
DOUG CHURCH
GREETINGSSSS!
OH MOLEY!
JUDGE DEATH!
JUDGE FIRE!
JUDGE MORTIS!
DOUG CHURCH
FEW RUN SSSO EAGERLY TO JUDGGGEMENT! YOUR ZZZEAL ISSS REWARDED!
DECAY IN PEACCE, LAWBREAKER!
THE GUILTY AWAIT!
STEAM ROOM
ALL MUSSST BE JUDGGED!
OH MY FLAB!

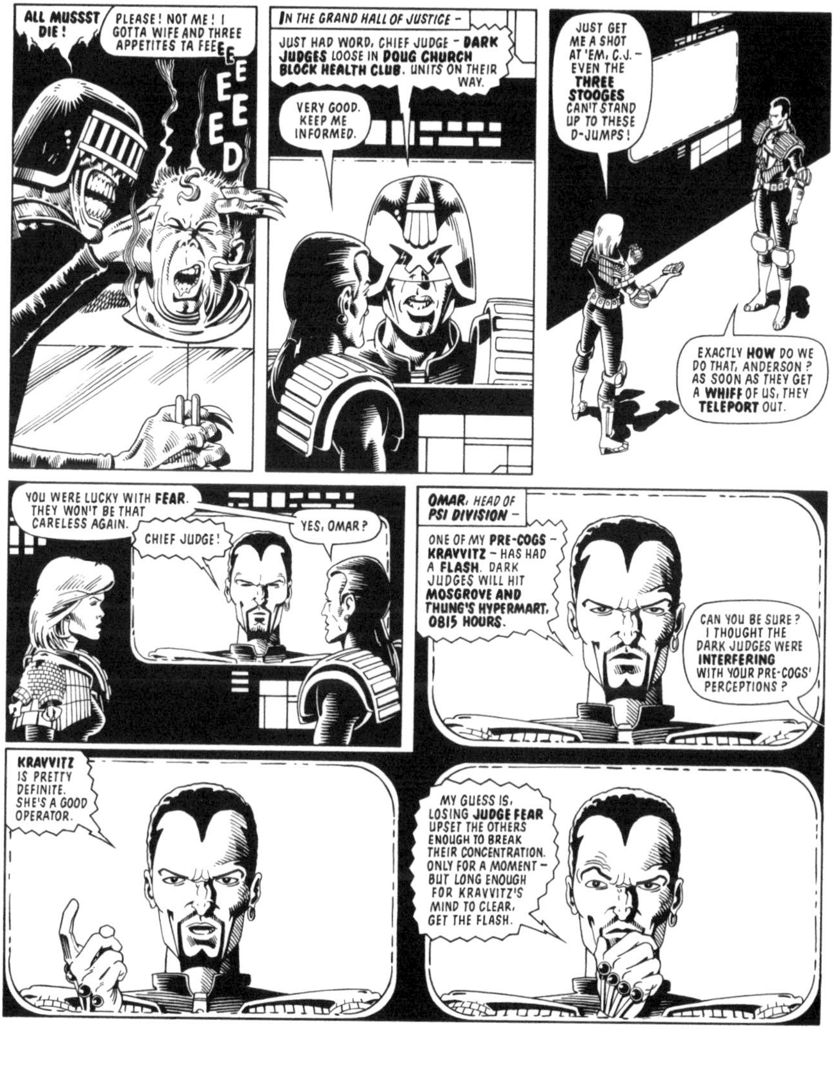
ALL MUSSST DIE!
PLEASE! NOT ME! I GOTTA WIFE AND THREE APPETITES TA FEEEEEEEED
IN THE GRAND HALL OF JUSTICE –
JUST HAD WORD, CHIEF JUDGE – DARK JUDGES LOOSE IN DOUG CHURCH BLOCK HEALTH CLUB. UNITS ON THEIR WAY.
VERY GOOD. KEEP ME INFORMED.
JUST GET ME A SHOT AT 'EM, C.J. – EVEN THE THREE STOOGES CAN'T STAND UP TO THESE D-JUMPS!
EXACTLY HOW DO WE DO THAT, ANDERSON? AS SOON AS THEY GET A WHIFF OF US, THEY TELEPORT OUT.
YOU WERE LUCKY WITH FEAR. THEY WON'T BE THAT CARELESS AGAIN.
CHIEF JUDGE!
YES, OMAR?
OMAR, HEAD OF PSI DIVISION –
ONE OF MY PRE-COGS – KRAVVITZ – HAS HAD A FLASH. DARK JUDGES WILL HIT MOSGROVE AND THUNG'S HYPERMART, 0815 HOURS.
CAN YOU BE SURE? I THOUGHT THE DARK JUDGES WERE INTERFERING WITH YOUR PRE-COGS' PERCEPTIONS?
KRAVVITZ IS PRETTY DEFINITE. SHE'S A GOOD OPERATOR.
MY GUESS IS, LOSING JUDGE FEAR UPSET THE OTHERS ENOUGH TO BREAK THEIR CONCENTRATION. ONLY FOR A MOMENT – BUT LONG ENOUGH FOR KRAVVITZ'S MIND TO CLEAR, GET THE FLASH.

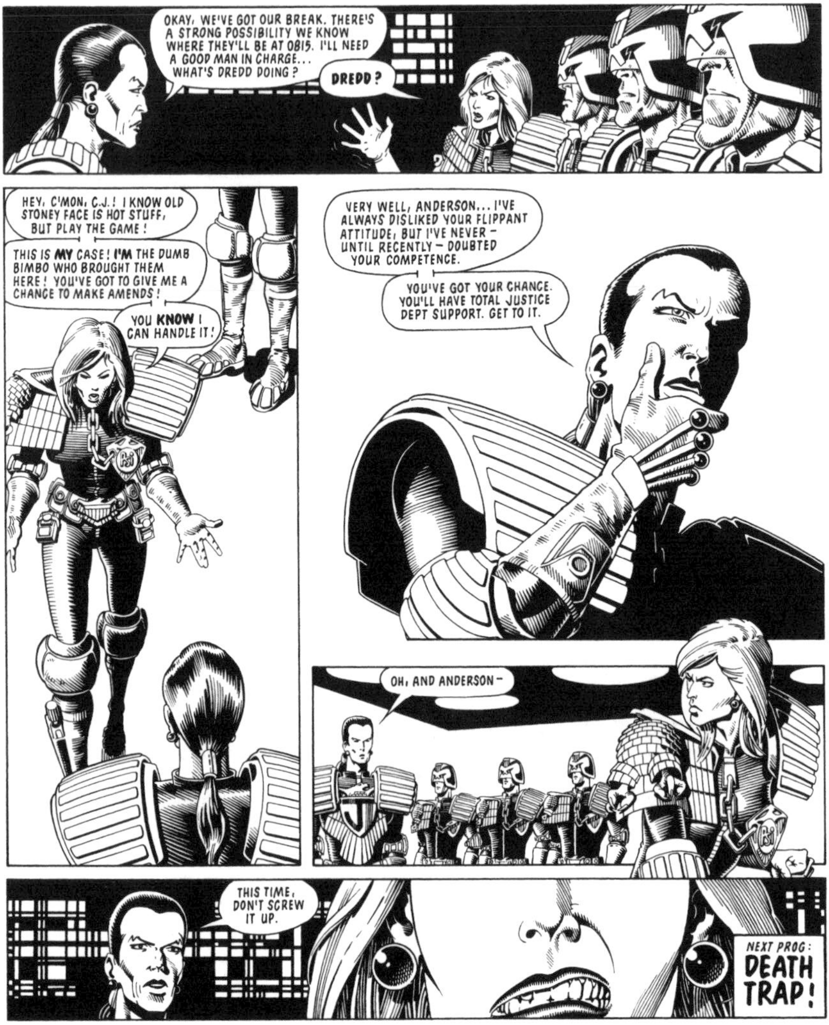
OKAY, WE'VE GOT OUR BREAK. THERE'S A STRONG POSSIBILITY WE KNOW WHERE THEY'LL BE AT 0815. I'LL NEED A GOOD MAN IN CHARGE... WHAT'S DREDD DOING?
DREDD?
HEY, C'MON, C.J.! I KNOW OLD STONEY FACE IS HOT STUFF, BUT PLAY THE GAME!
THIS IS MY CASE! I'M THE DUMB BIMBO WHO BROUGHT THEM HERE! YOU'VE GOT TO GIVE ME A CHANCE TO MAKE AMENDS!
YOU KNOW I CAN HANDLE IT!
VERY WELL, ANDERSON... I'VE ALWAYS DISLIKED YOUR FLIPPANT ATTITUDE, BUT I'VE NEVER — UNTIL RECENTLY — DOUBTED YOUR COMPETENCE.
YOU'VE GOT YOUR CHANCE. YOU'LL HAVE TOTAL JUSTICE DEPT SUPPORT. GET TO IT.
OH, AND ANDERSON —
THIS TIME, DON'T SCREW IT UP.
NEXT PROG: DEATH TRAP!

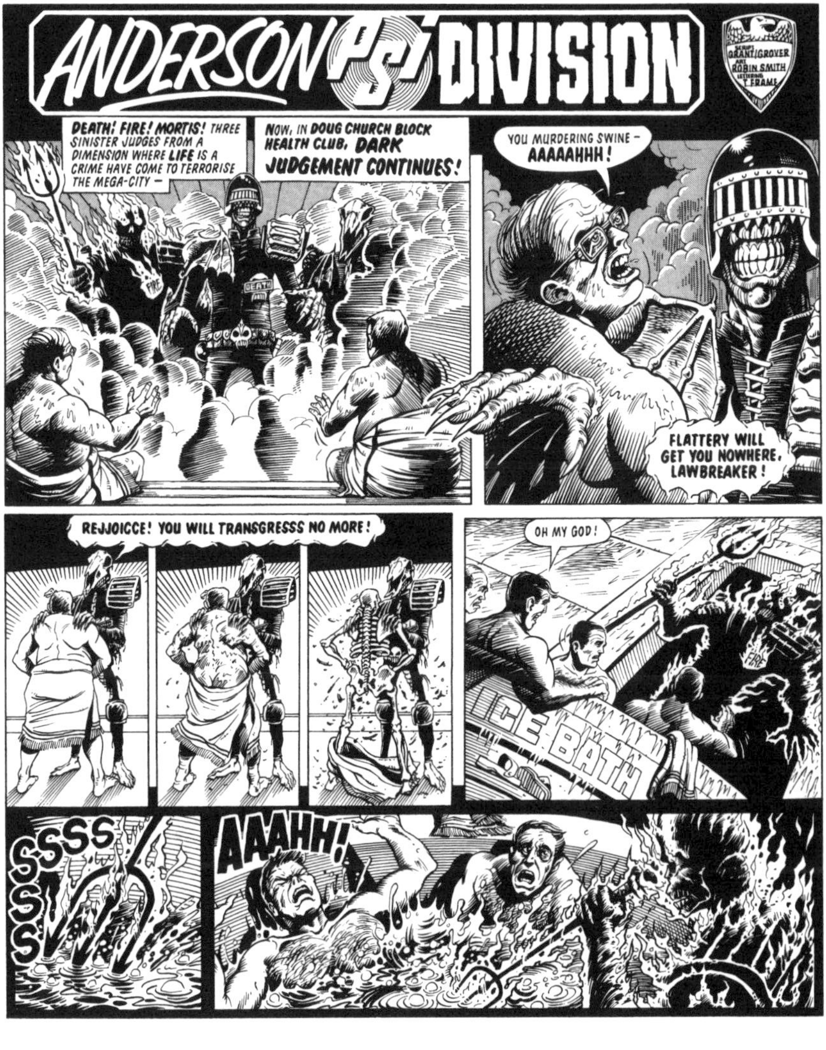
ANDERSON PSI DIVISION
SCRIPT GRANT/GROVER
ART ROBIN SMITH
LETTERING T FRAME
DEATH! FIRE! MORTIS! THREE SINISTER JUDGES FROM A DIMENSION WHERE LIFE IS A CRIME HAVE COME TO TERRORISE THE MEGA-CITY –
NOW, IN DOUG CHURCH BLOCK HEALTH CLUB, DARK JUDGEMENT CONTINUES!
FIRE
DEATH
YOU MURDERING SWINE – AAAAAHHH!
FLATTERY WILL GET YOU NOWHERE, LAWBREAKER!
REJJOICCE! YOU WILL TRANSGRESSS NO MORE!
OH MY GOD!
ICE BATH
FIRE
SSSSSSS
AAAHH!

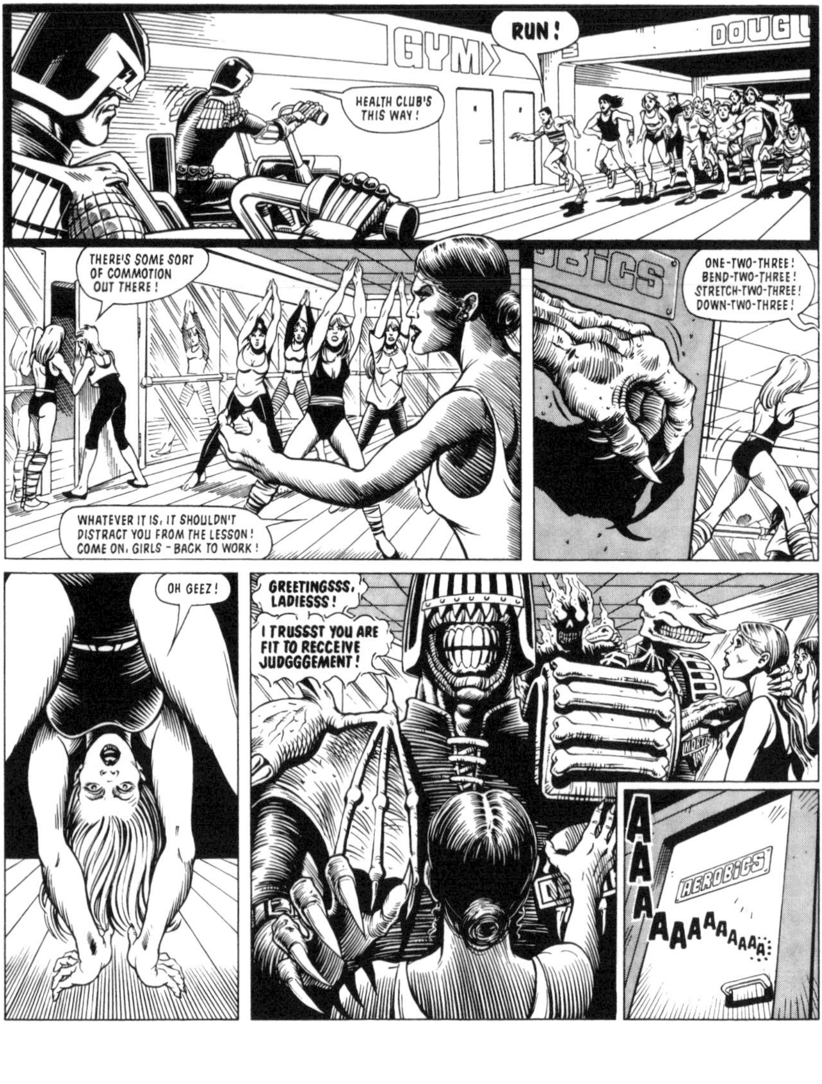
GYM
RUN!
HEALTH CLUB'S THIS WAY!
THERE'S SOME SORT OF COMMOTION OUT THERE!
WHATEVER IT IS, IT SHOULDN'T DISTRACT YOU FROM THE LESSON! COME ON, GIRLS - BACK TO WORK!
ONE-TWO-THREE! BEND-TWO-THREE! STRETCH-TWO-THREE! DOWN-TWO-THREE!
OH GEEZ!
GREETINGSSS, LADIESSS!
I TRUSSST YOU ARE FIT TO RECCEIVE JUDGGGEMENT!
AEROBICS
AAAAAAAAAAAA

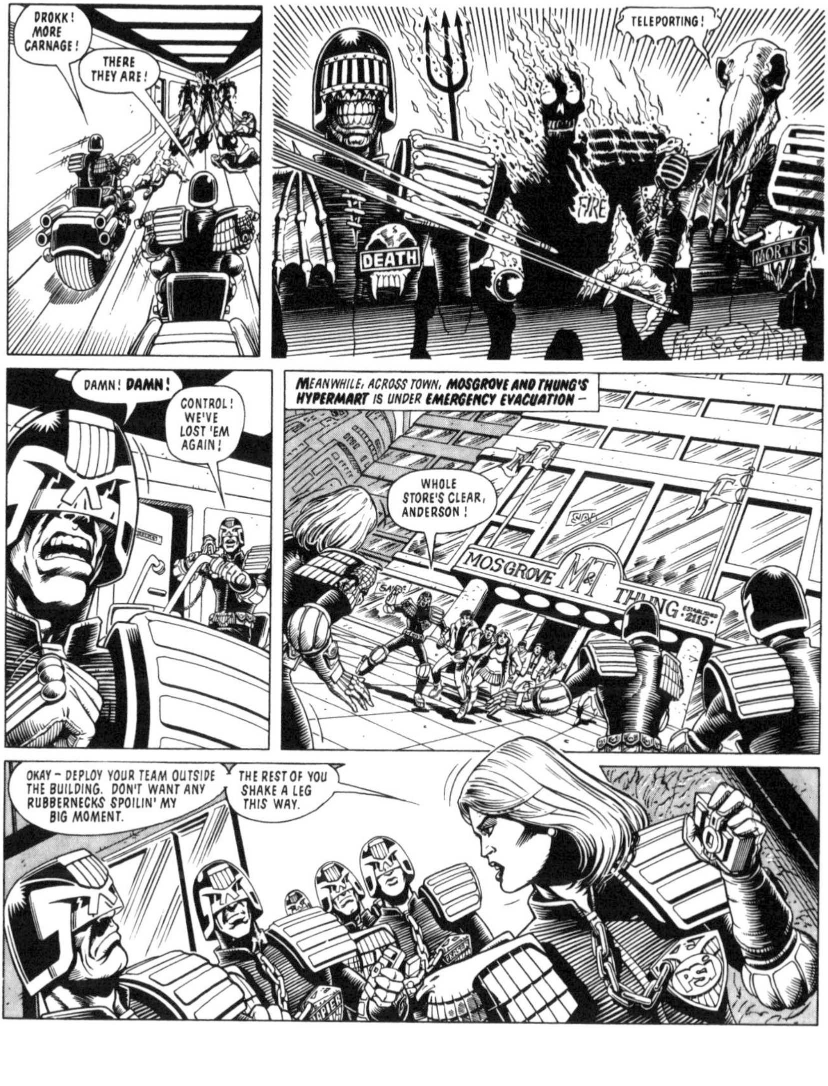
DROKK! MORE CARNAGE!
THERE THEY ARE!
TELEPORTING!
DEATH
FIRE
MORTIS
DAMN! DAMN!
CONTROL! WE'VE LOST 'EM AGAIN!
MEANWHILE, ACROSS TOWN, MOSGROVE AND THUNG'S HYPERMART IS UNDER EMERGENCY EVACUATION –
WHOLE STORE'S CLEAR, ANDERSON!
MOSGROVE M&T THUNG ESTABLISHED 2115
OKAY – DEPLOY YOUR TEAM OUTSIDE THE BUILDING. DON'T WANT ANY RUBBERNECKS SPOILIN' MY BIG MOMENT.
THE REST OF YOU SHAKE A LEG THIS WAY.
PSI

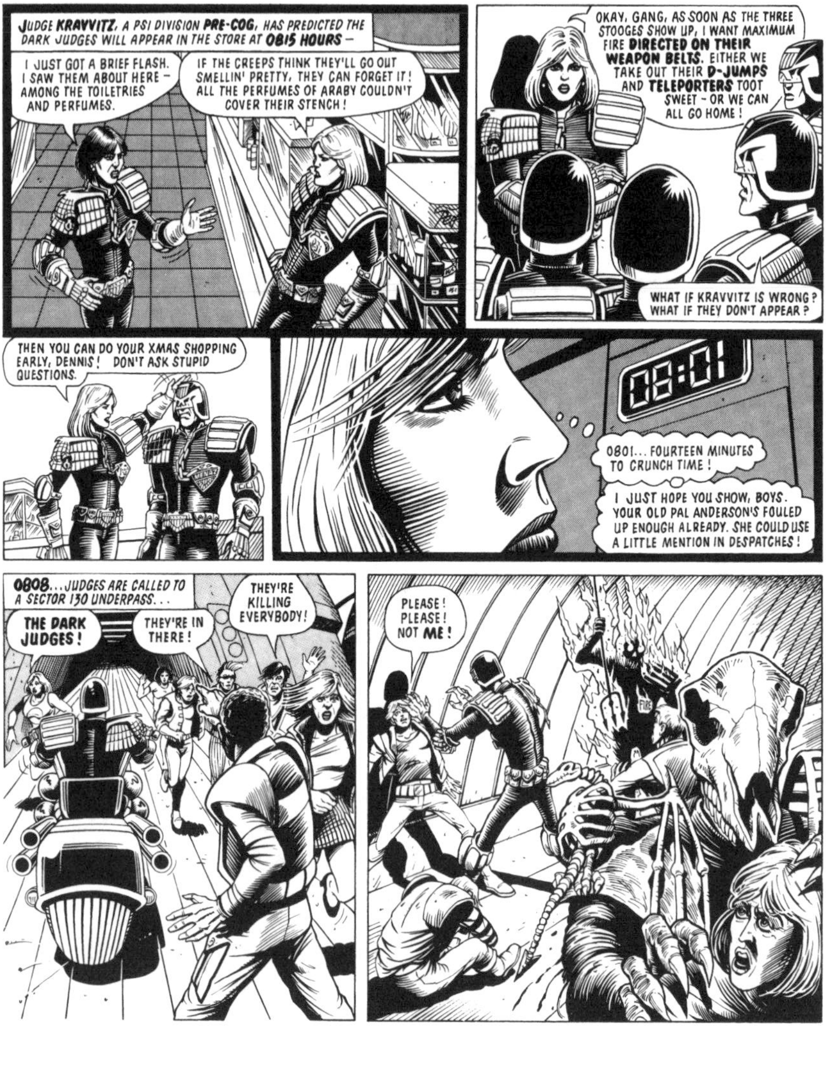
JUDGE KRAVVITZ, A PSI DIVISION PRE-COG, HAS PREDICTED THE DARK JUDGES WILL APPEAR IN THE STORE AT 0815 HOURS –
I JUST GOT A BRIEF FLASH. I SAW THEM ABOUT HERE – AMONG THE TOILETRIES AND PERFUMES.
IF THE CREEPS THINK THEY'LL GO OUT SMELLIN' PRETTY, THEY CAN FORGET IT! ALL THE PERFUMES OF ARABY COULDN'T COVER THEIR STENCH!
OKAY, GANG, AS SOON AS THE THREE STOOGES SHOW UP, I WANT MAXIMUM FIRE DIRECTED ON THEIR WEAPON BELTS. EITHER WE TAKE OUT THEIR D-JUMPS AND TELEPORTERS TOOT SWEET – OR WE CAN ALL GO HOME!
WHAT IF KRAVVITZ IS WRONG? WHAT IF THEY DON'T APPEAR?
THEN YOU CAN DO YOUR XMAS SHOPPING EARLY, DENNIS! DON'T ASK STUPID QUESTIONS.
08:01
0801... FOURTEEN MINUTES TO CRUNCH TIME!
I JUST HOPE YOU SHOW, BOYS. YOUR OLD PAL ANDERSON'S FOULED UP ENOUGH ALREADY. SHE COULD USE A LITTLE MENTION IN DESPATCHES!
0808... JUDGES ARE CALLED TO A SECTOR 130 UNDERPASS...
THE DARK JUDGES!
THEY'RE IN THERE!
THEY'RE KILLING EVERYBODY!
PLEASE! PLEASE! NOT ME!

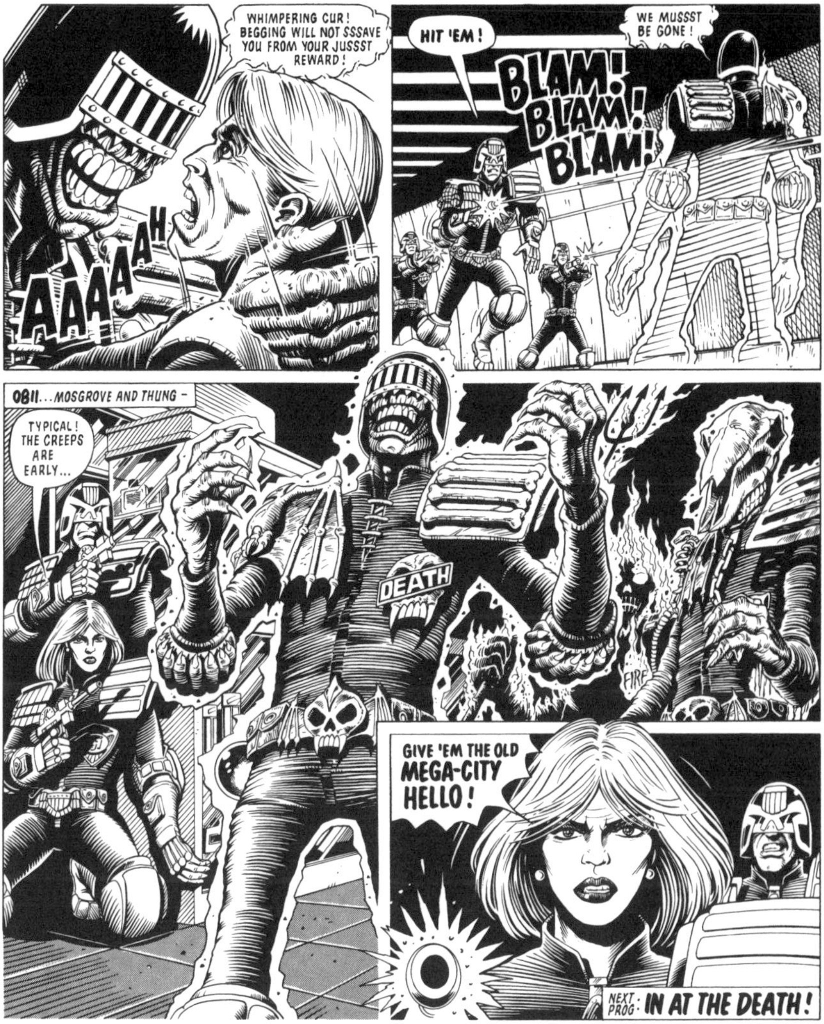
WHIMPERING CUR! BEGGING WILL NOT SSSAVE YOU FROM YOUR JUSSST REWARD!
AAAAAAH
HIT 'EM!
WE MUSSST BE GONE!
BLAM! BLAM! BLAM!
OBII... MOSGROVE AND THUNG –
TYPICAL! THE CREEPS ARE EARLY...
DEATH
FIRE
GIVE 'EM THE OLD MEGA-CITY HELLO!
NEXT PROG: IN AT THE DEATH!

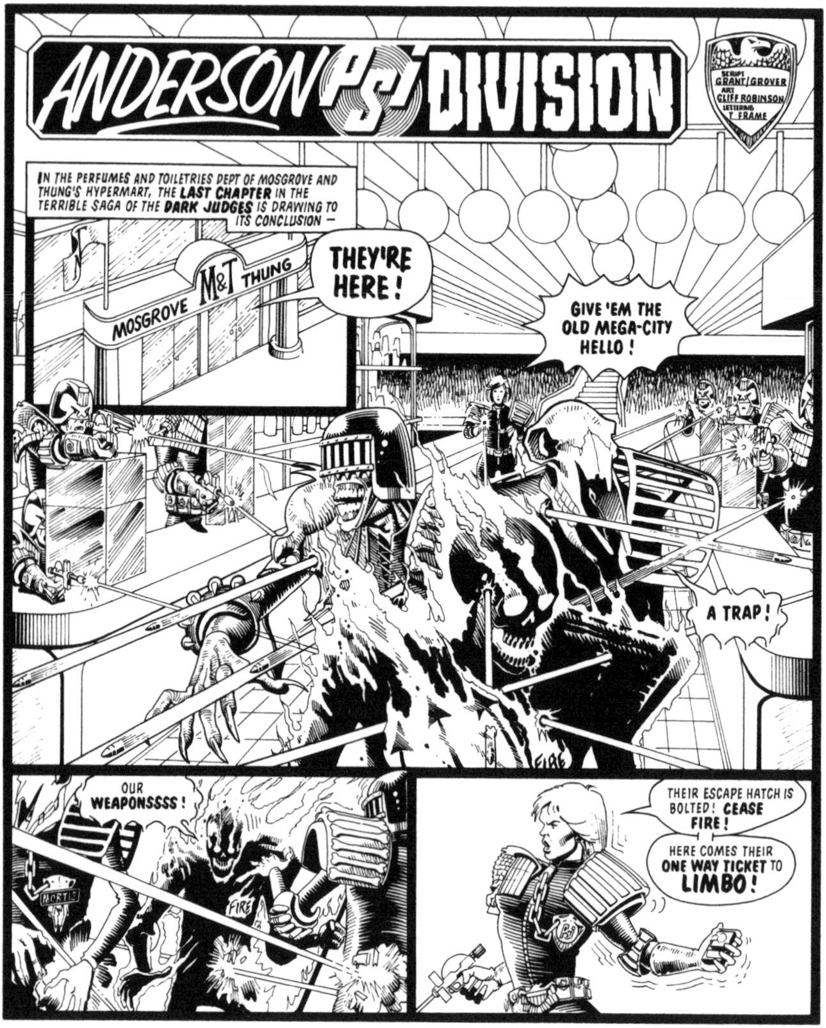
ANDERSON PSI DIVISION
SCRIPT GRANT/GROVER ART CLIFF ROBINSON LETTERING T FRAME
IN THE PERFUMES AND TOILETRIES DEPT OF MOSGROVE AND THUNG'S HYPERMART, THE LAST CHAPTER IN THE TERRIBLE SAGA OF THE DARK JUDGES IS DRAWING TO ITS CONCLUSION —
MOSGROVE M&T THUNG
THEY'RE HERE!
GIVE 'EM THE OLD MEGA-CITY HELLO!
A TRAP!
FIRE
OUR WEAPONSSSS!
MORTIS
FIRE
THEIR ESCAPE HATCH IS BOLTED! CEASE FIRE!
HERE COMES THEIR ONE WAY TICKET TO LIMBO!

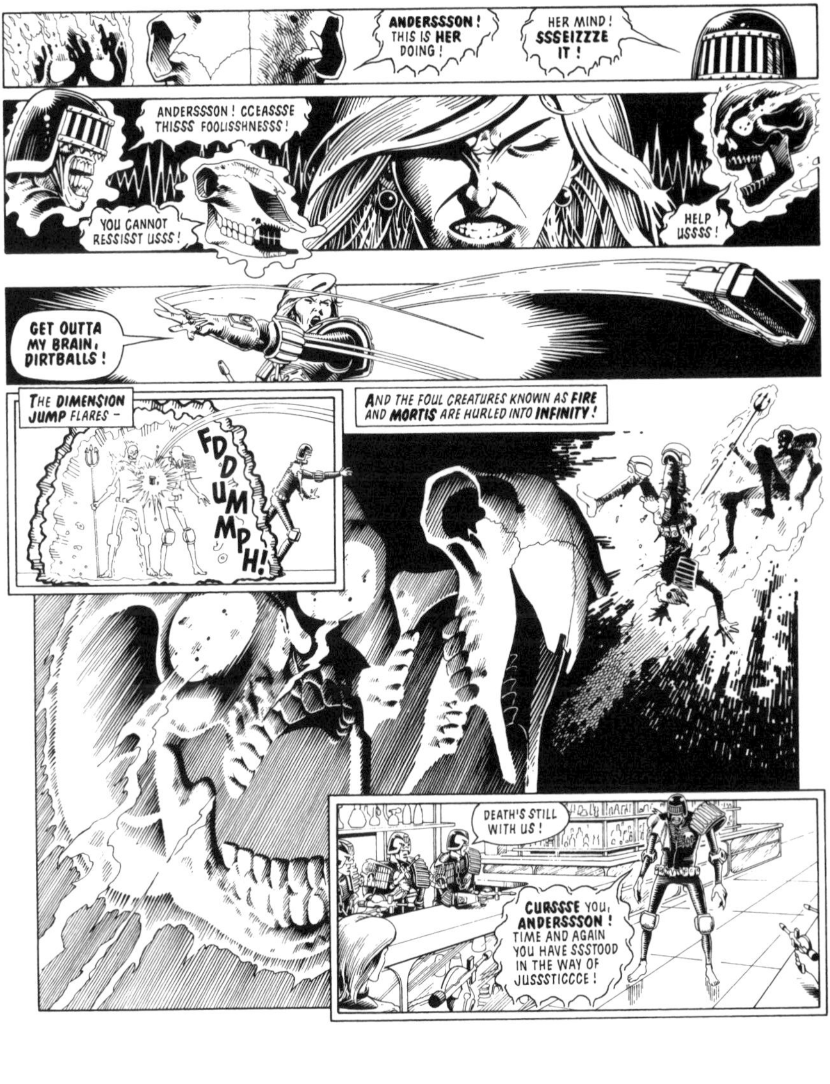
ANDERSSSON! THIS IS HER DOING!
HER MIND! SSSEIZZZE IT!
ANDERSSSON! CCEASSSE THISSS FOOLISSHNESSS!
YOU CANNOT RESSISST USSS!
HELP USSSS!
GET OUTTA MY BRAIN, DIRTBALLS!
THE DIMENSION JUMP FLARES –
FDDUMMPH!
AND THE FOUL CREATURES KNOWN AS FIRE AND MORTIS ARE HURLED INTO INFINITY!
DEATH'S STILL WITH US!
CURSSSE YOU, ANDERSSSON! TIME AND AGAIN YOU HAVE SSSTOOD IN THE WAY OF JUSSSTICCCE!

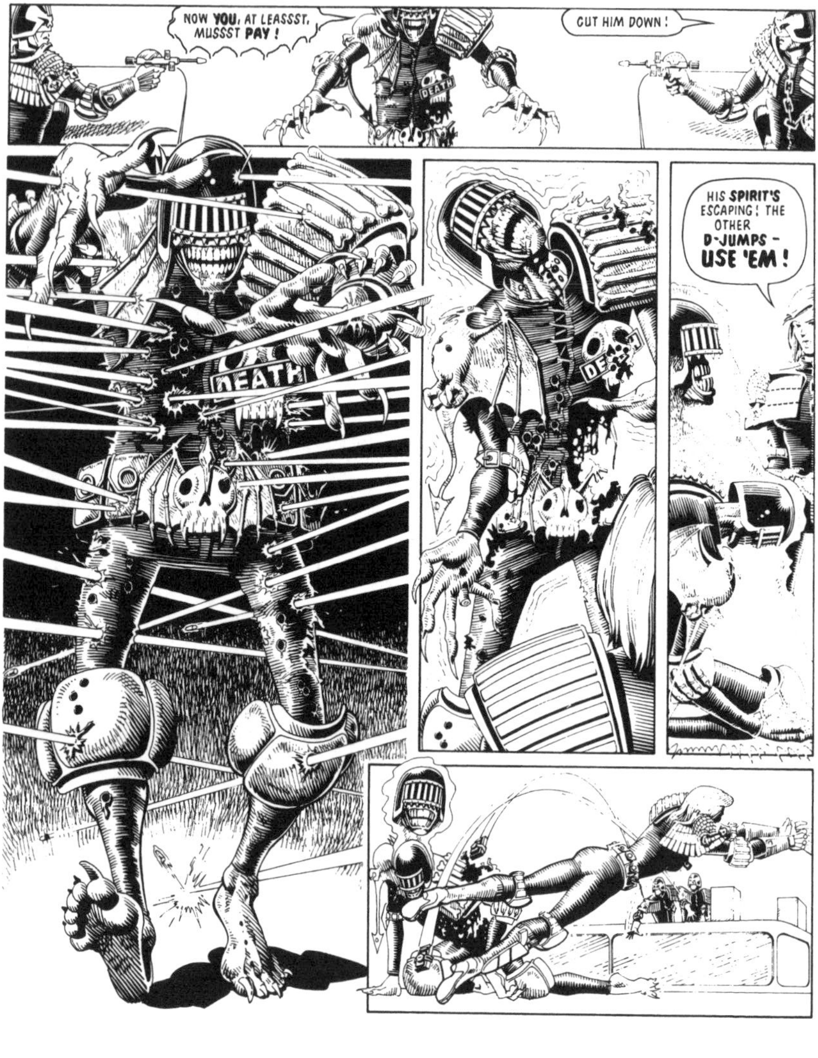
NOW YOU, AT LEASSST, MUSSST PAY!
CUT HIM DOWN!
HIS SPIRIT'S ESCAPING! THE OTHER D-JUMPS - USE 'EM!

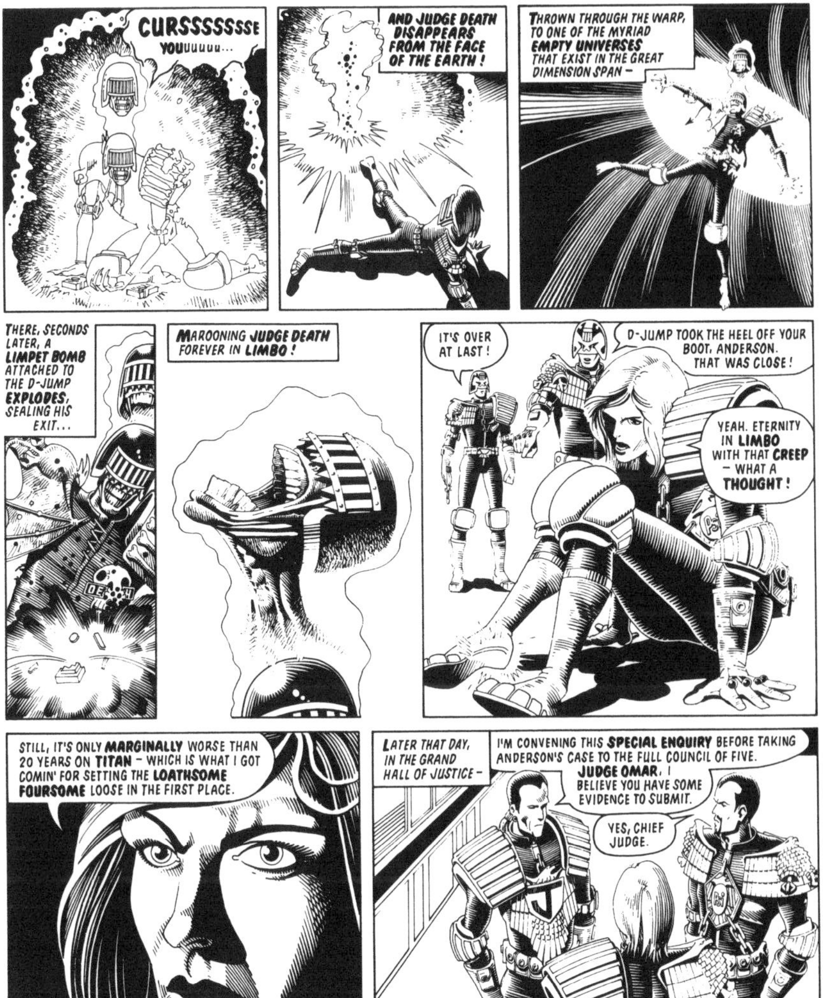
CURSSSSSSSE
YOUuuuuu...
AND JUDGE DEATH DISAPPEARS FROM THE FACE OF THE EARTH!
THROWN THROUGH THE WARP, TO ONE OF THE MYRIAD EMPTY UNIVERSES THAT EXIST IN THE GREAT DIMENSION SPAN —
THERE, SECONDS LATER, A LIMPET BOMB ATTACHED TO THE D-JUMP EXPLODES, SEALING HIS EXIT...
MAROONING JUDGE DEATH FOREVER IN LIMBO!
IT'S OVER AT LAST!
D-JUMP TOOK THE HEEL OFF YOUR BOOT, ANDERSON. THAT WAS CLOSE!
YEAH. ETERNITY IN LIMBO WITH THAT CREEP — WHAT A THOUGHT!
STILL, IT'S ONLY MARGINALLY WORSE THAN 20 YEARS ON TITAN — WHICH IS WHAT I GOT COMIN' FOR SETTING THE LOATHSOME FOURSOME LOOSE IN THE FIRST PLACE.
LATER THAT DAY, IN THE GRAND HALL OF JUSTICE —
I'M CONVENING THIS SPECIAL ENQUIRY BEFORE TAKING ANDERSON'S CASE TO THE FULL COUNCIL OF FIVE.
JUDGE OMAR, I BELIEVE YOU HAVE SOME EVIDENCE TO SUBMIT.
YES, CHIEF JUDGE.

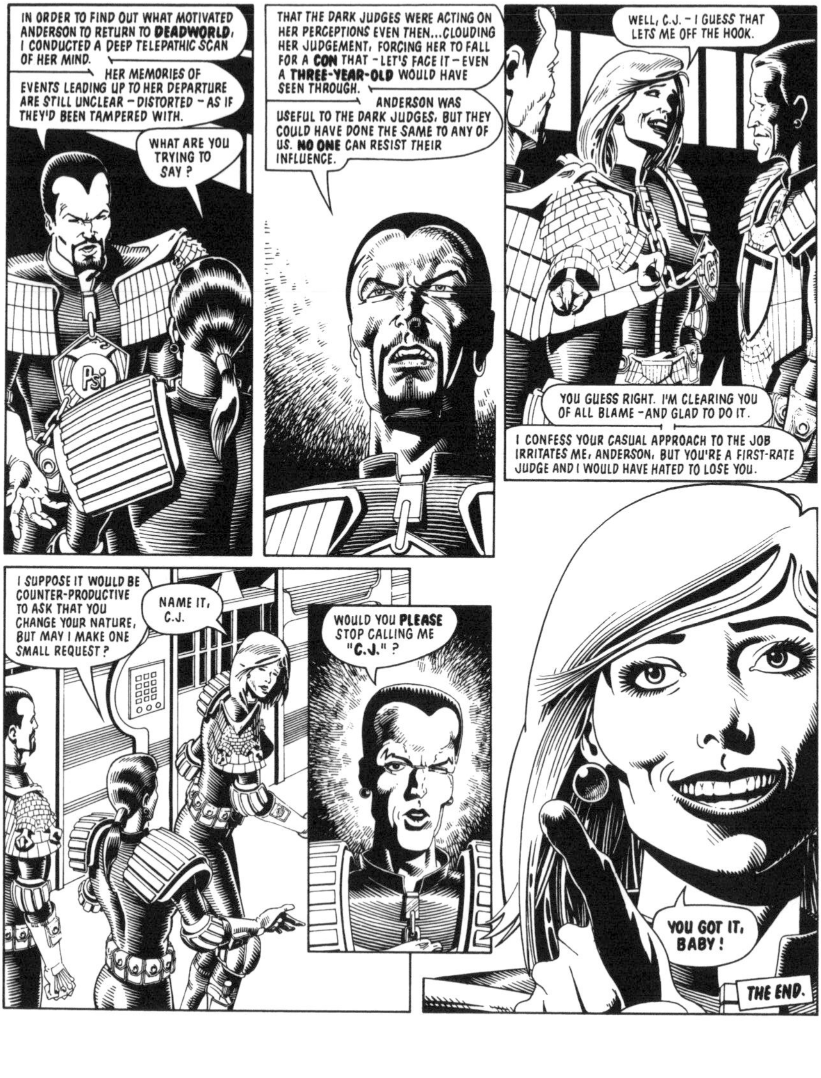
IN ORDER TO FIND OUT WHAT MOTIVATED ANDERSON TO RETURN TO **DEADWORLD**, I CONDUCTED A DEEP TELEPATHIC SCAN OF HER MIND.
HER MEMORIES OF EVENTS LEADING UP TO HER DEPARTURE ARE STILL UNCLEAR – DISTORTED – AS IF THEY'D BEEN TAMPERED WITH.
WHAT ARE YOU TRYING TO SAY ?
THAT THE DARK JUDGES WERE ACTING ON HER PERCEPTIONS EVEN THEN... CLOUDING HER JUDGEMENT, FORCING HER TO FALL FOR A **CON** THAT – LET'S FACE IT – EVEN A **THREE-YEAR-OLD** WOULD HAVE SEEN THROUGH.
ANDERSON WAS USEFUL TO THE DARK JUDGES, BUT THEY COULD HAVE DONE THE SAME TO ANY OF US. **NO ONE** CAN RESIST THEIR INFLUENCE.
WELL, C.J. – I GUESS THAT LETS ME OFF THE HOOK.
YOU GUESS RIGHT. I'M CLEARING YOU OF ALL BLAME – AND GLAD TO DO IT.
I CONFESS YOUR CASUAL APPROACH TO THE JOB IRRITATES ME, ANDERSON, BUT YOU'RE A FIRST-RATE JUDGE AND I WOULD HAVE HATED TO LOSE YOU.
I SUPPOSE IT WOULD BE COUNTER-PRODUCTIVE TO ASK THAT YOU CHANGE YOUR NATURE, BUT MAY I MAKE ONE SMALL REQUEST ?
NAME IT, C.J.
WOULD YOU **PLEASE** STOP CALLING ME **"C.J."** ?
YOU GOT IT, BABY !
THE END.

THE DARK JUDGES GALLERY

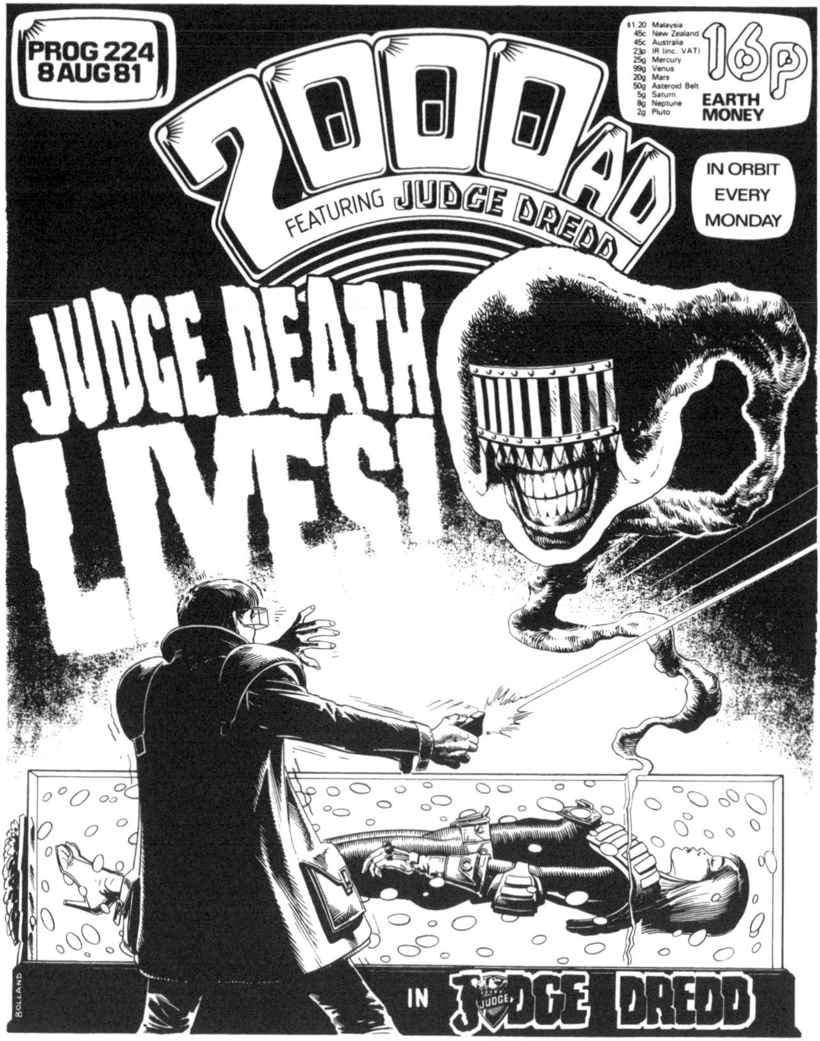
PROG 224
8 AUG 81
2000 AD
FEATURING JUDGE DREDD
$1.20 Malaysia
45c New Zealand
45c Australia
23p IR (inc. VAT)
25g Mercury
99g Venus
20g Mars
50g Asteroid Belt
5g Saturn
8g Neptune
2g Pluto
16p
EARTH MONEY
IN ORBIT EVERY MONDAY
JUDGE DEATH LIVES!
BOLLAND
IN JUDGE DREDD

2000 AD Prog 224: Cover by **Brian Bolland**

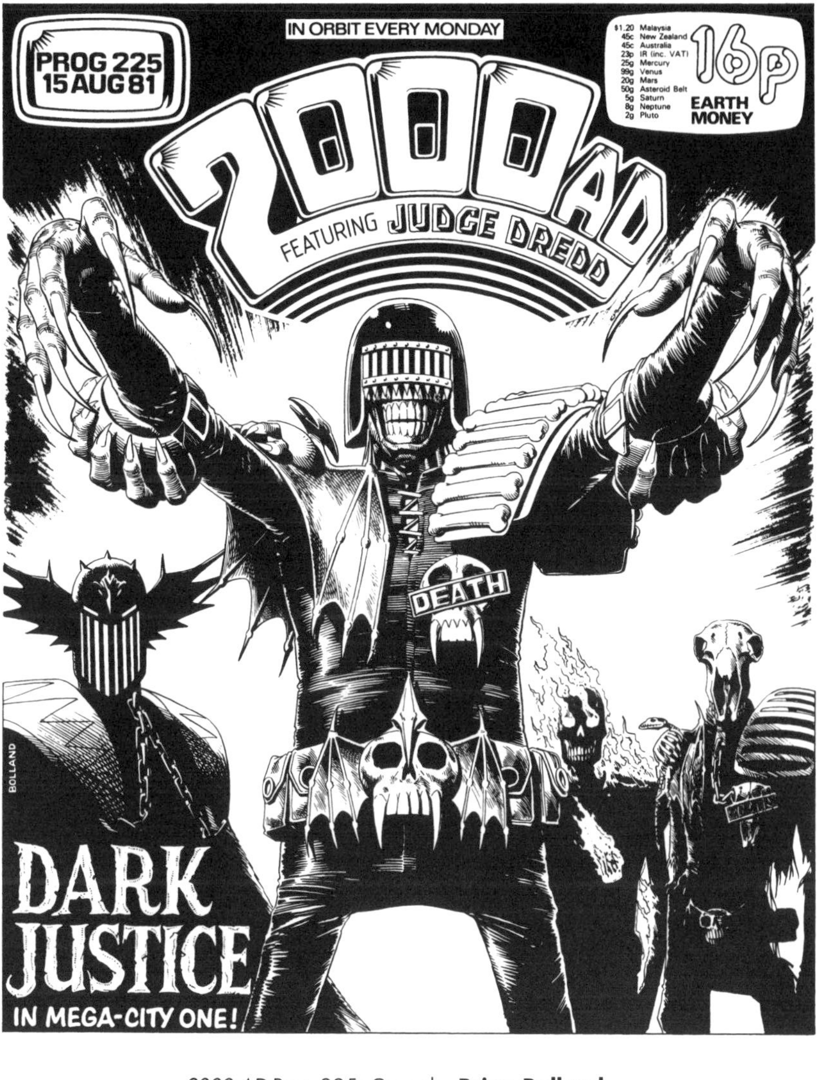
PROG 225
15 AUG 81
IN ORBIT EVERY MONDAY
$1.20 Malaysia
45c New Zealand
45c Australia
23p IR (inc. VAT)
25g Mercury
99g Venus
20g Mars
50g Asteroid Belt
5g Saturn
8g Neptune
2g Pluto
16p
EARTH MONEY
2000 AD
FEATURING JUDGE DREDD
DEATH
BOLLAND
DARK JUSTICE
IN MEGA-CITY ONE!

2000 AD Prog 225: Cover by **Brian Bolland**

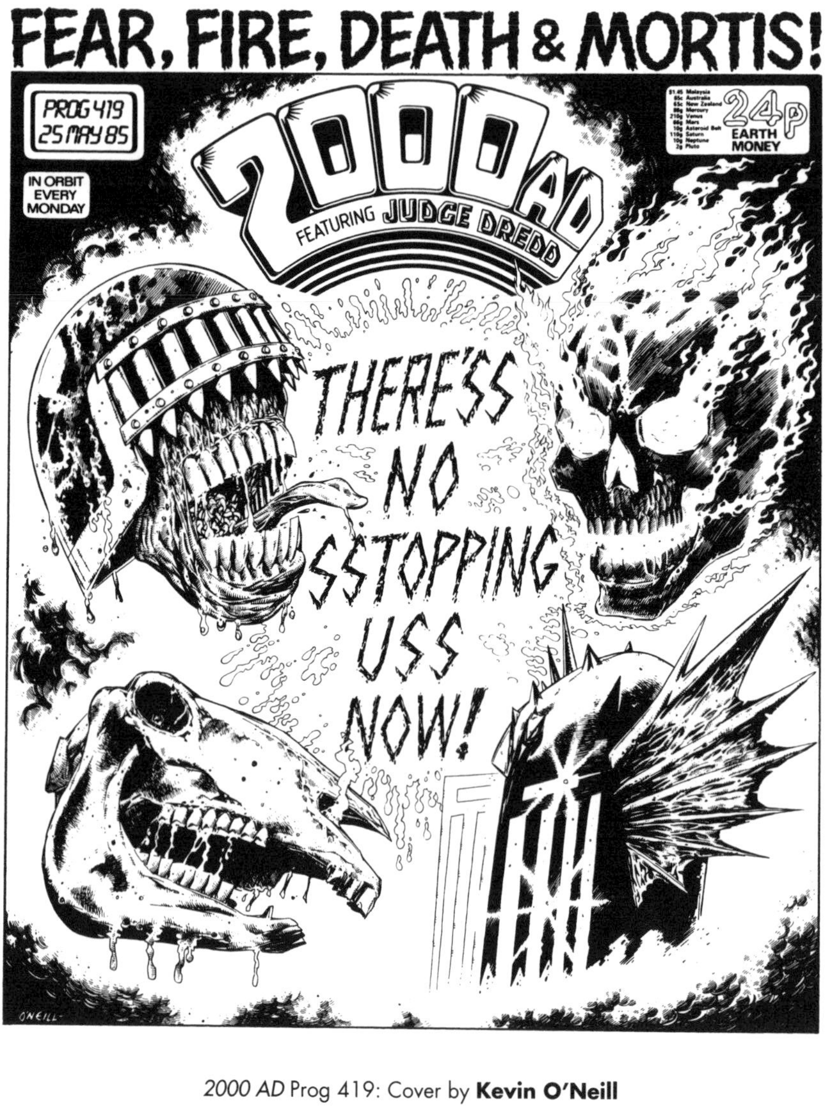
FEAR, FIRE, DEATH & MORTIS!
PROG 419
25 MAY 85
IN ORBIT EVERY MONDAY
2000 AD
FEATURING JUDGE DREDD
24p
EARTH MONEY
THERE'SS NO SSTOPPING USS NOW!
O'NEILL

2000 AD Prog 419: Cover by **Kevin O'Neill**

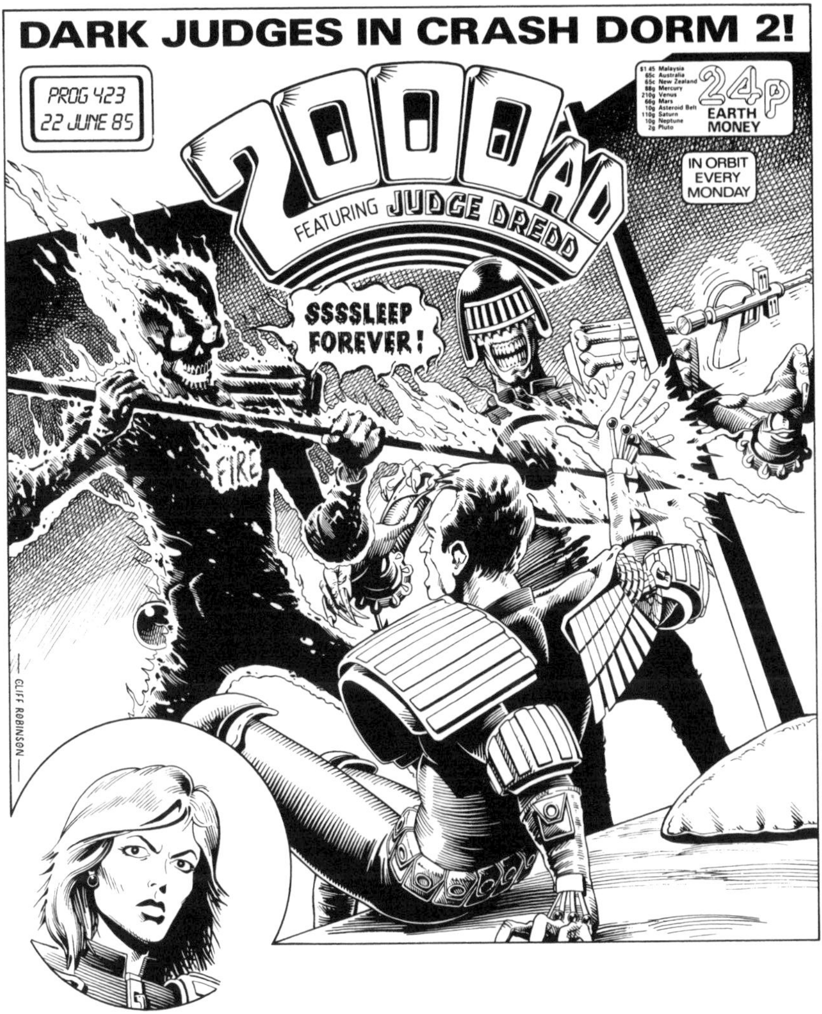
DARK JUDGES IN CRASH DORM 2!
PROG 423
22 JUNE 85
2000 AD
FEATURING JUDGE DREDD
$1.45 Malaysia
65c Australia
65c New Zealand
88g Mercury
210g Venus
66g Mars
10g Asteroid Belt
110g Saturn
10g Neptune
2g Pluto
24p
EARTH MONEY
IN ORBIT EVERY MONDAY
SSSSLEEP FOREVER!
FIRE
CLIFF ROBINSON

2000 AD Prog 423: Cover by **Cliff Robinson**

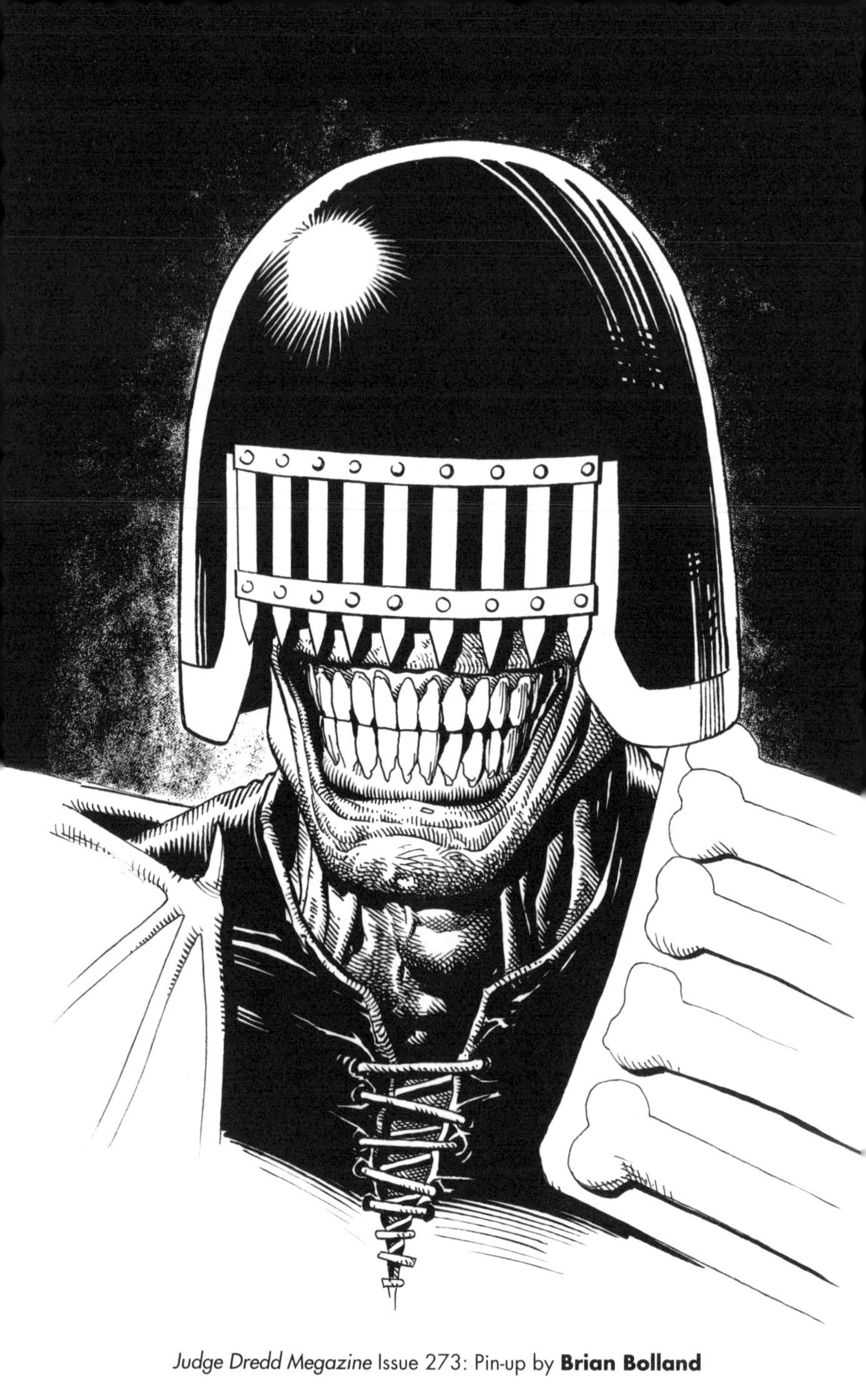

Judge Dredd Megazine Issue 273: Pin-up by **Brian Bolland**

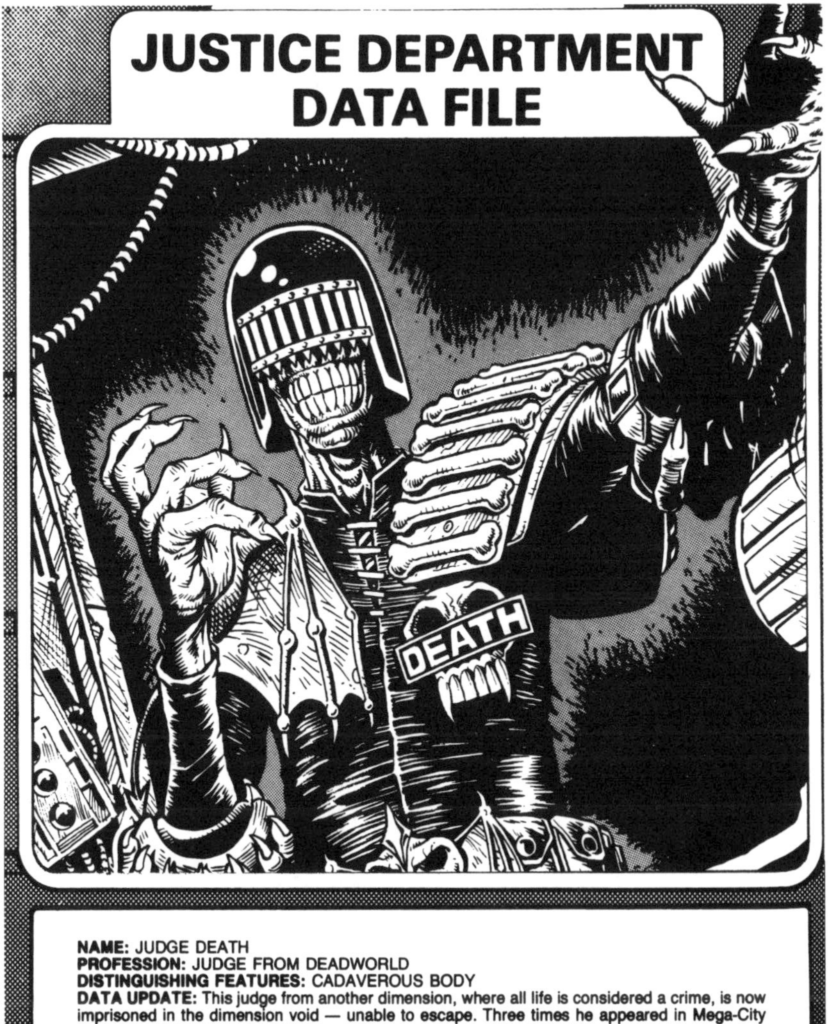
JUSTICE DEPARTMENT
DATA FILE
DEATH
NAME: JUDGE DEATH
PROFESSION: JUDGE FROM DEADWORLD
DISTINGUISHING FEATURES: CADAVEROUS BODY
DATA UPDATE: This judge from another dimension, where all life is considered a crime, is now imprisoned in the dimension void — unable to escape. Three times he appeared in Mega-City One, determined to carry out his warped brand of justice — exterminating the living in order to stop all crime. Three times he was defeated, the last being due to Judge Anderson's clever use of 22nd Century technology. She used a Dimension Jump to hurl Death into another dimension. A limpet mine attached to the device destroyed it before Death could use it to return.
PAUSE
EJECT
REWIND
WIND
START
STOP
FOCUS
VOLUME
80

Judge Dredd Annual 1986: Data File by **Brett Ewins**

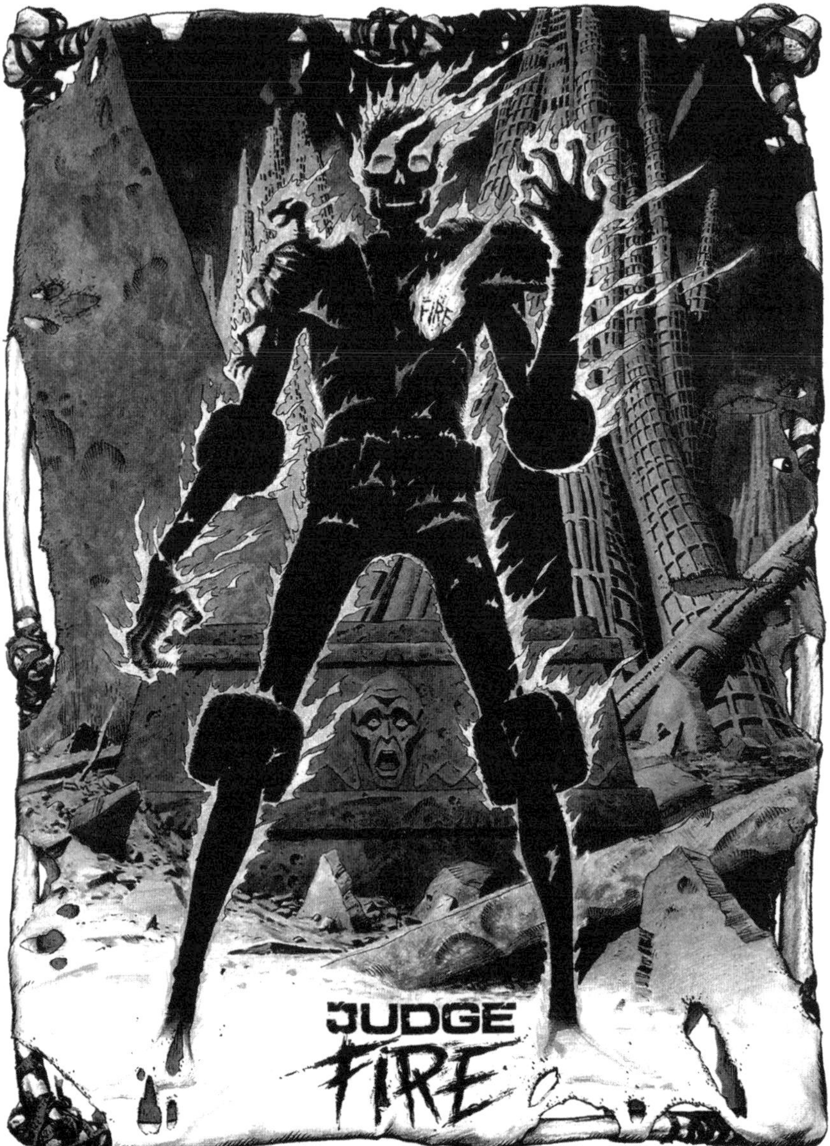
FIRE
JUDGE
FIRE

2000 AD Prog 555: Pin-up by **Garry Leach**

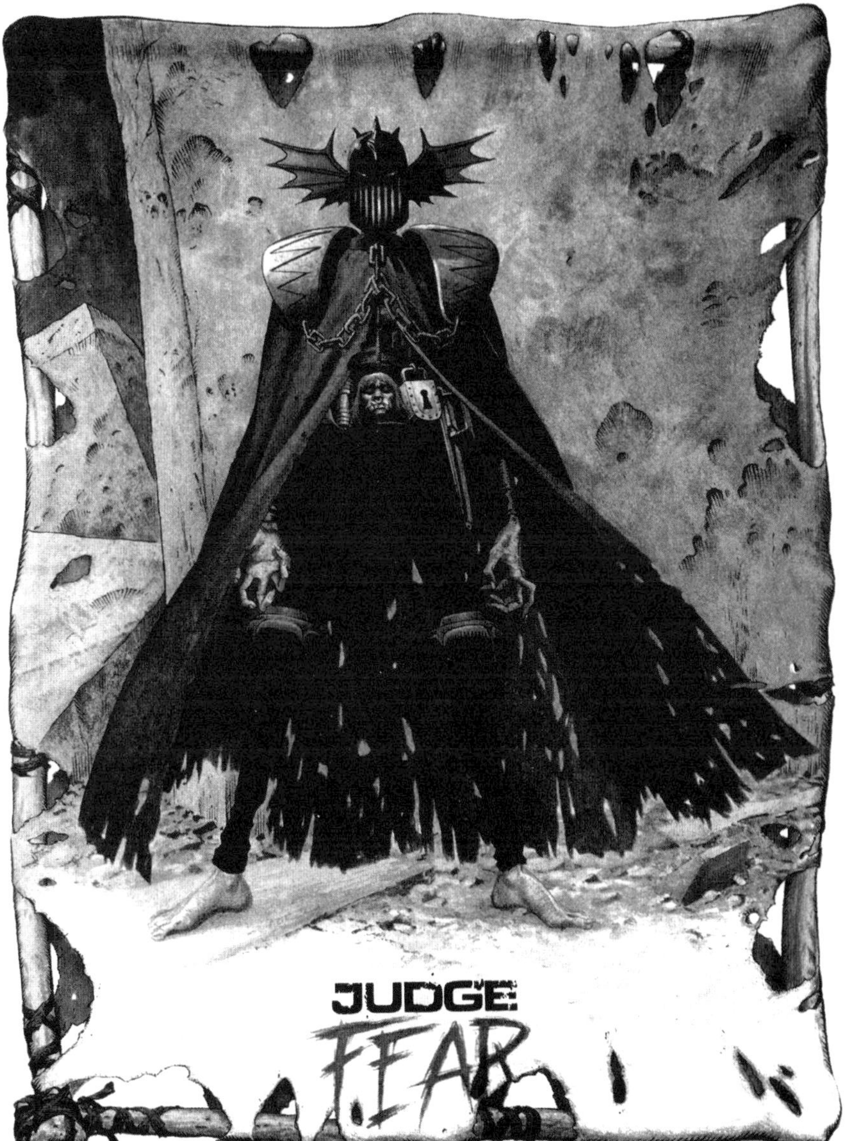
JUDGE
FEAR

2000 AD Prog 556 Pin-up by **Garry Leach**

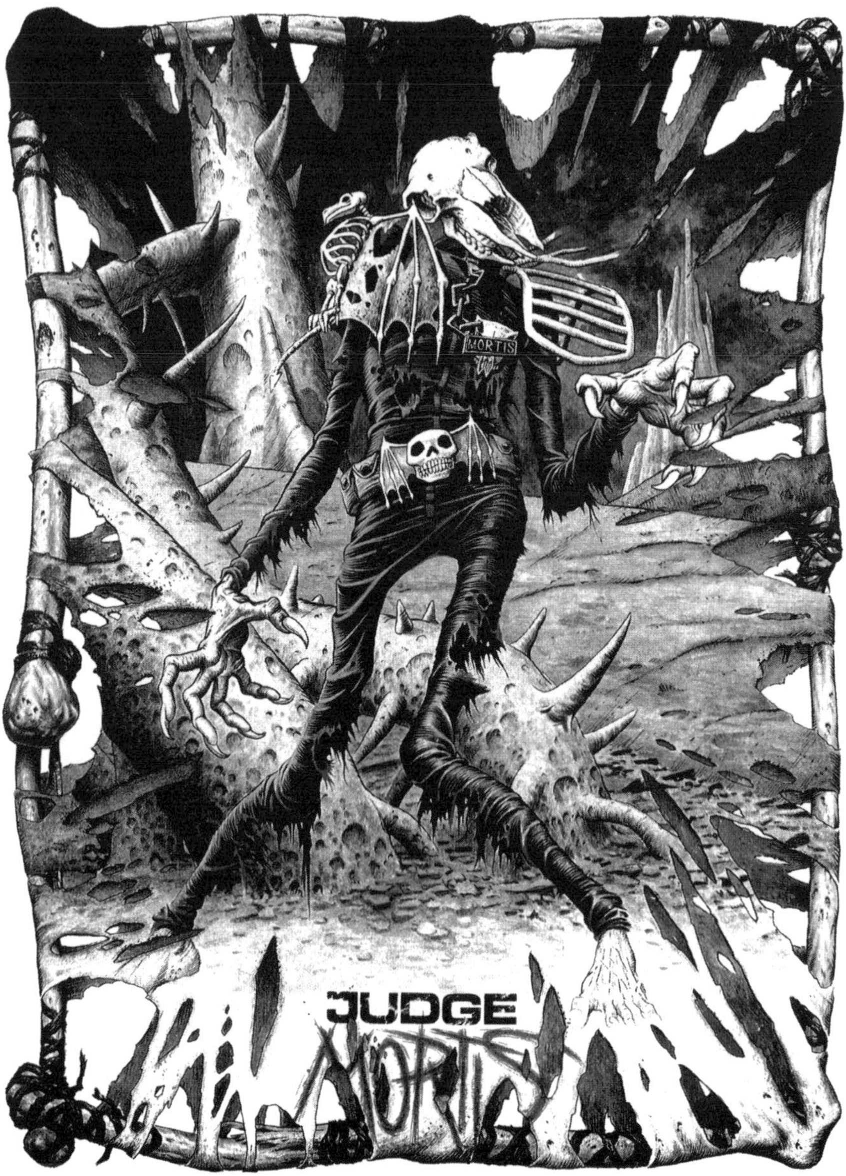

MORTIS
MORTIS
JUDGE
MORTIS

2000 AD Prog 557 Pin-up by **Garry Leach**

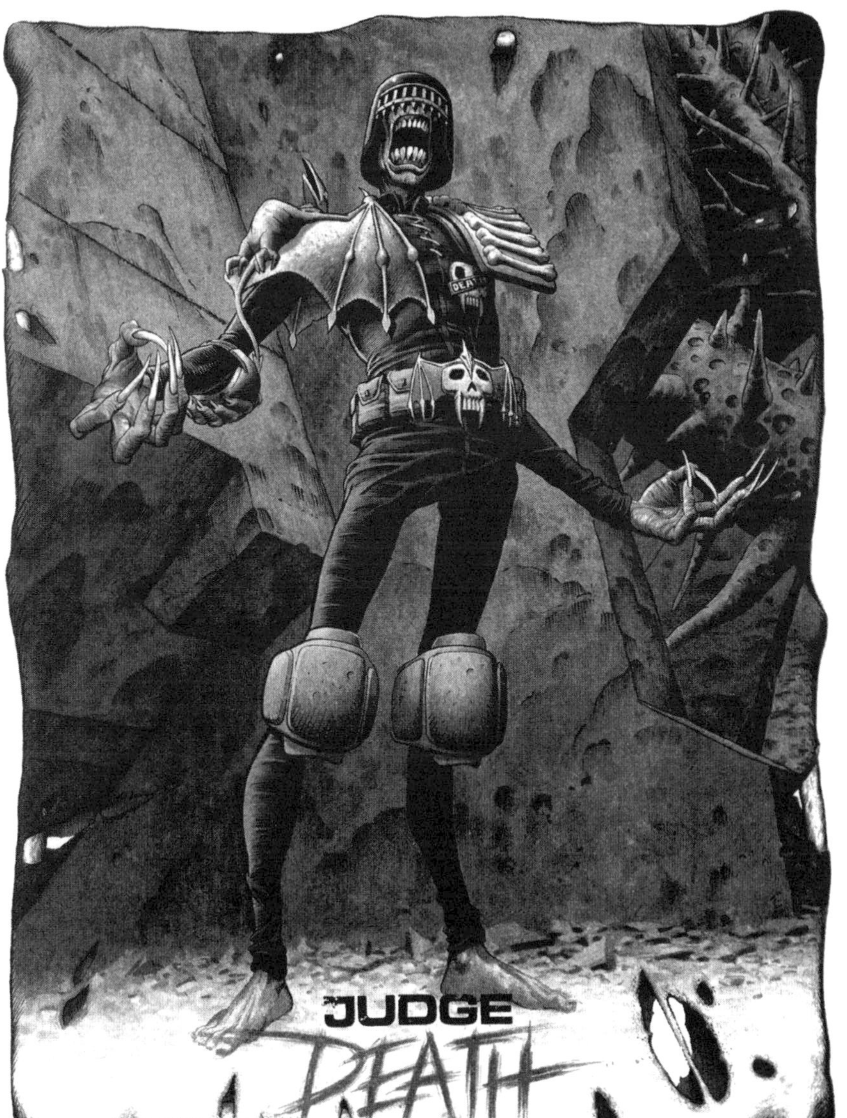
JUDGE
DEATH

2000 AD Prog 558 Pin-up by **Garry Leach**

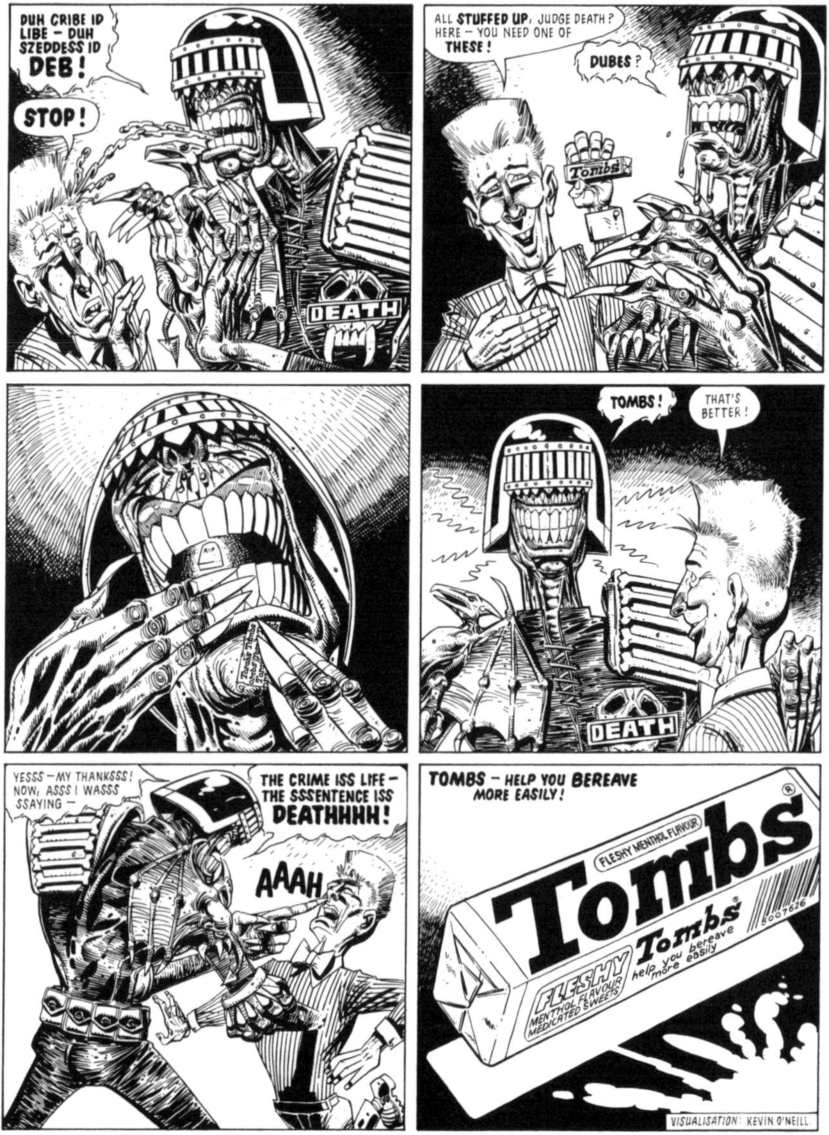
DUH CRIBE ID LIBE – DUH SZEDDESS ID DEB!
STOP!
ALL STUFFED UP, JUDGE DEATH? HERE – YOU NEED ONE OF THESE!
DUBES?
Tombs
DEATH
TOMBS!
THAT'S BETTER!
DEATH
YESSS – MY THANKSSS! NOW, ASSS I WASSS SSAYING –
THE CRIME ISS LIFE – THE SSSENTENCE ISS DEATHHHH!
AAAH
TOMBS – HELP YOU BEREAVE MORE EASILY!
FLESHY MENTHOL FLAVOUR
Tombs
Tombs
help you bereave more easily
FLESHY MENTHOL FLAVOUR MEDICATED SWEETS
5007626
VISUALISATION: KEVIN O'NEILL.

2000 AD Prog 521: Advertorial by **Kevin O'Neill**

ALSO AVAILABLE IN THIS SERIES

ALSO AVAILABLE IN THIS SERIES

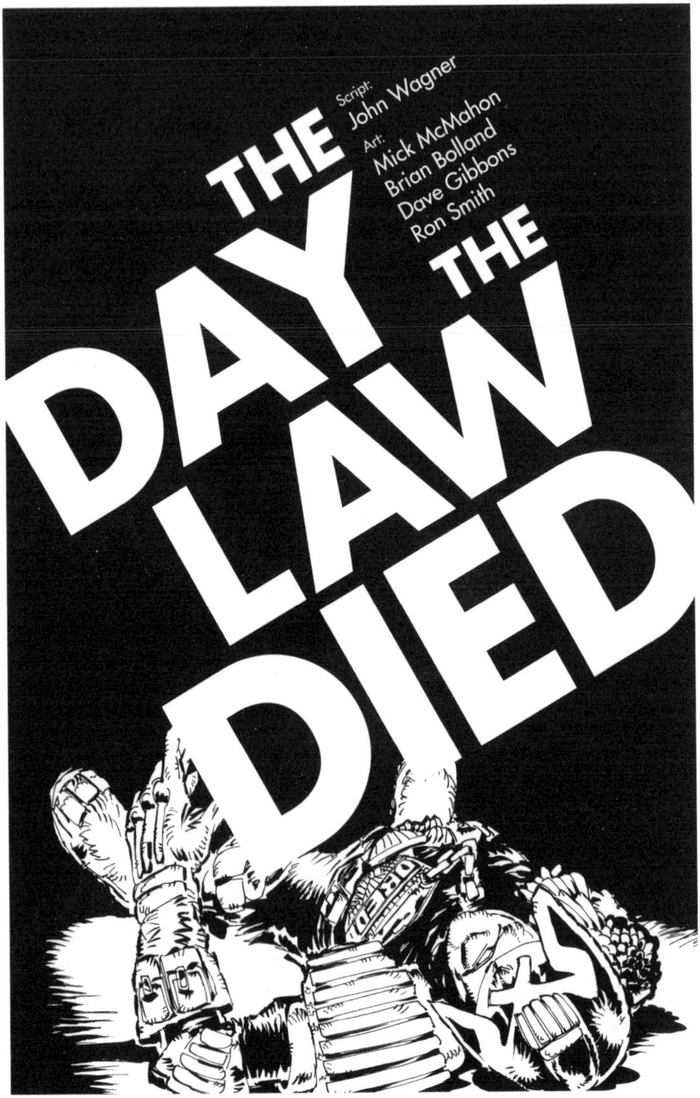

THE DAY THE LAW DIED
Script: John Wagner
Art: Mick McMahon
Brian Bolland
Dave Gibbons
Ron Smith

ISBN: 978-1-78108-009-2 • £.6.99

WWW.2000ADONLINE.COM